ORIGINS OF THE STATE

The Anthropology of
Political Evolution

ORIGINS OF THE STATE

The Anthropology of
Political Evolution

Edited by
RONALD COHEN
and
ELMAN R. SERVICE

A Publication of the
Institute for the Study of Human Issues
Philadelphia

Manufactured in the United States of America

Library of Congress Cataloging in Publication Data:

Main entry under title:

Origins of the state.

    Includes bibliographies and index.
    1. Government, Primitive—Addresses, essays, lectures. 2. State, The—
Addresses, essays, lectures. I. Cohen, Ronald. II. Service, Elman Rogers,
1915-
GN492.6.07   320.1'1   77-19091
ISBN 0-915980-68-1
ISBN 0-915980-84-3 pbk.

For information, write:

Director of Publications
ISHI
3401 Science Center
Philadelphia, Pennsylvania 19104
U.S.A.

Contents

Introduction

RONALD COHEN

The question of how and why states were formed involves anthropology in problems of social evolution and ultimately in fundamental issues of moral and political philosophy. In evolutionary terms, it forces us to ask what qualities inherent in the human condition propel societies toward more complex, more inclusive, more differentiated systems of social organization.[1] Give or take a few multinational corporations, the state is the most powerful organizational structure ever developed in the history of the planet. It literally moves mountains and redirects rivers, and it has on occasion sent untold thousands, even millions, to their deaths. How did such a thing happen? Why? These are issues to be dealt with in a study of the origins of states.

But there is more. As a sociopolitical system, the state permits greater inequity within its population than any known earlier form of association. Why do people give up, or why are they forced to give up, so much local and individual autonomy to become part of, and subordinate to, despotic, sometimes quite cruel forms of government? Do the benefits derived from such a development outweigh the costs for those who must accept the less advantageous positions? Why do those who create such systems attempt the task of reshaping their societies? From these empirical issues, it is but a small step to more philosophical ones concerning the nature of power, the nature of good government, and the problem of justice in human affairs. Although these matters are not resolved in this volume (how could they be?), it is important to realize that they underlie much of the discussion that ensues. If the benefits derived from membership in the state outweigh the inequities and cruelties it supports, we judge the morality of the state in one way. If, on the other hand, such benefits are delusions or

1

are less significant than the inequity and injustice, then we must judge the morality in quite another way. We cannot go into this issue in detail, but I raise it to alert the reader. There is more to the origin of states than simply facts and theories.

Problems of Definition

In its most general sense the term "state" refers to the temporal and spatial dimensions of an entity, including those qualities, quantities, and relations that determine and characterize these dimensional features. In this sense physical scientists speak of a "steady state" or a philosopher like Hobbes refers to the "state" of nature. In anthropology "state" in the broad sense refers to society or polity. Lowie (1927) never defines the word but clearly means any organized social system. Koppers (1963) speaks of "the state" as if it refers to any human group that occupies or controls a territory. Although too general to be useful, such a usage makes the worthwhile point that all human beings live out their lives within some form of social order. Within this framework, the state refers to any and all variations in power, authority structure, and values that support the organizational framework of society. However, equating all known political forms by lumping them under one term—"the state"—does nothing to explain the differences among them. Probably for this reason alone, the authors of the essays in this book accept the notion that the state and society are not synonymous. *Homo sapiens* has evolved a number of quite different and distinct political systems; one of these is the state.

From this baseline of agreement, our notions about what to emphasize in a definition of "state" begin to diverge sharply. Elsewhere (Cohen 1978) I have classified definitions into those based on (a) stratification, (b) authority structures and/or information processing, and (c) diagnostic traits. Let me go over each of these categories briefly.

Definitions based on stratification stress the correlation between the rise of states and the establishment of permanent social classes. In this view, stratification divides the population so that valued goods, services, and positions are differentially enjoyed; those in power are well-off relative to those over whom they have authority. Although this position goes back at least to Rousseau's *Discourse on Inequality*, today it is most commonly associated with Marx and Engels, especially with the latter's work on social evolution (Engels 1891). All of these writers see the state as the outcome of a formation of classes in which an upper or ruling class obtains control over the means of production. The state is an instrument for maintaining this control and for protecting the privileges of the ruling group (Krader 1968: 25). More recently Professor Fried has become the most widely cited Western scholar to espouse this position. In Fried's terms the state is a centralized governmental system that emerges inevitably from any system of institutionalized inequity in which the leaders, or ruling group, have special access to those resources that sustain and enhance life (1967: 186).

A second set of definitions focuses on the structure of the governmental system itself. This approach goes back to Herbert Spencer, Louis Henry Morgan, and Sir Henry Maine in the nineteenth century. It is applied more clearly by Hobhouse, Wheeler, and Ginsburg (1915), who define the state as a centralized and hierarchical system of authority relations in which local political units lose their autonomy, becoming districts whose local or regional heads or chiefs are subordinate to central government. With only minor additions this is the same approach used by Fortes and Evans-Pritchard (1940) in their division of African polities into state and non-state forms. Service (1975) also uses this approach, emphasizing as well the notion that the centralized government has a monopoly over the use of force.

A more recent version retains the notion of the state as a hierarchical and centralized political structure but focuses on the means by which information is processed (Wright and Johnson 1975) and/or energy is obtained and utilized in the system (Adams 1975). All social and political life is seen as a series of transactions or information flows in which higher levels of decision making affect lower levels of the authority structure. This approach allows archaeologists and others to obtain indicators—data on information transfers or on the harnessing and distribution of energy—and then classify organizational forms into different types on the basis of how they carry out these activities (see Price's essay in this volume). Linking these operations to known political systems has allowed researchers to define a state as that type of hierarchically organized polity in which there are three or more levels of hierarchy from the center of the system to its peripheries.

Finally, there are definitions that lump together certain common traits found among early centralized states.[2] It is noteworthy that none of the contributors to this volume use this type of definition. The reason is clear: it is next to impossible to obtain a set of traits that applies to more than a few societies. Early states do not, for example, universally practice human sacrifice (Murdock 1959: 38), nor do they necessarily demand that members either accept or reject state sovereignty, leaving no intermediate position of semi-subordination or hegemony (Krader 1968: 27). The more numerous and discrete the traits, the more difficult the list is to apply. Little wonder then that, with the notable exception of Lenski (1966: 157), very few researchers have adopted such definitions in their own work.

In one way or another all of these definitions place a discrete set of features against a continuous phenomenon. When non-states are compared to state systems, there is no precise, clear-cut dividing line. And yet it is widely, albeit not universally, agreed upon that not all structures that override local authority come under the definition. To be a "true" state the system should exhibit some stable or permanent hierarchy that can withstand the disruptive effects of succession struggles. Those who disagree with this position (e.g., Southall 1956; Claessen and Skalník 1978) would use the term "state" to refer to inter-mediate forms generally classified as "chieftaincies."

Elsewhere (Cohen 1971, 1978) I have argued that the key diagnostic feature is that of fission. All political systems except true states break up into similar units as part of their normal process of political activity. Hunting bands, locally autonomous food producers, and chief-taincies each build up the polity to some critical point and then send off subordinate segments to found new units or split because of con-flict over succession, land shortage, failure by one segment to support another in intergroup competition or hostilities, or for some other reason. These new units grow in their turn, then split again. The state is a system specifically designed to restrain such tendencies. And this capacity creates an entirely new society: one that can expand without splitting, incorporate other polities and ethnic groups, and become more populous, more heterogeneous, and more powerful, with no known upper limit on its size or strength.

The enormous potential of states compared to all earlier forms of organization that are known to us stems from the capacity of states to coordinate human efforts to carry out public policy. To do so, states evolve a "ruling class" or, in structural terms, a governing bureau-cracy. The officeholders oversee successions to high office, collect revenues, raise militia, adjudicate disputes, allocate scarce resources, and, as an official hierarchy, join the non-officeholders to the govern-ing regime.

Chieftaincies have such officeholders as well. However, their positions are not so clearly differentiated, nor do the very top office-holders feel responsible for the maintenance of the entire system. Instead, each nodal point in the structure has an exact replica of the officials at the center of the system. When pressures build up, seg-ments can break off, fully equipped to carry on the governing functions of the parent body. Contrarily, in the early state, many officeholders at the center carry out unique duties not shared by others in the system.

There is a state religion focused on the central ruler, and even though local authority structures may be modeled on that at the center, they are not identical to it. There are unique duties, functions, titles, and rituals at the apex of a state system that are not found in its segments. This is not so, or very much less so, for chieftaincies.

These then are states, or more precisely, early states. Our object in this volume is to examine the ways in which states have evolved out of previous forms, focusing attention on earlier types of organization or contemporary structures that are comparable. Without going into detail, we can simply assert that industrialization is a watershed dividing states into those that are committed to this mode of production and those that are not. Industrialization is associated with such radical changes in demography, economics, social organization, and the utilization of resources that wherever it develops it brings with it a new and recognizable way of life. We assume that it is also associated with fundamental changes in political organization.

Theories of State Formation

As Elman Service points out in his essay, theories of state origins can be divided into two schools: those that stress conflict and those that stress integration. The argument is reminiscent of a similar one discussed by Dahrendorf (1959) in his analysis of the failure of Marxian theory to predict the outcome of class conflict in industrial society. Like Service, Dahrendorf argues that all of social theory is either conflict- or integration-oriented. He equates the latter type with structural-functionalism and notes that it assumes all societies to be generally stable (not changing) systems of structured parts which are integrated to form functioning wholes based on a widespread consensus of values (Dahrendorf 1959: 161). He notes sympathetically that at any given point this description is reasonably valid for most societies not faced with rapid social change.

Those who use conflict approaches, says Dahrendorf, focus all their attention on change, on instability rather than stability. The approach assumes that dissent, not consensus, and conflict, not cooperation, are the fundamental features of social systems. Instead of integration and adaptive functioning, conflict theories see the opposite—increasing disintegration held in check by coercive forces of social control (Dahrendorf 1959: 162).

This is the Janus-headed quality of social theory. The two approaches are mutually exclusive attempts to comprehend a common social reality in which in fact conflict and integration coexist. Unfortunately, each theory has basic assumptions that are, as Morton Fried says in his chapter, "diametrically opposed."[3] It is therefore difficult to view the common reality from both points of view.

Applying the conflict approach to state origins, we theorize that increased centralization of governmental institutions arises out of competition between groups. Populations, or segments of them, vie for access to scarce resources, and ultimately this process leaves one group dominant, at least for a time. This can occur through conquest, through increasing population density that presses on resources forcing one group to take power, or through the possession by one or a few kin groups of traditionally privileged access to resources not granted to other groups. This unequal access is for Fried a prior condition, indeed *the essential* condition for the evolution of statehood. Those having such access have to protect it. To do so they must use force and stabilize the differential relations to resources by means of a system of centralized government that makes them into a ruling elite. As Fried puts it, the state receives its "key impetus" from the need to protect the stratification system. This is manifest in "the forward marshalling repressive sanctioning forces [of society] for the purpose of supporting an otherwise vulnerable system of stratification." And this fundamental competition for resources—a kind of bedevilled Darwinism—drives society toward a Rousseauistic civilization based on increasing inequity among the various classes of the polity.

In his previous work, Fried has made a distinction between primary states—that is, states formed in the absence of any other centralized polity—and secondary states. For him and others (see Price's chapter as well) the fact that other states are already present creates factors not present when states are formed in isolation. Conflicts between states and non-state polities may be the most significant cause of the emergence of secondary states. For this reason, Fried and those who follow him on this point maintain a distinction between the two varieties.

The opposite position, that stressing the integrative functions of the state, is taken by Service (1975). Holders of this view accept the demonstrable fact that state formation involves countless conflicts. However, they would follow Service in focusing attention upon the enormously increased capacities that state systems have for coordinating and organizing large numbers of people, often of different ethnic and ecological backgrounds. While conceding that in extreme situations such activity may involve coercive force or the threat of such force by a central government, the integrationist stresses the point that early state government generally receives widespread recognition and support from those who live under its sway. The theory is based, then, on the notion that states are formed by governments and their legitimacy among citizens. Centralized government offers protection and security, machinery for settling disputes, and access to sustenance in exchange for loyal acceptance of an overlordship that satisfies new needs in a changing situation. It is these kinds of benefits that bring people into this new form of political organization and lead them to accept its benign but demanding yoke. For integration theory, social stratification is coterminous with state formation. For conflict theory, stratification occurs first. Service's chapter in this book summarizes his own research on the topic (Service 1975) and reports that there are no known cases of social stratification prior to statehood. He argues instead that those conditions leading to centralized government bring with them the development of a ruling group or class. In this sense social stratification is a result, not a cause, of state formation.

In his chapter Fried clearly sees that the disagreement between Service and himself on this point is crucial. Accordingly he presents suggestive but not conclusive evidence that stratification was in fact an early feature of ancient societies in the Near East. He notes that stealing in Hammurabi's time was punishable with increasing severity depending on the social status of the individual or institution concerned. Unfortunately for the argument, Hammurabi's time was a post-state formation period. More important, thievery as a punishable offense is documented for both non-state and state societies. Therefore it cannot, in my opinion, be used as evidence for "invidious access" to resources. Similarly Fried's evidence that statehood produces hints of social rage and rebelliousness through its coercive rule is ambiguous. The rebels referred to in the early law codes could very well be other members of the ruling class and their lower-class followers who seek the replacement of one regime by another. Fried's passage also refers to "justice" and the "welfare of the people" and speaks out against oppression of the weak by the strong. Such "benefits," it seems to me, support Service's theory as well as Fried's.

And there it stands. Except for Barbara Price on secondary-state formation, the contributors to this volume avoid clear identification with one side or the other of this theoretical controversy. The reason, I believe, is a growing awareness that each side has some validity. The formation of states does result from competition over scarce resources when different groups have unequal access to the available supplies. States do clearly create benefits for their citizenry, who are in turn obligated to support a ruling class. People do also resent inequity and may even rebel against invidious privileges that deprive them of access to resources while granting access to others. Case material from history and ethnography can be found to support or refute all these positions and others as well (Cohen 1978).

Lately the examination of such material has led to a more synthetic position in which state origin is viewed as a systemic process. In this view, state formation is an "output" or effect of any one or more of a number of factors. The initial impetus could be population pressure or circumscription of a population, long-distance trade, warfare and military organization, conquest, defense, internal strife, protection of privileges by a higher ranking group, or the benefits to be derived from subordination to centralized authority. Elsewhere I have shown that none of these factors alone is sufficient to produce centralization or is consistently antecedent to state formation.[4] In many instances hypothesized causes can be shown to be consequences instead. The facts tend to disappoint anyone who emphasizes one causal nexus over another. It is now becoming clear that there are multiple roads to statehood, that whatever sets off the process tends as well to set off other changes which, no matter how different they are to begin with, all tend to produce similar results. It is this similarity of result, I believe, that has clouded the issue of causality. Similar results—the state—imply common antecedents. Unfortunately, as the data are compared, as more cases appear in the literature, historical sequences support the notion of multiple and varied causes producing similar effects.

The reason for this is clear. Once a society begins to evolve more centralized and more permanent authority structures, the political realm itself becomes an increasingly powerful determinant of change in the economy, society, and culture of the system. After the tendency to centralized control has been triggered, the hierarchical structure itself becomes a selective determinant that feeds back to all the sociocultural features to make them fit more closely into its overall pattern. Early states as far removed as Incan Peru, ancient China, Egypt, early Europe, and precolonial West Africa exhibit striking similarities. Thus the state as a form of organization is an emergent selective force that has sent humankind along a converging path.

Wright's chapter, the original version of which was written in 1970, as well as his other writings (see Wright and Johnson 1975), uses this synthetic approach. His goal is a model that will explain state formation as a process in which many variables are interlinked in ways that produce increased hierarchical and managerial control over decision making. The way in which his model-building and testing program has developed is a fascinating memoir in intellectual history. Because of his openness, flexibility, and lack of commitment to any particular set of assumptions, Wright has been able to show that for his material, the same general subject matter alluded to in Fried's essay, that of population increase, does not substantially affect state development. Nor do his data support the notion of increased inter-regional trade and militarism until *after* the state has been founded. These results have forced Wright to look at other factors of interethnic conflict and at societal reorganization rather than at circumscription and increased density of population.

The ethnographic case studies in this volume on Mexico, the Chad basin (Nigeria), and Baluchistan tend to support a synthetic view of state origins rather than one side or the other of the Fried-Service debate. For example, the Hunts' chapter, like other of their writings (e.g., Hunt and Hunt 1976), investigates what Wright calls "managerial theory" and what others refer to as the "irrigation hypothesis" (Wittfogel 1957). The chapter shows in excellent detail the kind of coordinating activity that is necessary when an area evolves an irrigation-dependent ecology. The Hunts demonstrate that, whether a cause of statehood or not, irrigation where it is present is a major focus of political action. Under conditions of scarcity, water for irrigation makes people competitive, dishonest, and quarrelsome. All water managers, no matter how they are recruited or what privileges they enjoy, are also political leaders. The Hunts theorize that this is inevitable because of the vital role of irrigation in local subsistence and the continuing disputes in which water managers must, willy-nilly, be involved. The situation makes irrigation a focus of politicization, and if and when a more centralized, more stratified society evolves, control of irrigation becomes an aspect of elite power.

On the other hand, irrigation can operate without hierarchy. The Hunts' essay shows that while irrigation strengthens centralized authority, it is neither a necessary nor a sufficient cause of state government. Indeed, we are told that farmers can develop their own system of water distribution, though they tend to use officials to settle disputes. Hunt and Hunt attribute Cuikatec statehood to population pressure and warfare. However, they also emphasize the benefits derived from the adjudicative, coordinating, and managerial functions of the elite. In other words, their interpretation of the factors that brought statehood to Cuikatec support both conflict and integrationist theories.

Philip Salzman's chapter examines irrigation agriculture within a complex pattern of interaction between sedentary agriculturalists and nomadic pastoralists. According to his interpretation, the centralization of Baluchi government is rooted in the geographical situation. Periodic droughts force nomads to become predatory raiders against the settled agriculturalists of the region, who use a supply of water to irrigate their farms. This conflict makes it difficult for the two groups to establish symbiotic exchange relations during wetter years. Ultimately—I would say inevitably—a major nomad group changes raiding into conquest, and its leader sets himself and his supporters up as overlords of the irrigated farm lands. The previous owners of the water are deprived of access. which goes to the rulers and their nomad followers. Thus the formerly free and autonomous farmers become serfs who exchange labor for their lost water. The now settled and monarchical nomad leader becomes an intermediary between the sedentary agriculturalists, whom he protects against nomad raids, and the nomads, whom he uses as a reserve militia to quell revolts and among whom he distributes the agricultural products he obtains as state revenue. The ramifying patrilineal linkages of nomadic segmentary descent systems (a widespread feature of pastoral nomads) give them capabilities for mobilizing militarily that are not available to the less unified farmers. Thus the nomads have an automatic advantage whenever trouble breaks out.

Fried could with some justification say that Salzman's case supports his theory. But the matter is not so simple. According to these data, it is not a ruling group that exerts force over a deprived population to form a state. Rather it is the deprived group—the nomads—that is moved ultimately to unite under a leader and *reverse* an invidious situation. This it does with a vengeance, turning former haves into have-nots in a centralized polity that provides new benefits to nomads, creates increased security for agriculturalists, and grants ruling monarchical status to the leader who mediates between nomads and sedentary populations.

The interesting feature of this case is neither the "invidious" pattern of access nor the "benefits" provided by state formation. Rather it lies in the interaction between factors of ecology, interethnic relations, and leadership functions that Salzman skillfully analyzes into an understandable process of state formation. Given irrigation, droughts, and relations between nomads and settled farmers, the end result of drought-produced raiding is conquest and a new form of more centralized control by a ruling group of nomads who become sedentary. Salzman extends his theory by suggesting that where a single population engages in both farming and herding, as in North Africa, mediating roles are less necessary and hierarchy less well developed.

In the chapter comparing the formation of three state systems in the Chad basin, I have isolated two distinct pathways to statehood. The first of these, exemplified by Borno and Fombina, is another instance of interaction between nomads and agriculturalists. These data add further support to Salzman's findings and Wright's theorizing that local supplies of farmer-controlled pasture or water may change to the disadvantage of nomads. In these cases intensified interaction and shortages led to mixed farming for some nomads, who then became more oriented toward hierarchy while maintaining contact with their nomad cousins. Increased demands from previous owners of the land for fees, tributes, and other exactions, in addition to cultural differences, produced tensions between the in-migrant nomads and the agriculturalists. In both cases nomads eventually triumphed and developed centralized institutions for dominating the region.

The second pathway is one in which sedentary agriculturalists aggregate into walled towns to defend themselves from attacks by neighboring state systems. Previous forms of dispute settlement through fission then become impractical, while increased population size and intensified land use increase the work load of the headmen and their councils of elders. This group develops into a noble or governing stratum, abrogates exogamy rules if such exist, and becomes an upper class within the nascent state.

In terms of benefits versus conflicts over unequal access to resources, the nomad-agriculturalist path is similar to that described by Salzman. On the other hand, the sedentary agricultural route to statehood leans more in the direction of benefits than of conflict. Although the movement toward statehood is set off by conflict and defensive reactions, in such situations ordinary people eagerly give up rights in order to benefit from the advantages of town life and the functions performed by the ruling group. Indeed, it is increased demands for adjudication and leadership by the rulers that force the classes to separate.

The three cases from Nigeria, Salzman's Baluchistan case, and the irrigation ethnography by Hunt and Hunt all refer in one way or another to "secondary" states. Even ancient Borno was formed by leaders who were aware of the Islamic law and political theory of the state systems of North Africa. Barbara Price addresses the problem of secondary states in her chapter on state formation in Middle America. Assuming the distinction between primary and secondary states to be a useful and significant one, Price goes on to develop hypotheses as to why some societies opt for secondary state formation, while others do not.

Using her materials from Middle America, Price theorizes that where early states exist, they tend to expand toward areas whose resources they wish to control. This competitive pressure sets off processes of state formation, including intensified use of resources as well as demographic changes among local peoples. If, in Price's terminology, the target society has a "weak infrastructure" for harnessing energy, then the resulting secondary state will be unstable; if the infrastructure is weaker still, "tribalization" will result. The most common determinant of infrastructure stability, she suggests, is irrigation agriculture. The greater the capability to harness energy, the greater the tendency for both primary and secondary states to develop urban centers. Price suggests that nonurban states are *always* secondary, while *all* primary states have urban centers.

Why all this should occur as it is described, or whether such patterns of state development are widespread, is not clear. From other research it appears that irrigation enhances centralized governmental institutions but is neither a necessary nor a sufficient cause of their development (cf. Hunt and Hunt 1976). The West African materials are instructive here. In a number of cases (Harris 1965; Netting 1972; Cohen 1976) pressure from neighboring polities has led to patterned reactions by those receiving such pressures. These include running away to more remote areas, being conquered and absorbed as an ethnically distinctive group of subject-citizens, and setting up of a "secondary" state in reaction to continuous attacks. Irrigation is not involved, nor are previous infrastructure differences. In the West African cases referred to above (Mbembe, Kofyar, and Bura) each polity that evolved greater degrees of hierarchy did so amidst other quite similar groups that remained politically less complex. Researchers have found that differential hierarchical organization has resulted from varying degrees of outside attack (Mbembe) and/or a differential need to utilize leaders for dispute settlements (Kofyar, Bura). As Price suggests, the latter development stems from the narrower population distribution occasioned by defensive needs. But in the West African cases neither irrigation nor infrastructure variation has been observed to explain variations in the degree of centralization.

Another problem raised by Price's chapter, and discussed in my own, is whether the distinction between primary-state and secondary-state formation is a fruitful one. Fried's position on this point is well-known, and he reiterates it here. Secondary states are propelled into existence by primary states in their region. This basic distinction in provenience makes the two types distinct. Khazanov (1978) agrees with the position and argues strongly for it. So does Price, but she also notes that once the process has been initiated, "secondary" states go through changes similar to those of primary states and for similar reasons. In other words, primary and secondary states differ in the way they are set into motion: the triggering events are dissimilar. But the internal interactions necessary to transform a non-state society into one recognizable as a state do not vary significantly from one kind of state to the other. In their concluding analysis of twenty-one detailed case studies of state formation, Claessen and Skalník (1978: Conclusion) accept the idea that states may be traced to pristine (primary) or secondary provenience, but then note that both types go through gradual and similar developments.

Weissleder's essay resuscitates the tradition of earlier writers like Herbert Spencer, Louis Henry Morgan, and Sir Henry Maine, whose classical backgrounds were better than those of most contemporary scholars. It is clear that studies of state formation must ultimately bring us back to the classical materials. Western history must be part of any world sample and theory of social evolution. Weissleder's skill with classical Greek and his philosophical and anthropological training give him a unique set of tools for reexamining state formation from Aristotle's own point of view—that of a scholar whose society had undergone such a process in the remembered past.

Aristotle saw the state as a means by which a people could achieve an autonomous existence. He viewed it as an association of differing groups based on reciprocity or mutual benefits among individuals and groups, who accepted inequities of status and power. The basic unity of this political system lay not in the family, as has been supposed, but in a complex, potentially large domestic organization based on a controlling or founding patrilineage. The unit included an extended patrilocal family with ramifying cadet lineages, slaves, and other servile non-kin members and their families. For Aristotle the city-state consisted of an organized political system governed by leaders drawn from the headships of these domestic units. By contrast, the pre-state was based on scattered domestic groups related primarily by marriage and descent. He theorized that the state evolved when population became more compact and when specialization of labor, trade, and scholarship created coordinating needs that made kinship an inadequate means for organization. Weissleder interprets Aristotle as conceiving of the process in "evolutionary" terms. Out of the household organization, adapted and expanded superior-subordinate role dyads evolve to relate household heads to one another and to the authority structure of the city-state.

Aristotle's state is, in Weissleder's depiction, a beneficent one. Cruelty, injustice, and an increase in power result from bad situations, poor rulers; they do not inhere in the institutions of statehood itself. As I read Weissleder's interpretation, Aristotle's idea of the state supports Service's theories but not those of Fried. In my view, this stems from an overgeneralized conception of social stratification in the latter's work. Horizontal strata are not organized as such in Aristotle's conception of the early state. Instead they are cross-cut by bundles or sets of hierarchically organized units, which are in turn organized into the city-state. These units may cooperate and compete, and within them people may obtain rewards or "access to resources" in return for service and loyalty. Such access can be differential depending on age, sex, wealth, descent, and slave vs. free status. In such a conception, for example, slaves are viewed not only as a separate class, but as additional members of large domestic organizations. This is more akin to recent work on slavery in traditional Africa (Meirs and Kopytoff 1977) than to conceptions of society in which horizontal strata separate more and less privileged groups.

The final chapter in this volume takes a "macro" perspective on state formation. Carneiro sees the process as a continuing one in which states are still forming, absorbing one another, and dying out. He asks what the overall trend of this process is. The data are clear: states are getting bigger and fewer, and the trend is exponential. Carneiro suggests that it follows the direction set by the biological principle of mutual exclusivity. This principle states that species using the same resources must eventually compete and conflict; in the process some species win, others lose, and the victors enjoy the spoils. Balances may be struck, but shortages are inevitable and so therefore is conflict and ultimate "exclusion." On this basis, using some suggestive data, Carneiro predicts a world state by A.D. 2300.

As he notes, others have considered a similar idea and come up with similar results—for differing reasons. Adams (1975), however, has rejected the notion, noting instead that nations require complementary and opposite units if they are to survive. They persist, he says, partly as reactions to like units. Therefore, in his view the trend will continue until the world contains two states; then the situation will stabilize. Extrapolation is difficult for phenomena we understand much better than state formation. And it is therefore difficult to take sides in this matter. But the overall trend is important. Carneiro has described the long-term fate of most nations—extinction as separate entities and incorporation into larger units. How and why this extinction and incorporation occurs and what effects it will have are matters that call for more research and more concern.

Some Concluding Remarks

This volume does not cover every bit of research and theory related to the origins of states. The authors have instead elected to present major theories and new data that shed light on these explanations. Although each theoretical position includes elements of the other, each tends to stress different causes and effects. Fried is impressed with the needs of those in power to control access to scarce resources and believes that the state emerges out of actions by the powerful to restrict access to resources and sustain their control. Disputing this view, Service has shown that in the course of history situations arise that demand the larger-scaled coordination of population units. People would not accept the unequal privileges brought on by such increased hierarchy, and its enforced subordination, if they saw in it little of benefit to themselves. Using this theory, non-ruling groups are not seen to be primarily an exploited class. In a number of cases they give up previous autonomy voluntarily in order to gain security and social-political opportunities open to them only through subordinate or lower-status membership in the state. Where Fried's views lead one to think of instances of conquest and enforced subordination, Service's suggest cases of states forming in local areas through more peaceful processes of social growth and change.

The two positions have been somewhat oversimplified. Neither Fried nor Service is so naive or so lacking in subtlety as to deny any validity to the other's position. Each admits that there are both costs and benefits to all members of a polity that evolves from a pre-state to a state system. But each represents, as Service suggests in his chapter, a different tradition of social analysis.

Somewhere between the approaches of Fried and Service, but closer to that of Service, is a systems approach, espoused by field workers like Wright in archaeology and myself in social anthropology. We see state origin as a multiple feedback system in which pre-state polities in various situations respond to selective pressures by changing some of their internal structures, or by subduing a competing group, or by establishing themselves as dominant in a region, or by gaining control of water resources, or whatever. This initial shift sets off a chain reaction of other changes that leads ultimately, whatever the beginning, to a similar end—the state. The view is similar to Service's in that the state is seen as a solution to problems that demand more centralized coordination of the polity. (Whether people accept more control willingly or unwillingly is an empirical question.) The view is similar to Fried's in that it accepts conflict and power seeking as a basis for "selective pressures." It differs from his approach in not seeing stratification as a necessary precondition for state formation.

I believe that the case studies in this volume, with the exception of Price's, tend to support a more eclectic, non-doctrinaire position than either Fried's or Service's. Although conflict is present in some way in

most of the cases of actual state formation described here, so are benefits, problem solving, conquest, and a host of other factors. But the
votes are not all in. Clear-cut hypothesis testing should now be the
rule. We have enough theories and propositions, including contradictory ones, to keep us busy for the next decade. The job ahead is to con-
front our theories with the facts.

In this regard, it is important to keep in mind some important
issues that have not been treated in this volume because of our attempt
to remain within contemporary theoretical constructs. Two substantive issues that come immediately to mind are (a) the sacralization of
the monarch as statehood emerges, and (b) the state as an expression
of emergent ethnicity. In both Service's (1975) treatment of state origin
and Claessen and Skalník's (1978) comparative analysis, it is clear that
as the state emerges from a non-state background the leader of the
emerging dynastic family is endowed with supernatural powers that
help him or her to nurture the welfare of the state, to adjudicate fairly
among factions and disputants, and to triumph over foreign enemies.
The necessary political duties of state leadership are sacralized. This
sacred dimension often develops from the supernatural powers previously held by local headmen, but there need not be a precursor. It is a
function of the awesomeness of state power and the magnification of
power differentials that accompany the emergence of a stable, non-
fissioning centralized government. One of the conundrums for those
who see the state as "exploitative" is the fact that in many early states
voluntary tributes to the monarch *increase* during times of shortages.
The people demand of the monarch that he conduct prayers and rituals
for their welfare—and emphasize this through their tributes.

While little is said in this volume about the state as an emergent
ethnic entity, the topic is one that anthropologists most especially
should consider. As I have noted (Cohen 1978), the state creates a new
role, that of citizen-member. In so doing it has the capability of uniting
differing ethnic groups under one centralized polity. However, no matter how disparate its segments are ethnically, the polity tends to be a
culture-creating social entity; given enough time and not too many
infusions of new ethnic groups, the state becomes more culturally
homogeneous, creating a "polity-induced" ethnicity. The process is
continuous and never-ending. The state not only creates a new form of
stratified polity; it is also a constant stimulus for the creation of new
ethnic units. *E pluribus unum* is a political statement, but it has had
undeniable cultural effects.

Finally, and underlying much of the debate that circulates around
the topic of state origins, are questions of epistemology and philosophy that tend to determine which types of theories are more appealing.

Those who see the state as a solution to problems that offer no alternative except more centralization of power are more positivistic, more "objective" in their analyses and theories. For them (e.g., Service, Wright, and myself in this volume) the state is neither good nor bad. It is a natural phenomenon, like hunters and gatherers. Like all cultural entities it must be understood in its own context, on its own terms. For this purpose we can describe it, classify it, analyze it into parts and relations, but we do not judge it as good or evil compared to other political forms experienced by humankind in social evolution. This does not mean that we should rule out cost/benefit analyses that attempt to assess what gains it has produced and what its evolution has cost in human lives and values. Nor should we rule out studying the inequities associated with power differentials and think about designing ways to improve such matters. Those who see the state as adaptive do not see it as perfect; indeed, adaptation means the task is never done, because the environment being tracked is also evolving and changing.

Those who espouse a more Rousseauistic or Marxian type of conflict theory combine political analysis with moral accounting. From this perspective state origins are seen first as a drama that reveals the moral nature of political order. State systems are associated, once they evolve, with an impressive magnification of power differences and inequity in stratified sociopolitical systems. This feature of early states stimulates indignation in many conflict theorists and empirical researchers, giving their work a direction and moral purpose absent in other approaches. The "integrationists" as described by Service, and the systems analysts referred to above, are the descendants of earlier exponents of cultural relativism; practitioners of a so-called non-evaluative social science. Underlying the theoretical and substantive debates of this volume, therefore, is another more emotional issue: how we should address our data. On the one hand are detached, dispassionate "objectivists"; on the other are those whose research into social evolution gives them an opportunity to comment on basic issues of justice, equity, and humane social organization. This fundamental difference in approach is, I suspect, what makes a rather esoteric subject so fascinating and what provides the passion and enthusiasm manifest throughout this book.

Acknowledgments

This introduction was written during 1976-1977 while I was a Fellow at the Center for Advanced Study in the Behavioral Sciences, Palo Alto. While the views expressed in it are my own responsibility, the Center was responsible

for conditions of collegial stimulation and delightful tranquility under which
it was written. Funds for the Fellowship came from the National Science
Foundation. The writer is grateful for this support as well as previous grants
by NSF and The National Endowment for the Humanities for the fieldwork
phase of this research.

I also wish to thank Henri J. M. Claessen for a number of useful criticisms and clarifications, and both Claessen and co-worker Peter Skalník for
the opportunity to read manuscript drafts of their work on the early states.

Notes

1. This does not mean that I accept a Spencerian definition of evolution which
   decrees it to be a set of changes and processes involving increasing complexity and differentiation (Carneiro 1973). In my view, evolution is simply
   "descent with modification" (including zero modification!). This view is
   more in line with Wilson's (1975) conception of evolution as an interaction
   between a system and environment. It includes as well, therefore, the possibility that a society will become simpler or become extinct.

2. The previous definitions do not require any separate classification of preindustrial and industrialized states. However, the trait list definitions
   clearly require such a separation, since almost all such lists include statements about the economic organization of society.

3. Although Fried uses this phrase to characterize the relation of his position
   to that of Service, it can of course be applied as well to the relations between
   conflict and integration based theories in social science as a whole.

4. This statement and what follows paraphrase the conclusion to my detailed
   examination and reformulation of the problem of state origins in Claessen
   and Skalník (1978).

References

Adams, R. N.
  1975   *Energy and Structure: A Theory of Social Power*. Austin: University
          of Texas Press.
Carneiro, R. L.
  1973   Classical Evolution. In R. Naroll and F. Naroll (eds.), *Main Cur-
          rents in Anthropology*. Englewood Cliffs, N.J.: Prentice-Hall.
Claessen, H. J. M., and P. Skalník (eds.)
  1978   *The Early States*. The Hague: Mouton.
Cohen, R.
  1971   The Political System. In R. Naroll and R. Cohen (eds.), *Handbook
          of Method in Cultural Anthropology*. New York: Natural History
          Press.
  1976   The Natural History of Hierarchy: A Case Study. In T. R. Burns and
          W. Buckley (eds.), *Power and Control: Social Structures and Their
          Transformation*. London: Sage.
  1978   State Origins: A Reappraisal. In H. J. M. Claessen and P. Skalník
          (eds.), *The Early States*. The Hague: Mouton.

Dahrendorf, R.
  1959   *Class and Class Conflict in Industrial Society.* Stanford: Stanford University Press.
Engels, F.
  1891   *The Origin of the Family, Private Property, and the State.* Reprint edition, E. B. Leacock, ed., 1972. New York: International Publishers.
Fortes, M., and E. E. Evans-Pritchard (eds.)
  1940   *African Political Systems.* London: Oxford University Press.
Fried, M. H.
  1967   *The Evolution of Political Society.* New York: Random House.
Harris, R.
  1965   *The Political Organization of the Mbembe, Nigeria.* London: HMSO.
Hobhouse, L. T., G. Wheeler, and M. Ginsburg
  1915   *The Material Culture and Social Institutions of the Simpler Peoples.* London: Chapman and Hall.
Hunt, R. C., and E. Hunt
  1976   Canal Irrigation and Local Social Organization. *Current Anthropology* 17: 389-411.
Khazanov, A. M.
  1978   Some Theoretical Problems of the Study of the Early State. In H. J. M. Claessen and P. Skalník (eds.), *The Early States.* The Hague: Mouton.
Koppers, W.
  1963   *L'origine de l'état.* Sixth International Congress of Anthropological and Ethnological Sciences 1960, vol. 2, pp. 159-168. Paris.
Krader, L.
  1968   *Formation of the State.* Englewood Cliffs, N.J.: Prentice-Hall.
Lenski, G.
  1966   *Power and Privilege; A Theory of Social Stratification.* New York: McGraw-Hill.
Lowie, R. H.
  1927   *The Origin of the State.* New York: Harcourt, Brace, and World.
Meirs, S., and I. Kopytoff (eds.)
  1977   *Slavery in Africa.* Madison: University of Wisconsin Press.
Murdock, G. P.
  1959   *Africa: Its Peoples and Their Culture History.* New York: McGraw-Hill.
Netting, R. McC.
  1972   Sacred Power and Centralization: Aspects of Political Adaptation in Africa. In B. Spooner (ed.), *Population Growth: Anthropological Implications.* Cambridge, Mass.: MIT Press.
Service, E. R.
  1975   *Origins of the State and Civilization: The Process of Cultural Evolution.* New York: Norton.
Southall, A.
  1956   *Alur Society.* Cambridge, Mass.: Heffer.
Wilson, E. O.
  1975   *Sociobiology: The New Synthesis.* Cambridge, Mass.: Harvard University Press, Belknap Press.

Wittfogel, K.
   1957   *Oriental Despotism: A Comparative Study of Total Power.* New
           Haven: Yale University Press.
Wright, H. T., and G. Johnson
   1975   Population, Exchange, and Early State Formation in Southwestern
           Iran. *American Anthropologist* 77: 267-289.

Classical and Modern Theories
of the Origins of Government

ELMAN R. SERVICE

Although the whole of the Western world's thought on the origins of government may not be adequately represented in Table 1, it seems that all of the major nontheological theories—that is, classical secular-philosophical and modern scientific—can be usefully delineated with a brief discussion.

There are two major types of theories, each including several subtypes. The major types may be labeled *conflict theories* and *integrative theories*. It should be remarked that in actuality conflict and integration are not mutually exclusive as factors in a society's equilibrium;[1] but here we are concerned with characterizing *theories*, not actuality.

Conflict Theories

INDIVIDUAL CONFLICTS

Conflicts between individuals, seen as the catalyst for the creation of forms of government that would curb the ensuing social disruption and threats to the security of individuals and their possessions, have been the basis for two major kinds of theories: (a) social contract theories; and (b) social Darwinism.

(a) Social contract theories are best exemplified by the writings of Hobbes, Locke, and Rousseau. These three, distinct in many important respects, are nevertheless traditionally classified together as a sort of school because of their common assumption that "society" (government, more accurately) originated in a contract, or some form of

21

TABLE 1   *State Origins: An Outline of the Major Theories*

Conflict Theories	Integrative Theories
Individual Conflicts	*Circumscription*
Social Contract	Geographical Barriers
Social Darwinism	Military Barriers
Inter-societal Conflicts	*Organizational Benefits*
Conquest	Redistribution
Darwinian Selection	War Organization
	Public Works
Intra-societal Conflicts	
Class Struggle	
Kin-group Struggle	

agreement, among discrete individuals who removed themselves from an anarchical "state of nature" in order to live together under law and justice. However, we need not accept this agreement as an actual theory of the origin of the state.

According to a prime authority (Kendall 1968: 376):

> . . . none of the three committed himself unambiguously to the "historic-ity" of a freely negotiated contract among men in the act of emerging from a state of nature. Hobbes, for example, was willing for the subscribers to his "contract" to be bludgeoned into participation by any strong man capable of forcing their compliance. Locke was willing for the partici-pants to be nursed into compliance by a "godlike" king. Rousseau placed great stress on the role of a "founder," or legislator, in midwifing the contract into existence over a long period of time.

In actuality, therefore, these were arguments about the *nature of society,* not about the origin of government. The problem these men addressed had to do particularly with the relation of individual persons to the society (or government). And here the three men were alike in making a clean break with the prevailing and long-standing Aristo-telian (Augustinian-Thomistic) theory of the individual's dutiful subordination to a God-given immutable social order. The social con-tract emphasized a *right* rather than duties—the right of self-preserva-tion—and this was revolutionary. From the social contract school, we have inherited various notions of good statecraft that embrace legiti-macy (with its allied idea of the consent of the governed), a political morality involving protection of "inalienable" human rights, majority rule, even equality before the law.

But, to repeat, these theories have to do with the nature of ideal society, not society's origin or its actuality. Above all, they lie outside our field of interest because they bypass the major political problems: the relation of *groups* to each other within a society as a feature of statecraft, and the related conduct of the society itself in foreign affairs. In terms of the evolution of political theory, the greatest significance of the social contract theories lies in the extraordinary break with the prevalent Aristotelian and theistic philosophy of government.

(b) Social Darwinism has taken several forms, but the one to be mentioned at this point has to do with the conflict that arises out of the competition of individual entrepreneurs (and individually guided, independent firms). Although Herbert Spencer and other social scientists (especially Malthus) anticipated Darwin in important respects, it was the wide and powerful impact of the idea of natural selection as promulgated by his work *On the Origin of Species* that was so catalytic in our intellectual history. At any rate, the theory eventually best known as social Darwinism involved the assumption that out of conflict in the competitive economic arena would arise the economic and then the social and political preeminence of superior persons. Essentially, then, this was a justification of stratification, classes, inequality—if based on relatively free competition. The most usual force counterposed to this rise of the superior was the action of the state itself in limiting free competition and in its socially ameliorative activities. But, as in the case of the social contract theories, social Darwinism has little relevance to our problem of the origin of the state, since it deals essentially with the relations of *individuals* to each other and to the state and vouchsafes some opinions about what the state ought to be or become—but little about its basic nature or origin. (But it should be quickly remarked at this point that there is another form of Darwinian theory that is *supra*-individual, and which rewards further attention. This will be discussed in the next section as Darwinian selection.)

INTER-SOCIETAL CONFLICTS

"Inter-societal conflicts," as a convenient rubric, introduces two types of theory that are much more modern in outlook but also less philosophical and more "materialist-economic" than individual conflict theories. These are conquest theory and Darwinian selection.

(a) Conquest theory is the form of conflict theory that is much more closely related to modern sociological thought than social contract thinking and social Darwinism precisely because it is concerned with the relations of whole groups and societies. As first promulgated convincingly by Ibn Khaldun in *The Muqaddimah: An Introduction to History* (1377), the "conquest" version of conflict theory was concerned with the dynamic relations between nomadic and sedentary societies. Later, and apparently independently, Jean Bodin continued this preoccupation with conflict—and, it should be emphasized, with secular, materialistic, and geographic determinants of societal forms, considered comparatively and inductively, in contradistinction to the social contract theorists.

Bodin's theory has provided the basis for a more modern sociological school of conflict theorists, represented particularly by Ludwig Gumplowicz, Franz Oppenheimer, Albion Small, and Lester Ward. All these men were impressed with "Darwinian" conflict and the idea of survival-of-the-fittest, but in the present context we wish to note their emphasis on *conquest,* the permanent subjugation of losers by winners that gives rise to the basic repressive forms of the state.

Although Herbert Spencer's more usual emphasis was on the selective process by which winners survived losers in evolution, he sometimes seems to say that if the compounding of a society by conquest and forceful subordination of parts is to become permanent, it is an important factor in promoting centralization of the regulating agency. But this situation remains unstable; ". . . it tends toward stability in proportion as the regulating agents, major and minor, are habituated to combined action against external enemies" (Spencer 1967: 37). This latter point, in part at least, is reminiscent of the ideas of other conquest theorists in that it presupposes that the military organization is the model for the political organization (in its centralizing aspect, certainly)—that the military hierarchy and its insistence on discipline and subordination are, when carried over into peacetime, the basis of government. But to Spencer this carryover results not precisely or only from conquest but from the *prevalence* of intersocietal conflict; the army, so to speak, remains on guard consistently over time, and the population is mobilized under it as it becomes both political and military.

(b) The notion of the prevalence of inter-societal conflict also suggests Darwinian selection. By this term we mean something other than the social Darwinism discussed above. We mean competition among whole societies, not among individuals, groups, and firms within a given society. Whole social systems *do* compete, and the "survival of the fittest," in Spencer's terminology, must have been an important factor in political evolution.

A contemporary of Spencer's, Walter Bagehot, was the first avowed social Darwinist. He also applied the idea of selection to the problem of the origin of the state—most cogently in his small book

Physics and Politics (1872). He argued, in essence, that warfare among societies in early stages of societal evolution would "naturally select"—as survivors or victors—those with the best leaders and the most obedient populace. As he phrased it, "the tamest are the strongest." Bagehot also addressed himself to what he believed was a main problem in political evolution: how to perpetuate leadership, how to make an "official" out of a hero. In early times this must have become accomplished by creating an "office" of headship which would be passed on from father to son.

INTRA-SOCIETAL CONFLICTS

Intra-societal conflicts are of two basic kinds: class struggle and kin-group struggle. The first of these is the basis of the theory of state origin so widely promulgated by Marxists. The second is a refinement of it advanced by some anthropologists who found the original Marxist theory to be inadequate in certain respects because of some erroneous assumptions about the economics of primitive society.

(a) The class-struggle theory of the origin of the state first achieved fairly wide currency with the publication of *Ancient Society* by Lewis Henry Morgan (1877). This book described the probable stages of social evolution and, of particular interest here, characterized primitive society as basically communistic, lacking commerce and entrepreneurs, private property, classes of rich and poor, and despotic rulers. Toward the end of the book, Morgan argued that increased productivity (brought about by technological improvements) eventually led to private property, economic classes, and the state. Marx and Engels were much impressed with this book, and after Marx's death Engels published their joint appreciation of Morgan as *The Origin of the Family, Private Property, and the State* (1891).

Engels' book expands on some of the important ideas suggested by Morgan. It holds that as certain primitive collectivistic (or communistic) societies improved their technological means of production and increasingly traded the surplus products that resulted, their economies changed from production for use to production of commodities; with this kind of production there rose middlemen, entrepreneurs, capital, and thus differences in private wealth—culminating in economic classes. The repressive state attends to the political buttressing of this kind of society, erecting a structure to preserve the class interests of the rich. The succession of stages which culminated in modern types of state apparatus was "ancient" to "feudal" to "bourgeois" (in Europe, that is; the "oriental epoch" was seen as outside the experience of Western civilization).[2] In a nutshell, the difficulty with the class-struggle theory is that we cannot find anywhere in the primitive world even a suggestion that commodity production and private wealth were likely preconditions for the class system or the primitive state.

(b) "Kin-group struggle" is my label for the result of attempts by some modern anthropologists to correct the shortcomings—now so obvious—of the class-struggle theory. The first attempt was the interesting work of the famous British archaeologist V. Gordon Childe, who, though not wholly successful, at least made a more anthropologically sophisticated (and more complicated) scientific analysis of the actual rise of the state and civilization in the classical archaic regions.

Childe's fame rests on two notable achievements: his scientific reanalysis and his pathfinding work in archaeology itself. With respect to this latter point, it should be pointed out that most, if not all, of the archaeologists excavating the classical sites (mostly in the Middle East, on the Mediterranean islands, and in Greece and Rome) were not sophisticated in anthropology—their "science" had to do with excavating techniques, and their major intellectual effort was concerned with the history of classical art and architecture. Childe was the first important classical archaeologist to attempt broad-gauged, comparative, evolutionary-functional analysis of the archaic materials, and a whole generation of modern anthropological archaeologists thank him for it.

Childe described the "urban revolution" as the hallmark of civilization and the feature which attended the birth of the original civilizations. His latest statement of his theory (1950) indicates that "urbanism" is not the sole cause of civilization but a useful rubric suggestive of several factors that seem to come together. Of these, the most important was the progressive techno-economic changes affecting the economic structure and social organization of communities. Mainly the economic changes consisted of greater production, which in turn allowed the greater demographic size and density of societies suggested by the term "urban." But, in addition, the greater productivity created a "social surplus" of food which made possible the rise of a nonproducing class of military and political bureaucrats, craftsmen, priests, and entrepreneurs. Here Childe retains a residue of Marxism; and, more important, he also sees the state arising as a repressive structure functioning to preserve this class structure (which includes many non-entrepreneurial elements). This aspect of his theory still allies him basically with the class-struggle aspect of Marxism, however more sophisticated his exposition.

Childe's "urban" conception has been mostly superceded; we

know now that some archaic civilizations lacked cities, while others became states before their cities developed. As Robert McC. Adams says (1972: 73), "truly urban agglomerations depend upon the institution of the state as a political form, and the emergence of the latter is but an aspect in turn of the formation of stratified class societies." This statement is a good summary of the more modern view of the relation of urbanism to the state. It almost reverses Childe, as it were, about the significance of urbanism, but it also returns us to Childe's rewriting of the Marxist class-conflict theory of the repressive state. Several modern anthropologists have modified the argument by having "stratification" of kin groups rather than entrepreneurial individuals forming classes of rich over poor, as in the original Morgan-Engels version. But this modification retains the essence of the original theory: that the state was formed to settle the conflict caused by the repression of the masses by some kind of upper stratum or aristocracy. This thesis has been argued at the greatest length and most convincingly by the ethnologist Morton Fried, a contributor to this volume.

According to Fried, a stratified society is one with "genuine socioeconomic classes associated with markedly contrasted standards of living, security, and even life expectancy" (1967: 225). In primitive society these strata are not formed by rich capitalists and poor workers but by whole kin groups, some of which have better access to strategic resources than others. The magnitude of internal disputes and conflicts caused by this inequality is so great that the kin-organized social system cannot cope; hence an increasing emphasis is placed on non-kinship repressive mechanisms. "It is precisely these mechanisms that mature, coalesce, and form the state" (*ibid.*). "The primary functions of the state [are] internal and external maintenance of a specific order of stratification . . ." (p. 235). Stratification is thus so closely coterminous with the state as to be virtually synonymous with it. This presumably is the reason that Fried cannot provide us with any instances of a stratified society that has not yet acquired its state apparatus or that seems to be in the process of forming it.

Integrative Theories

Theories of state formation stressing factors that counter the normal centrifugal forces that threaten societies may be called integrative theories, so as to make clear their differences from the conflict theories. There is little doubt that every human society has propensities which in certain circumstances will result in conflict between component groups that is likely to have centrifugal effects. And there is also little doubt that all successful societies have countered these propensities with numerous kinds of integrative devices. The state itself, of course, is—according to both conflict and integrative theories —the supreme integrative apparatus above the level of kinship institutions. The question is, why and how does it integrate societies? In conflict theory it prevents disintegration by repressions of various kinds; such repressions are its main function and, thus, why it comes into being. In integrative theories, the government counters disintegration by doing *other things*—performing functions that are not directly countering disintegration so much as benefiting society and thereby indirectly fostering integration. One is tempted to suggest parallels such as the contrast of punitive with rewarding "sanctions," or negative with positive "reinforcements."

CIRCUMSCRIPTION

Circumscription theory emphasizes environmental influences that counter centrifugal tendencies by making the leaders of potentially dissident groups prefer maintenance of their *status quo* within the society to any other alternative. These circumscribing circumstances are of two kinds, geographical and military.

(a) Geographical barriers as a necessary condition for the formation of successful states have been emphasized by Robert Carneiro (1970). He has described regions in which areas of unusually good land are surrounded by areas of very poor land, such as deserts, or by unproductive mountains, or by the sea. When population pressure results in increased competition and warfare in such regions, the weaker, or vanquished, groups cannot simply move away, as they typically do in regions where resources are less differentiated. When *very* rich land is tightly circumscribed, subordinated groups become absolutely tied down in their lower-class or caste status. The constant military dominance that would maintain this situation would in time become structured as a repressive state—much as Spencer would have it. Certain archaic civilizations do manifest these geographical extremes: the river valleys of Egypt and coastal Peru are probably the best examples, since both are imprisoned within true deserts. All others so improved their habitats by water control and terracing that the cultivated areas were very much preferable to the wastelands outside. One problem is that these improvements must have been in some measure contingent on the prior development of some kind of governmental leadership and control. Certainly, however, such circumscription must have been a powerful factor in the continuance and further development of the society. It is interesting that the two most drastically circumscribed societies, Egypt and Peru, were also those with the longest epochs of peaceful development.

(b) Military barriers must sometimes have played an important circumscribing role in much the same way as deserts, mountains, or sea. The integrative forces in this case reside in the protection a successful government may provide against the threat from outside enemies.

The outside military threat may be of either of two kinds. One is the threat from a rival society of a roughly similar sort, as in the case of the quarreling independent city-states of lower Mesopotamia. The more usual kind, and the one that presents the best case for circumscription, however, is the threat from raiding nomads, often simply professional predators and thieves who keep the society in a continual state of apprehension or near-siege. The simultaneous rise of defensively walled city-states and nomadic pastoralists in northern China is probably the best example of this latter kind of circumscription.

The defense against persistent nomadic raiders is likely to lead to permanent installations such as walls, hilltop forts, and citadels, and to increased urbanism. It is difficult to make treaties and alliances or even to maintain peaceful trade with mobile groups that combine and subdivide, join new leaders, topple old ones, and in general are not permanently governed; hence no long periods of peace can be expected. Such circumstances, it may be added, lead not only to defensive agglomerations but to an intensification of agriculture.

ORGANIZATIONAL BENEFITS

Organizational benefits have an integrative effect because rebelling against the society that provides them means exchanging them for a much less favored or uncertain future outside the society. Organizational benefits are of three basic kinds: a redistributional economic system, a successful war organization, and public works.

(a) Redistributional systems have to do with the mobilization of both natural resources and persons in production and consumption. A complex administrative machinery can arise as more and more specialized workers are subsidized (professionalized) and as more diversified ecological zones are exploited. The products of the skilled workers and diversified zones are brought together and used to support the court, bureaucracy, priesthood, and army; but these benefits are also given to some extent to the citizens at large, at least when they are not self-supporting, as in some kind of emergency.

Long-distance trade is frequently an important aspect of the redistributional organization. The products to be exported must be acquired, carriers or shippers subsidized, protection arranged for them, and the goods accepted in return stored and at some point redistributed. Such trade helps a government by benefiting the leaders of the subsidiary component chiefdoms, for they in turn can redistribute valued goods to their own followers. The integration achieved is of course due to the organismic division of labor (by skills and regions) so emphasized by the sociologists Spencer, Weber, and Durkheim.

(b) A war organization that has been successful is often a notable integrative feature of a society. Success in war not only confers benefits by bringing in wealth of various kinds (booty, captives, tribute) but greatly enhances the "national pride." And, other things being equal, it is the government that in the end is credited with the victories of the army.

(c) Public works are usually seen as of two major types, religious and secular. Of the first, the most common and most notable are monumental temples and tombs (sometimes huge pyramids). The most important of the secular are complex systems of water control. All the classic civilizations built huge temples and tombs, and all except the lowland Maya had complex hydraulic systems.

It seems obvious that the various regions of a society are strongly integrated to the extent that they depend on participation in the network of canals that nourish their fields. Centrifugal tendencies of any of the parts are therefore counteracted. Karl Wittfogel (1957) wrote an interesting book describing the tremendous governmental power that results from bureaucratic control of the water system. The problem of relating this power to the *origin* of the state, however, is not simple, since the state seems in some cases to have antedated the water system. Furthermore, it can be argued that some, at least, of the water systems were built by accretion, begun through some kind of local initiative of families and extended by cooperation. But certainly once both state and hydraulic system are in existence, the system is a very important support to the bureaucratic organization of government.

It is tempting for us, as products of the Industrial Revolution, to rate a secular system of public works as a more important integrative device than a religious system of public works. This could be a mistake in a consideration of the archaic civilizations, for they were all intensely theocratic. A. M. Hocart says (1936: 217):

> It would be an error to put such works [as irrigation canals] in a category by themselves as "utilitarian" in opposition to "religious" works such as temples. Temples are just as utilitarian as dams and canals, since they are necessary to prosperity; dams and canals are as ritual as temples, since they are part of the same social system of seeking welfare.

In theocracies religion pervades all activities, and the public monuments and temples where the ceremonies take place, built by the corvee labor of the society, pertain to the whole society. In reading about classic theocracies, one realizes that of course the redistributional system must have worked, of course the wars must have been won and the ditches dug and maintained—that is, the secular duties of the state must have been successfully accomplished. But the power of religion is manifest. Its positive as well as its negative conditioning seems to be by far the most direct and pervasive cause of the "consent of the governed." And here, too, is the best context for that consent to be "engineered." How comfortable to know that your own society's gods are the greatest in the universe and that the representatives of those gods on earth are their holy descendants. For then you are truly a chosen people!

Conclusion

I have presented integrative theories in such a way as to suggest that they are not mutually exclusive. All of the six archaic civilizations (Mesoamerica, Peru, Mesopotamia, Egypt, Indus, and China) were somewhat, if not thoroughly, circumscribed by geographic and/or military barriers. All exhibited, as well, the organizational benefits of a complex bureaucracy administering a redistributional economy, the military order, and great public works. A theory that singles out any particular one of these to the exclusion of the others—as most notably in the cases of Carneiro's geographic circumscription and Wittfogel's hydraulic public works—must be oversimplified.

On the other hand, the various conflict theories are too heterogeneous to be thrown together. For our purposes, theories about individual conflicts can be dismissed out of hand, simply because they are about individuals rather than societies. Theories about intersocietal conflicts come closer to our subject and seem more plausible, but there is abundant evidence in history and ethnology that pre-state societies do *not* truly conquer and absorb an enemy, creating a repressive state in the process. If this were the most important means by which the first true civilizations, the six pristine classical empires, came about, there should be some evidence of such a process somewhere—if not in the archaeology of the civilizations themselves, then among the many instances of conflict known to ethnology. But always a successful conquest followed by integration was accomplished by a preexisting state.

However, the other factor in inter-societal conflict, Darwinian selection, must indeed have been a matter to reckon with. In a context of inter-societal conflict, the best-governed society would be the strongest and would tend to prevail and probably even to grow in power as weaker societies joined it. This selective factor would be important in assuring the continuation and growth of the superior society; but it would not account for its origin. In other words, the competition-selection factor only attests to the significance of good government; it is not its cause. It is, in other words, an important setting for an evolutionary episode.

Intra-societal conflicts, based on the struggle between classes or strata in the society, no longer seem plausible enough to argue about. All the archaic civilizations, and the ethnologically known primitive states, for that matter, did have strata: basically there were two, the *governors* and the *governed,* sometimes phrased as "aristocracy" and "peasantry." But nowhere, even in the simplest, most primitive cases, were these strata based on differences in wealth, forms of property, or "differential access to strategic resources." The difference was in political and religious *power,* and this power was so absolute that it needed no buttress such as economic advantage.

The question thus turns on the origin of this political power. Darwinian selection is important in a certain context, a set of competitive circumstances, and provides impetus once the power structure embarks on the road to civilization. Similarly, circumscription, geographic or military, is a condition that powerfully modifies the centrifugal tendencies of such a society. But the nature of the power structure itself is not revealed by a consideration of those circumstances.

Fortunately, we do have a great deal of evidence from a range of simple to complex ethnological instances that spells out the likely course of events. Essentially, the road to civilization was the developmental route taken by a few simple bureaucracies formed by hereditary (institutionalized) leaders and their relatives. Under rather unusual environmental conditions (competitive-selective and eventually circumscribed) this development fulfilled the tremendous potentialities that lay in centralized leadership. Redistribution (and especially trade), military organization, and public works were all basic in the classical civilizations, but all must have had small beginnings in the simple attempts of primitive leaders to perpetuate their social dominance by organizing such benefits for their followers. These organizational benefits, growing ever more complex, more useful, and finally necessary to the society, assured the continued maintenance and defense of the society—*and* the continued growth in power of the bureaucratic organization itself.

Notes

1. As Simmel (1908) and Coser (1956) argue, certain kinds of conflict can play reinforcing roles in integration, as we shall see later. These men are the most frequently cited by sociologists, but I cannot forbear emphasizing that as early as 1767 Adam Ferguson wrote brilliantly on the positive integrative functions of conflict in cultural evolution—and for that matter in individual psychology.

2. This simple version is not quite fair to Marx himself, for unpublished sketches (*Grundrisse*) he left show that he was aware of the complications in moving from particular historical types of precapitalist societies to general evolutionary stages (see Marx 1965). But it is Engels' book which holds the stage and which, therefore, must be cited here.

References

Adams, R. McC.
  1972   Patterns of Urbanization in Early Southern Mesopotamia. In P. J. Ucko, R. Tringham, and G. W. Dimbleby (eds.), *Man, Settlement and Urbanism*. London: Duckworth.
Bagehot, W.
  1872   *Physics and Politics: Thoughts on the Application of the Principles of "Natural Selection" and "Inheritance" to Political Society*. Reprint edition, 1956. Boston: Beacon Press.
Carneiro, R. L.
  1970   A Theory of the Origin of the State. *Science* 169: 733-738.
Childe, V. G.
  1950   The Urban Revolution. *Town Planning Review* 21: 3-17.
Coser, L. A.
  1956   *The Functions of Social Conflict*. Glencoe, Ill.: The Free Press.
Engels, F.
  1891   *The Origin of the Family, Private Property, and the State*. Reprint edition, E. B. Leacock, ed., 1972. New York: International Publishers.
Ferguson, A.
  1767   *An Essay on the History of Civil Society*. Reprint edition, D. Forbes, ed., 1966. Chicago: Aldine.
Fried, M. H.
  1967   *The Evolution of Political Society*. New York: Random House.
Hocart, A. M.
  1932   *Kings and Councillors*. Reprint edition, 1970. Chicago: University of Chicago Press.
Ibn Khaldun
  1377   *The Mugaddimah: An Introduction to History*. 3 Vols. Reprint edition, 1958. New York: Pantheon.

Kendall, W.
   1968   Social Contract. *International Encyclopedia of the Social Sciences*,
           vol. 14, pp. 376-381.
Marx, K.
   1965   *Pre-Capitalist Economic Formations*. Trans. by J. Cohen; ed. and
           with an Introduction by E. J. Hobsbawm. New York: International
           Publishers.
Morgan, L. H.
   1877   *Ancient Society*. Reprint edition, 1964. Cambridge, Mass.: Harvard
           University Press, Belknap Press.
Simmel, G.
   1908   *Soziologie: Untersuchungen über die Formen der Vergellschaftung*.
           4th ed., 1958. Berlin: Duncker and Humblot.
Spencer, H.
   1967   *The Evolution of Society*. Ed. and with an Introduction by R. Car-
           neiro. Chicago: University of Chicago Press.
Wittfogel, K. A.
   1957   *Oriental Despotism: A Comparative Study of Total Power*. New
           Haven: Yale University Press.

The State, the Chicken, and the Egg; or, What Came First?

MORTON H. FRIED

When I presented the original version of this essay at the 1975 annual meeting of the American Anthropological Association, I began with a quote from a novel by Saul Bellow. It now seems much more appropriate to begin with some words from A. E. Taylor's translation of the *Timaeus:*

> If then, Socrates, we find ourselves in many points unable to make our discourse of the generation of gods and the universe in every way wholly consistent and exact, you must not be surprised. Nay, we must be well content if we can provide an account not less likely than another's.

It is of consequence that I found these words quoted in an article published by Thorkild Jacobsen about twenty years ago. Jacobsen was attempting to reconstruct the forms of political organization at the time of transition from prehistory into history and during the centuries that followed. The substantive ideas offered by Jacobsen are obviously of relevance to the subject of the present chapter but cannot receive critical attention here. Let me note only that outstanding scholar's general attitude toward the possibility of achieving a completely satisfactory solution of the riddle of the ancient Mesopotamian political structure. Considering the kinds of evidence to which he had access, Jacobsen said that we "must of a necessity relax the stringent claim of 'what the evidence obliges us to believe' and substitute for it a modest 'what the evidence makes it reasonable for us to believe'" (Jacobsen 1957: 95).

Few problems in the repertory of social science are at once more provoking and less accessible to direct research than those concerned

35

with the evolution of the political organization of human society in general and with the origins of the state in particular. Some scholars have seemingly avoided some of the most difficult questions by arguing the congruence of political organization and the state, but their approaches either fail to satisfy or provide identical frustrations when we seek to learn how incremental changes in political economy became qualitative shifts in the evolution of new levels of complex society. In this context, it seems advisable to identify myself as one of that company that sees the political state not merely as emergent from a long process of demographic, ecological, and economic development but as a source of revolutionary transformation of culture in general. I mean by that at least two things: that the emergence of the state transformed those sociocultural entities among which it appeared as an endogenous product, and that it sooner or later caused transformations in all other sociocultural aggregates with which it came into contact.

Fundamental to this conception is the notion that the state is something more than formally organized society, or even an aggregate of institutions and apparatus of social control at some specified level of complexity. Central to the concept of state on which this essay is based is an order of stratification, specifically a system whereby different members of a society enjoy invidiously differentiated rights of access to the basic productive necessities of life. It is not enough that the society should provide different or even grossly unequal levels of prestige for its members; it is essential that such differences of rank be intertwined with inequalities of economic access. Indeed, the state needs something more than this—a formal organization of power including but going beyond the social control functions of kinship. This formal organization of power has as its central task the protection (and often extension) of the order of stratification.

Although it seems fair to say that the foregoing assertions narrow the problem and remove some of the egregious fuzziness with which the question has been surrounded, enormous difficulties remain. On the side of archaeology, for example, resides continuing uncertainty in the identification of sure signs of stratification, particularly the distinguishing of markers of rank from the indicators of invidious differentiation of rights of access. On the side of the study of the most ancient documentary materials is an equally irritating lack of closure. As Samuel N. Kramer has sadly noted: "The Sumerian men of letters, as is well known, wrote no learned sociological and anthropological treatises. . . . [O]f systematic generalizations about their society and its institutions there is not a trace in their writing" (Kramer 1971: 1). Fortunately, the situation, while difficult, is not quite so dark. Indeed, Kramer is able to dig out quite a few things from the textual remains of myths, epics, hymns, lamentations, and "wisdom compositions" that help us in our quest. It is certainly true, however, that the ancients left no self-conscious history of the evolution of their earliest states.

One other difficulty must be mentioned at this preliminary moment. The foregoing caveats have been directed at the evidence pertaining to the emergence of those original states whose development was in a real sense *sui generis,* from endogenous stimuli, usually with no more advanced models present. These are what I have previously called "pristine states"; I find it essential to distinguish them from "secondary states," whose origins can be attributed to pressures from already existing states and which often use parts or all of the organization of some prior state as the model for emulation or improvement. These characteristics of secondary states create a tremendous difficulty for the student of political evolution who would use data derived from the study of such states as a source of information about pristine states. This difficulty is most conspicuous with reference to the problems of origins, since the bases of the former are in previously existing examples of the latter. Under such circumstances even the best documented case of secondary-state formation tells us little or nothing about pristine-state formation.

Apart from the problem of extrapolating pristine-state formation from understandings gained from the study of secondary states, other difficulties must be faced. The view of the state as the product of the accumulation of tiny variations over time has its own epistemological consequences. Consider the position put forth several decades ago by a widely read political scientist writing in the shadow of the work of Sumner and Keller:

> It is no longer possible to think of the State as a conscious invention, suddenly introduced as an antidote to confusion and chaos. The State must have evolved from rudimentary and inchoate beginnings, by a process of growth that was so slow as to have been all but imperceptible. . . . Even if the full record of that development were available, we would not be able to say precisely when the State began [Sait 1938: 105].

The view of evolution implicit in Sait's statement is fundamentally statistical and resembles the molecular biologist's conception of evolution as "change in gene frequencies." Once again, by adopting the definitional approach to the state proposed a few paragraphs back, certain difficulties may be eased. We can opt for the much larger-scale and only partially congruent approach in which evolution is viewed in terms of the appearance of new forms. Unfortunately, the second alternative brings in its train greater difficulty in objectifying the markers of evolution. It is evidently much easier to obtain agreement about an essentially mathematical statement of frequency than it is to achieve consensus about what constitutes a new form. However, it can both help and comfort us to realize that even in the "harder" biological sector, the gene-frequency approach tends to be most applicable to data derived from contemporary, living populations. It is less usefully applied historically and is least efficient in paleontological contexts. Indeed, in dealing with paleontological data, a reversal occurs, speculation about gene frequencies becoming less reliable than consensus recognitions of typological differences. The analogy seems particularly appropriate in view of the paucity of finely meshed data on the earliest evolving states.

Adoption of a typological approach to the problem of the evolution of the state returns me to my earlier remarks about the pivotal nature of the definition of the central phenomenon. Placing stratification at the core of that definition risks assuming at the outset precisely what is to be proven in the course of investigation and analysis. An alternative position has recently been presented by Elman R. Service, whose view of the state as a mature social institution does not differ too much from mine, agreeing with it in the critical elements of exploitation, class division, forceful control, and tendencies to external aggression. Significantly different in Service's approach, however, is his view of the genesis of the state, which is almost diametrically opposed to that I have presented. The debate can be focused on our contrasting identifications of the critical independent variable that appears constantly in a field of important but shifting dependent variables as one surveys the accumulated evidence of the emergence of state structure and organization. The feature selected for prime attention by Service is best introduced in his own words: "I . . . call it . . . the factor of governance by benefit. This general factor is, so far as I can see, a universal in the formation of all persevering power relationships" (Service 1975: 223).

Service criticizes an earlier statement in which I asserted, in terms similar to those already introduced above, that the state was rooted in stratification—in differential access to strategic resources which, I had theorized, could have arisen out of a variety of ecological pressures affecting economic and social organization. To this positing of a key role for the developing disparity of socioeconomic statuses, Service issued a direct rebuttal: "I do not agree with the notion that these inequalities were a naked exploitation of the disadvantaged by the advantaged, with institutions based on physical violence arising to protect this stratification" (*ibid.*: 285). Where I would argue that the state comprises the formal marshaling of the repressive sanctioning forces of society for the purpose of supporting an otherwise vulnerable system of stratification, from which it follows that the need for protecting the stratification system supplies the key impetus for the evolution of the state, Service finds a more reasonable explanation of the evolution of state polities to lie in "the immense benefits of fitting . . . different niches and skills into a centralized redistributional system . . ." (*ibid.*).

Service does not deny that the emergence of the state is accompanied by the evolution of significant social classes, but his concept of "class" resembles what I have elsewhere treated as "rank," which is concerned with status differences having no bearing on access to strategic resources. (For fuller discussion of these distinctions, with ethnographic illustrations, see Fried 1967.) This is the way Service puts it:

> In all of the archaic civilizations and historically known chiefdoms and primitive states, the creation and extension of the authority bureaucracy was also the creation of the ruling class, or aristocracy. The "stratification" was thus mainly of two classes, the governors and the governed— political strata, not strata of ownership groups [*ibid.*].

In the same context Service adamantly states his conviction that the state emerged from conditions of mutual benefit. Although he does not take kindly to the labeling, I will refer to this as a kind of contract theory, seeking thereby to emphasize Service's conception of peaceful mutuality. Again, he puts the matter bluntly:

> Nowhere in the cases discussed [in his book] do we find the power of force used in the maintenance of the position of the governing strata over the ordinary masses. At least this is not recorded in the historical cases, nor is it visible in the archaeological record. In other words, there apparently was no class conflict resulting in forceful repression [*ibid.*].

Probably the single most critical case that can be scrutinized for the illumination it might shed on the controversy is that of the rise of the state in the ancient Near East. In the light of present knowledge, it is this area in which we find the most pristine-state formations. It is also fascinating because our knowledge of the region continues slowly but steadily to enlarge, partly because of the contributions of archaeologists and partly because of a continuous flow of new information from cuneiformologists and other specialists in the analysis of the most ancient documentary evidence in the world.

It is appropriate to begin with Service's demurral to the thesis which Robert McC. Adams adapted from Lewis Henry Morgan, that "class stratification . . . was the 'mainspring' and 'foundation' of

political society" (Adams 1966: 80, citing Morgan 1963: 224). The
thrust of Service's criticism is that Adams sees socioeconomic
classes where, at most, there exists only a sociopolitical class division. Service sees inequalities to be sure, but these are basically
aspects of the division of labor, having nothing to do with a division of
ownership or rights of access to productive resources.

While it remains impossible, as was suggested at the outset of
this essay, to offer completely satisfying proof supporting either the
Adams position or that of Service, it seems to me that the former is
supported by the greater weight of evidence, some of which has become
more widely known since Adams provided us with *The Evolution of
Urban Society.* In the remainder of my remarks I will allude to some of
the newer material but also to some previously cited by Adams.

We may begin with some remarks by Samuel Noah Kramer, whom
we have already quoted in a pessimistic mood concerning the possibility of discovering significant details of early Mesopotamian political organization from literary fragments of diverse kinds. In fact,
Kramer used his knowledge of such fragments to make the following
conclusions regarding the early third millennium B.C.:

> Normal life in Lagash, it is not unreasonable to surmise, was far from
> ideal, classless and equalitarian; the slave was no doubt often made to
> feel the lowliness of his position; the strong lorded it over the weak;
> justice was honored largely in the breach; the orphan and the widow were
> at the mercy of the rich and the powerful; the woman was treated as a
> second class citizen that could not inherit the property of her parents,
> even when there was no male heir [Kramer 1971: 4].

The passage is certainly grossly impressionistic and the final reference to problems of female inheritance in a strongly patrilineal system
does not adequately deal with the status of women. (Cf. Adams 1966:
82 for mention of cases of women as heads of households, ceremonial
donors, administrators, and long-distance traders.) What impresses
me is the clear-cut feeling of invidious economic distinctions: that
between slave and non-slave is most obvious, but, as we shall see,
there is considerably more. Most important, however, is the clear
implication of the importance of some kind of property that is held by
individuals or small kin groups and is alienable.

This is emphatically the view of I. J. Gelb, whose summary statement is worthy of citation at length:

> The basic unit of the agricultural economy of Mesopotamia from the
> oldest periods down to and including the Ur III period was the *é bitum,*
> "the estate, manor, household." . . . The estates represented the collective

patrimony of a family, which included the lord of the manor, his younger brothers, and his descendants. Parts of the property could be sold by one family to another. As buyers of property appear individuals, representing private families, and kings, representing royal families. . . . There is no need to waste time proving the fallacy of the "Templewirtschaft" theory, according to which all land was owned by the temples in the Pre-Sargonic period, or of the "etatistic" theory ("Staatssozialismus"), according to which all land was owned by the state in the Ur III period.

. . . Three classes of people lived on an estate: a) the free class . . . b) the semi-free class providing the main labour force for the estate, and c) the much less numerous slaves. The existence of these classes provides evidence of a stratified society already in the earliest periods of Mesopotamia [Gelb 1962: 225-226].

Stratification in historic Mesopotamian society is manifested in clear evidence of differential access to such strategic resources as arable land, housing sites and housing, agricultural tools, domestic animals, wagons and boats, feed grains, and various media of exchange. It is somewhat curious, therefore, to find Service stating flatly that "neither the presence nor the absence of a propertied merchant class by the time of Hammurabi can be proved" (Service 1975: 221). Indeed, Service believes there was not such a class. Even if there were, he says, it came late in the game and cannot reflect on the presence of stratification a thousand or more years earlier when the state took shape.

Admittedly, answers to these problems are not altogether satisfying, but Professor Service does not have things all his own way. No one, to my knowledge, has argued that the state develops out of capitalism, yet that is the formulation Service seems to be attacking. On the other hand, the central question is one of the alienation of rights of access from portions of the social community and one aspect of such alienation is the private transacting of critical economic activities. In this context it is interesting to note the legal practices of the ancient city state of Nuzi, which flourished near the present site of Kirkuk and is known for its legal tablets dated to the middle of the fifteenth century B.C. Nuzi recognized the status of slavery and also provided for at least two forms of indenture, each associated with different rights of access to strategic resources and to legal recourse. A recent study provides information on specific individuals:

that Tehib-tilla son of Puhi-senni was one of the most economically influential people in Nuzi, that he owned vast real estate, that he was in need of obtaining the services of others, strengthens the assumption that Tehib-tilla utilized the institution of a personal *tidennutu* as a means of securing a long-term labor force by using the *tidennutu* transaction to gain indentured servants [Eichler 1973: 46].

The *tidennutu* was a pawning of persons or property. As a pawning of one's own person, it is succinctly defined by Eichler: "The self-*tidennutu* contract represents a loan transaction that an impoverished Nuzi citizen, in need of obtaining definite capital, is forced to make" (*ibid.*: 47). It differed from a *hapiru* contract, "a form of commendation in which the indigent *hapiru*, because of his status as an 'outsider,' is compelled to become a dependent of a patron *in order to obtain the basic necessities of life*" (*ibid.*, emphasis added).

I agree with Service that the period of Nuzi history to which the literary materials in question pertain is much too late to be of direct consequence to an inquiry about the origins of the state. Significant, however, are the conclusions reached by Eichler, that antichretic institutions, which is to say the pawning of persons or objects so that their labor or use provides a source of profit to the creditor in lieu of interest payments, existed at least from the Old Babylonian period, going back to the beginning of the second millennium B.C., and perhaps three centuries earlier. Furthermore, according to Eichler, institutions similar to those demonstrated to have been in existence near modern Kirkuk some 3500 years ago were present at even earlier dates throughout central and southern Mesopotamia (*ibid.*: Ch. 3).

Actually, there is somewhat harder evidence of stratification in quite early historic (i.e., literate) periods, evidence that not merely shows differential access and individual ownership and property alienation but refers specifically to commercial activities. Petr Charvat has recently provided a summary of the social organization of Adab during what he calls the "kingdom-making" period, somewhere about 2600 B.C. Adab was just to the north of Sumer and seems because of its location to have been less subject to incursions from other developing states. Be that as it may, though fundamentally agricultural, the economy of Adab was such that "[t]rade and commerce contributed to the wealth of Adab citizens" (Charvat 1974: 161). Land could be bought and sold, although it is likely that transactions were complex, having to satisfy not individuals but the collective memberships of unilineal kin groups (*ibid.*: 162). Most interesting is the evidence that indicates the presence of a class of persons who may have originated from places outside Adab and occupied a special status. According to Charvat, "it seems clear that a group of Adab inhabitants possessing no landed property was transferable for services elsewhere," the services not being described. We do know, however, that these people were administratively differentiated from the general populace, being directly attached to the ruler and receiving rations from him (*ibid.*: 162).

Returning to a point made above, I wish to emphasize that the argument that stimulates a preexisting condition of stratification in the evolution of the state does not thereby require that the forms of stratification include an ancient capitalism. Confusion about this matter can destroy our capacity to deal with the central question. Capitalism is a set of rather precise forms of stratification associated in special ways with the ownership and mobilization of resources, labor, media of exchange, technology, markets, credit, and a host of other institutional variables, a few of which were anticipated to some extent in early forms of economic organization that did not take on the familiar, distinct overall pattern until relatively recent time. Far from being a phenomenon associated with pristine-state formation, capitalism, it seems, cannot emerge in such a state, but is the product of second-, third-, and even later-generation states. In this context it is interesting to take note of the suggestions of Vladimir Jakobson, a critic of some of the views put forth by his colleague I. M. Diakonoff. Jakobson objects to the notion that the price of land in ancient Mesopotamia could stand for capital; he argues instead that this would be true only if land were a freely marketable commodity in the context of a range of investment options. As Jakobson notes, it was to be at least another 3500 years after the period of his concern that the institutions implied in such a range of transactions would finally come into being (Jakobson 1971: 36-37).

The same author also offers an ideal-type scheme of five stages to describe the evolution of landed property in ancient Mesopotamia. He begins with an association of land and "the god of the community," which he differentiates from the apparently secular association of the entire membership of the community with the land. The third stage comprises a more restricted ownership by kin units that do not make up the whole community, and this leads, in turn, to ownership by much smaller domestic units led by patriarchs and finally to individual private property (*ibid.*: 33). Without commenting on the soundness of these "stages," I should like to observe merely that the point at which stratification emerges in this scheme is somewhat indefinite. Indeed, it may well be somewhat variable, depending on microecological conditions. In any event, it is quite sufficient to my conception of stratification that there be within a community some members, whether individuals or kin groups, who suffer invidious limitations on their rights of access to strategic resources.

Having disposed of capitalism as a condition of stratification, I now turn the other way and suggest that the rarity or special nature of transactions in immovable property is of little consequence to my general finding of the presence or absence of stratification. Information about the frequency and relative difficulty of effecting such transactions provides a more detailed view of the precise nature of the stratification system but is not involved in the simple test of presence or absence of stratification. The decisive thing is that some such transactions should have occurred at all.

This is the view expressed by Igor Diakonoff in his reconstruction of Old Babylonian society and in his speculations on the preceding social arrangements of the third millennium B.C. In Diakonoff's opinion, "non-temple and non-royal land existed everywhere in Southern Mesopotamia alongside of temple land" (Diakonoff 1971: 1-16). Transactions in non-temple land were likely to see ultimate ownership by "members of the administration, or usurers" (ibid.: 18). Having long known about the weak property characteristics of what Marx called "the Asiatic Mode of Production" and Wittfogel calls "Oriental Despotism," we are not surprised that such concentrations of wealth and property as may exist will end up in the hands of those who run the government, whether priests, generals, or civil administrators. It is enough for the present argument that invidious distinctions exist with regard to access to strategic resources.

While the earliest known legal materials come from periods a millennium and more removed from the events of first-state formation, those fragments we possess throw interesting light on the questions here discussed. This is the more so if it be granted that the institutions reflected in those earliest "codes," such as those of Eshnunna, Lipit-Ishtar, or Hammurabi, must have had a reasonable period of development prior to the period of the early second millennium B.C., when they are found fully articulated.

The codes impel me to question Service's assertion that "there was apparently no class conflict resulting in forceful repression" (Service 1975: 285). I find that statement incompatible with, for example, the twelfth and thirteenth laws of Eshnunna:

> A man who is caught in the field of a *muskenum*[1] in the *crop* during daytime, shall pay 10 shekels of silver. He who is caught in the *crop* [at ni]ght, shall die, he shall not get away alive. . . . A man who is caught in the house of a *muskenum*, in the house, during daytime, shall pay 10 shekels of silver. He who is caught in the house at night, shall die, he shall not get away alive [Pritchard 1950: 162].

A similar point may be made by citing various provisions of the later code of Hammurabi—for example, the eighth provision, which, in one translation, reads:

> If a seignor stole either an ox or a sheep or an ass or a pig or a boat, if it belonged to the church [or] if it belonged to the state, he shall make thirtyfold restitution: if it belonged to a private citizen,[2] he shall make good

tenfold. If the thief does not have sufficient to make restitution, he shall be put to death [*ibid.*: 166].

Just as it is not necessary to discover capitalism in order to find institutions involving invidious distinctions of access to strategic resources, so it seems unnecessary to seek self-conscious expressions of class conflict and class warfare in fledgling states. After all, class consciousness and class warfare are far from universal or even particularly acute in much of the bourgeois world today. On the other hand, I do expect to find some evidence of inchoate social rages in such manifestations as crime, problems with slaves, and even some very early or incipient peasant rebellions. The prologue to the code of Lipit-Ishtar is illuminating in this respect:

> When Anu and Enlil had called Lipit-Ishtar the wise shepherd whose name had been pronounced by Nunamnir—to the princeship of the land in order to establish justice in the land, to banish complaints, *to turn back enmity and rebellion by force of arms,* and to bring well-being to the Sumerians and Akkadians . . . [Steele 1948: 434; emphasis added].

The Code of Hammurabi, in its prologue, states the basis of the polity in ideological terms that strike a modern chord:

> Anum and Enlil named me to promote the welfare of the people, me, Hammurabi, the devout, god-fearing prince, to cause justice to prevail in the land, to destroy the wicked and the evil, that the strong might not oppress the weak . . . [Pritchard 1950: 164].

And in the epilogue a curse is pronounced on whatever usurper might seek to scorn and overturn Hammurabi's social order and the laws that supported it:

> May Enlil, the lord, the determiner of destinies . . . *kindle revolt* against him in his abode which cannot be suppressed. . . . May Inanna, the lady of battle and conflict . . . shatter his weapons on the field of battle and conflict; *may she create confusion [and] revolt for him* [*ibid.*: 179; emphasis added].

Teasing a coherent picture of the past out of bits and scraps is particularly dangerous when the would-be manipulator is dealing exclusively with secondary and tertiary materials. Yet the specialists do not write merely for their most immediate colleagues, and we in somewhat disparate fields have the duty and responsibility to read what they have produced and use it to the best advantage, at times triumphantly noting the support such materials provide for our

favorite theories, at other times announcing glumly the demise of yet
another beautiful theory before the onslaught of some freshly discovered facts. Neither the archaeological nor the historical evidence is
yet sufficient for decisive conclusions about the nature of pristine-
state formation, particularly about the role of stratification in such
development. I think, however, that I have been able to show that the
thesis offered by Elman Service in his recent book is not yet fully con-
vincing in the light of contending evidence. Indeed, some of the most
important scholars presently considering the question come out close
to the other side of the debate, which asserts a leading role for a prior
condition of stratification.

Acknowledgments

The author wishes to thank Elman Service for his many constructive criticisms, not all of which could be properly assimilated in the time available for
this revision. It is also a great pleasure to acknowledge the considerable
bibliographic help provided by Dr. Norman Yoffee, an anthropologically
oriented cuneiformologist. The generosity of these scholars does not mean
that they are in any way responsible for the opinions here expressed or for the
errors of omission or commission that may be discovered.

Notes

1. At the time of the laws of Eshnunna the *muskenum* was probably a palace
   or temple hierarch.
2. It is of interest that the term translated by T. J. Meek in this passage as
   "private citizen" is *miskenum*, the same as that referred to in the previous
   note, which represents the gloss of F. R. Steele, a translator of the code of
   Lipit-Ishtar. Meek believes that by the time of Hammurabi the word had
   altered its meaning to "a man of the middle class, a commoner"; in the
   specific context rendered, Meek feels that "it manifestly refers to a private
   citizen as distinct from the church and the state" (Pritchard 1950: 166, n. 44).

References

Adams, R. McC.
    1966   *The Evolution of Urban Society: Early Mesopotamia and Pre-
            hispanic Mexico.* Chicago: Aldine.
Charvat, P.
    1974   Pre-Sargonic Adab. *Archiv Orientalni* 43: 161-166.
Diakonoff, I. M.
    1971   On the Structure of Old Babylonian Society. In H. Klengel (ed.),
            Beiträge zur Sozialstruktur des Alten Vorderasien. Berlin: Akademie-
            Verlag.

Eichler, B. L.
 1973   *Indenture at Nuzi: The Personal Tidennutu Contracts and Its Mesopotamian Analogies.* New Haven: Yale University Press.
Fried, M. H.
 1967   *The Evolution of Political Society.* New York: Random House.
Gelb, I. J.
 1962   *Social Stratification in the Old Akkadian Period.* Trudy Dvadtsat' Pyatogo Mezhdunarodnogo Kongressa Vostokvedov (Proceedings of the 25th International Congress of Orientalists), vol. 1, pp. 225-226. Moscow.
Jacobsen, T.
 1957   Early Political Development in Mesopotamia. *Zeitschrift für Assyriologie und Vorderasiatische Archeologie,* N.F., 18: 91-140.
Jacobson, V. A.
 1971   Some Problems Connected with the Rise of Landed Property (Old Babylonian Period). In H. Klengel (ed.), *Beiträge zur Sozialstruktur des Alten Vorderasien.* Berlin: Akademie-Verlag.
Kramer, S. N.
 1971   Aspects of Mesopotamian Society: Evidence from the Sumerian Literary Sources. In H. Klengel (ed.), *Beiträge zur Sozialstruktur des Alten Vorderasien.* Berlin: Akademie-Verlag.
Pritchard, J. B.
 1950   *Ancient Near Eastern Texts.* Princeton: Princeton University Press.
Sait, E. McC.
 1938   *Political Institutions: A Preface.* New York: Appleton-Century.
Service, E. R.
 1975   *Origins of the State and Civilization: The Process of Cultural Evolution.* New York: Norton.
Steele, F. R.
 1948   The Code of Lipit-Ishtar. *American Journal of Archaeology* 52: 425-450.

Toward an Explanation
of the Origin of the State

HENRY T. WRIGHT

This essay is concerned with research strategies for the investigation of the origin of the first states. The strategic problem is complicated by the type of explanations required and the samples available to test them. Most explanations that have been proposed, and no doubt those that will be proposed in the future, involve the interaction of a number of variables, regardless of whether a proponent chooses to specify one such variable as critical. Faced with such interaction, the laboratory scientist can create experimental situations in which some variables can be controlled so that the behavior of a few others can be observed. In contrast, field surveyors can obtain large samples that permit them to control statistically the behavior of most variables in order to consider the behavior of some others. Unfortunately neither of these avenues is easily followed by those who seek to explain state origins. Primary states are no longer evolving and could not be experimentally manipulated even if one wished; in the past only a few dozen primary states evolved and this number is insufficient for multivariate statistical studies. If neither experiment nor statistical control is feasible, how are multiple variable explanations to be tested? Before

---

This paper is another version of one prepared for an Advanced Seminar at the School of American Research in Sante Fe and published in *Explanation of Prehistoric Change*, edited by James N. Hill (University of New Mexico Press, 1977). The author and editors wish to express their gratitude to the School of American Research for its support of the conference and for permission to publish the article.

attempting to answer this question, let us consider some proposed explanations of the origin of the state.

Traditional Theories of State Origin

Past explanatory theories are useful because they indicate both the classes of variables and the types of variable linkage that have been, to some extent, concordant with the evidence. The typology of such efforts adopted below makes explicit the classes of variables that may be useful in the future. The examples chosen are predominately recent, not because they are structurally better than those of the nineteenth century but rather because the empirical evaluation of nineteenth-century explanations by recent workers has both increased and ordered our knowledge of early states. The later attempts of each type must account for this more comprehensive body of knowledge.

MANAGERIAL THEORIES

These involve certain activities whose complexity or structure requires certain kinds of management in the common sense of the term. Such activities might include irrigation or trade. Changes in management might involve increasingly professional administrators or increasingly despotic rulers.

Karl Wittfogel's influential general theory of Oriental or hydraulic societies, those in which the ruling class and the managing bureaucracy are identical, was first proposed in the 1930s and finally given full explication in *Oriental Despotism* in 1957. His propositions relevant to the origin of the state, defined as a professional government (Wittfogel 1963: 239), may be diagrammed as in Figure 1. In this and succeeding diagrams the numbers represent pages in the cited edition. Such diagrams are admittedly my interpretation of the various authors' longer and far more subtle presentations.

INTERNAL CONFLICT THEORIES

Internal conflict theories involve differential access to wealth, conflict or threat of conflict, and the subsequent emergence of the state as a mediating and dominating institution. An early example of this approach is that of Engels (1884). In 1957, I. M. Diakonoff published an explanation specifically concerning the formation of the state, defined as the administrative machinery of a class society, in Mesopotamia (Diakonoff 1969: 185). This explanation is diagrammed in Figure 2. There is an implication that the increased wealth of the ruling classes is invested in the means of production.

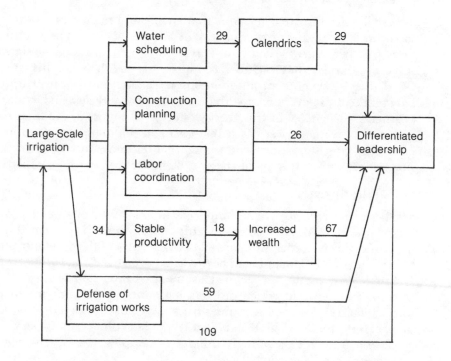

FIGURE 1

A Managerial Theory of State Origins (Wittfogel 1957)

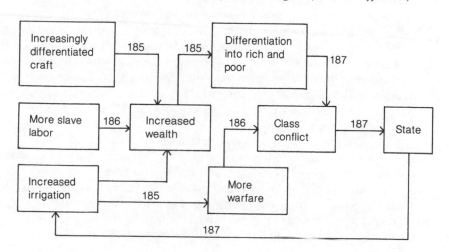

FIGURE 2

An Internal Conflict Theory of State Origins (Diakonoff 1969)

EXTERNAL CONFLICT THEORIES

These theories involve conditions that enable and require one society to control the means of production in another society. The institutions that permanently maintain this dominance constitute the state. Robert L. Carneiro has recently elaborated a general theory of this type. He defines a state as an autonomous territorial and political unit having a central government with coercive power over men and wealth (Carneiro 1970: 733). In this theory, shown in Figure 3, population growth is a prime mover. Each increment in population leads to increasingly larger and more centralized organizations. Once supra-local integration occurs, the rise of states and empires follows inexorably.

SYNTHETIC THEORIES

Synthetic theories involve the interrelated operation of several processes at once. A recent example of this type of theory is presented in the work of Robert McC. Adams. A specific theory of the development of the state in Mesopotamia can be extracted from his *The Evolution of Urban Society*. States are defined as hierarchically and territorially organized societies in which order is maintained with monopolized force (1966: 14). Figure 4 illustrates his analysis of Mesoamerica. Both managerial problems and external conflict are explicit factors here.

From these four seemingly different examples, four useful generalizations can be drawn:

1. States are variously defined as either a kind of government (that is, specialized and hierarchical) or a kind of society with such a government. Some authors add that the state maintains a monopoly of force.

2. All examples of theories involve the interaction of a number of variables, even if one is specified as a prime mover.

3. All examples involve implicit or explicit positive feedback processes leading to growth, but none involves stabilizing negative feedback processes. Specifically, the government makes investments in irrigation in the constructs of Wittfogel, Diakonoff, and Adams and strengthens military capacity in the construct of Carneiro; these actions lead to stronger government. However, the factors which limit the growth of primary states for periods of time or which lead to their decline have yet to be dealt with.

4. The connections between certain elements are neither specified nor obvious. For instance, how and why managerial needs or class conflict leads to specialized, hierarchical government is unclear.

Future general theories must involve carefully specified, multiple variable relationships governing both growth and stability. These relationships should express interrelations between management, internal conflict, external conflict, and other processes.

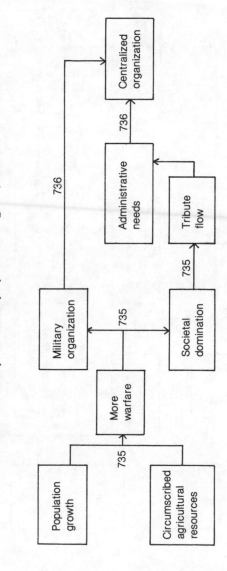

FIGURE 3

An External Conflict Theory of State Origins (Carneiro 1970)

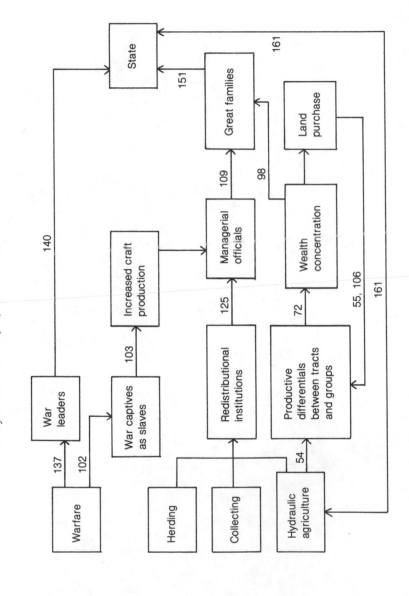

FIGURE 4

A Synthetic Theory of State Origins (Adams 1966)

Explanation and Test

In this essay an explanation of a variable's behavior will be the place of that variable in a tested theory. We seek explanations of complex cultural processes such as state evolution for quite practical reasons: at present the ramifications of planned changes in the cultural systems in which we participate often cannot be predicted. The type of explanation I seek should make specific explanation possible. But how are testable consequences to be generated from a proposed theory involving variable interaction, given the limited data available on state origins? Such consequences can be generated with a theoretically based systemic model.

By a *model* I mean a set of statements of dimension and variable definition and of variable relationship which represent a specific phenomenon, in our case a specific area of state development. Models need not be general and need not be theoretically based. Those that are so based can involve more than one theory. For instance, a model might involve tested theories drawn from plant ecology, geology, and communication science. A *system* is here considered a set of variables related in such a way that varying any one through its full range of values results in changes in all others. Note that a system is here defined as a type of formulation, not a phenomenon. Such a definition has a number of useful properties (Von Bertalanffy 1968: 55-77). It enables one to show which variables operate in a given system, even in systems with hierarchical or specialized regulatory subsystems that operate only under extreme conditions. Once a theoretically based systemic model has been constructed, consequences can be generated by providing initial values for the variables and successively transforming the various input conditions. Such generation is *simulation*. The end product of a simulation or the variable changes during a simulation can be tested with data from appropriate phenomena. Repeated testings of different simulation models against different cases should lead to progressive improvements in the theory and to increasingly better explanations.

States as Societies and States as Systems

States have been defined in many ways. Some definitions—for instance, those referring to legitimate force or property holding—deal with specific features sometimes found in societies far too simple to be considered states. The definition I am using refers to general features of social organization which necessitate other features considered definitional by others. For my purposes a *state* can be *recognized* as a society with specialized decision-making organizations that are receiving messages from many different sources, recoding these messages, supplementing them with previously stored data, making the actual decision, storing both the message and the decision, and conveying decisions back to other organizations. Such organizations are thus internally as well as externally specialized. Such societies contrast with those in which relations between the society's component organizations are mediated only by a generalized decision maker and with those in which relations between component organizations are exclusively self-regulating. In contrast, a state can be *conceptualized* as a sociocultural system in which there is a differentiated, internally specialized, decision-making subsystem that regulates varying exchanges among other subsystems and with other systems. Regulation involves information flow, even if it is expressed in flow of material items.

The conceptual definition has several implications of interest. First, information flow obeys the principle of channel capacity (Quastler 1955). For instance, individuals can perceive, reason, and communicate accurately only at a certain rate. Therefore, if an administrator is called on to handle information at a faster rate, either his organization ceases to operate effectively, or another administrator must be added to help carry the burden. If two administrators are required, a higher-order administrator *may* be needed to coordinate these two. With increasing information flow, more levels of hierarchy may be added, with the higher-order administrators making only a few general decisions about lower-order specific decisions. (These points are developed in Wright 1969: 1-6.) Traditional management theories such as those diagrammed in the first section of this chapter may be subsumed under such a formulation.

A second implication of the conceptual definition is that information flow cannot exist by itself. It is conveyed in the form of materials or energy. For instance, people, objects, food, and so on are needed to maintain specialized decision-making subsystems. Taxes, corvée, sinecured estates, and fines are all devices used in states for extracting such material support from other subsystems.

A third implication is that materials and human resources usually seem limited relative to the demands of the system. Therefore decision makers will usually engage in whatever competition and/or collusion might be possible without destroying the system in order to maintain their segment of the hierarchy. Such political action will further define the internal structure of the decision-making subsystem. Traditional internal conflict theories may be subsumed under such a formulation.

Given these definitions and implications, it follows that if one wished to test theories of state development, one would have to define the subsystems operating in a given case of state development and to devise some means of measuring the major flows into, within, and between these subsystems during this period of development. With such measurements and a body of theory, one could then attempt to predict changing patterns in the organization of the decision-making subsystem and proceed to test these predictions.

Now let us consider the problems that have arisen and the progress achieved in pursuing such a general strategy in one single case of state development.

Southwestern Iran as an Example of Research Strategy

Among all the areas where one could study early state development, Mesopotamia has a unique advantage. From earliest times, daily administrative records were kept on relatively durable clay tablets. These records enable one to test many kinds of hypotheses about administrative organizations. In my first research project in Mesopotamia, under the guidance of Robert McC. Adams, I worked not with state origins but with the structure of a developed Early Dynastic state in southern Iraq, using archaeological and textual data. Following the principle of channel capacity, this work demonstrated that the number of levels of administrative hierarchy in an organization was a function of the rate at which that organization had to process information concerning the activities it conducted (Wright 1969). It seemed logical that higher-order state governmental institutions might also have arisen in response to such information-processing problems. But what were the causes of such problems? Nearby southwestern Iran presented a practical natural laboratory for the study of the bases of state development.

Archaeologically attested state developments cover such vast areas and spans of time that it is difficult to investigate their organization in a season or two of fieldwork. For example, state development in southwestern Iran involved a number of interacting processes occurring during a period of almost ten centuries and in a diverse region covering more than 20,000 square kilometers. The work of Hole, Flannery, Neely and Helback (1969) provided an understanding of pre-state developments, and the work of the Délégation Archaeologique Français en Iran (summarized in Le Breton 1957) and the general survey of Robert McC. Adams (1962) provided a basic framework for the period of state development between 4000 and 3000 B.C. However, when I began my work in the spring of 1968, I had little accurate evidence of the variables that might be considered as elements in subsystems of a systemic model. I conceived of my work with this case of state development as being composed of two stages, each involving a number of field projects.

In the first stage, each project would be directed at elucidating two or more potential subsystems and structured in terms of one or more traditional hypotheses explaining state development. The end result of this procedure should, in the first place, be a set of tested hypotheses, some rejected and some accepted. The confirmation of any of the traditional particularistic hypotheses, derived from proposals such as those discussed in the first section of this essay, would not be conclusive given the standards we have set for useful explanation. Most of these hypotheses fail to explain at least one case of early state development. However, even if increased irrigation, population, or trade occurred in every case of state development, one would still have to demonstrate exactly how such changes determined the organization of decision making. In the second place, there should be demonstration of the relative changes in and relations between key variables in the potential subsystems. We should move from a position in which we know a potential subsystem existed, as we knew that rural population existed because there were small sites from the successive periods between 4000 and 3000 B.C., to a position in which we could demonstrate at least relative changes in key variables, such as aggregate population, average size of rural settlement, and the spacing of rural settlements. Furthermore we should be in a position to test hypotheses about the mechanics of these potential subsystems, such as the hypothesis that decrease in rural population involved agglomeration into more central settlements rather than the uniform decline of all settlements. At the end of this first stage we could begin assembling the systemic models within whose context possible explanations could be tested. Let me emphasize that such possible explanations are not simply generated or suggested by the fieldwork. They are generated by constant attempts to make explicit and question one's own assumptions in the light of the efforts of other workers in one's own and related fields. However, without the models, which can be constructed only with the aid of such fieldwork, there would be no way to provide exact tests of hypotheses dealing with such abstract concepts as channel capacity.

In the second stage each project would focus on the absolute measurement of one or more of the critical variables operating in the developed systemic model. In the case of certain variables, such as those relating to population, the measurements may require little or no additional data collection. In the case of others, such as those relating to agricultural production, the measurements may require the more extensive application of methods and research designs utilized in the first stage. In yet other cases, such estimation might require the application of new methods and research designs. In this second stage of research there would be a shift from predominate concern with the productive subsystems to predominate concern with the decision-making subsystems and with regulatory links between them and the other subsystems. The end result would be one test of a synthetic theory of state development utilizing a comprehensive systemic model of southwestern Iran between 4000 and 3000 B.C.

At the present moment three field projects contributing to the first stage have been completed, and one additional project has been planned. Direct evidence of the mechanics of population growth and decline, rural agriculture production, craft production and local exchange, and interregional exchange has been obtained. There is yet little direct evidence of transhumant herding, of higher-order decision-making, and of relations between various emerging states throughout Mesopotamia. Let me utilize aspects of the three field projects as examples of the strengths and problems of the approach outlined above.

In 1968 I planned an excavation project on a small town in the Deh Luran Plain, a valley marginal to the main area of state emergence on the Susiana Plain. I hoped to elucidate changing organization for warfare and for interregional exchange. The working model from which hypotheses were to be derived is diagrammed in Figure 5.

I argued that because of the town's marginal location, it would bear the brunt of any competition between states, and because of its location on the traditional trade route between southwestern Iran and Iraq, it would have evidence of changing flows of wood, stone, and other commodities being transported into lowland Mesopotamia. The specific hypotheses to be tested were (1) that competition over agricultural land, perhaps dictated by increasing population and decreasing land quality, required fortified towns and specialists in military administration, and (2) that increased participation in interregional exchange, whose growth was perhaps dictated by the increasing population of Greater Mesopotamia, required specialists in economic administration both to organize local export production and to redistribute imports.

No positive evidence of military competition was recovered in the excavations. Given the probably elementary level of warfare, such negative evidence means little. Patterns of competition were monitored in 1971 with survey methods. The data relevant to interregional exchange were most useful (Wright 1972). The reorganization and growth of early trade, beginning at about 3200 B.C., followed the appearance of administrative specialists. Therefore trade did not

FIGURE 5

The Working Model of 1968

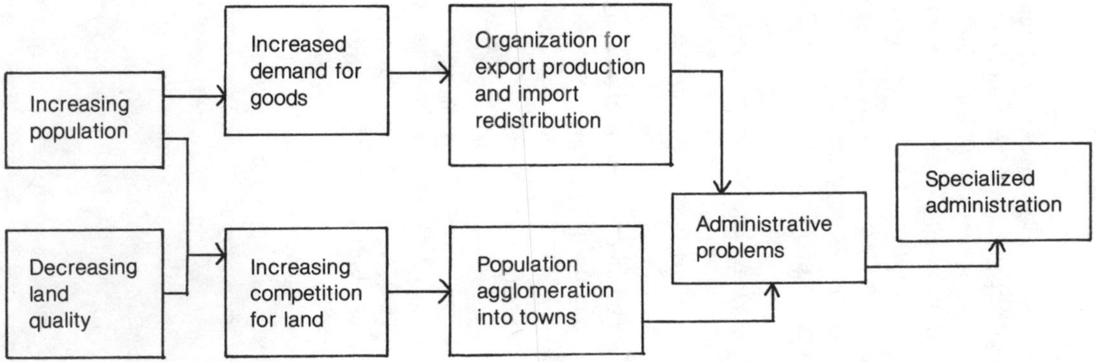

cause administrative specialization, and the second hypothesis could be rejected. Evidence from other sites throughout southwestern Iran made available since 1968 confirms this rejection. Furthermore there was a regular proportional relationship between changes in the relative values of imports and of exports. Some of the mechanisms of administered interregional trade were thus explicated. As is usually the case in archaeological research, some of the data not immediately relevant to our problem proved interesting. For instance, we improved the local ceramic sequence, which will be useful for dating settlements in future surveys, and we added to the stock of subsistence remains which will someday be needed to attack the problems of agricultural and herding organization.

In the spring of 1969 I planned a brief general survey project to provide complete settlement pattern maps for most of the foothill valleys hitherto unsurveyed. In that same season Frank Hole and James Neely were also conducting surveys. A portion of the working model was altered to the form shown in Figure 6. In the light of the previous season, I separated exchange and the state. Indeed I viewed increasing interregional trade and agglomeration into towns as changes occurring after state formation. I continued naively to assume population increase. The hypothesis that structured the season's work was that military competition for the fruits of a complex interregional economy forced craftsmen and other workers into the towns at about 3000 B.C.

The results of the various surveys were surprising for three reasons. First, the settlement data from three of the component plains of southwestern Iran showed no evidence of simple population increase. Population oscillated throughout the fourth and third millennia B.C. Second, the data indicated that towns grew up rather abruptly around 3500 B.C. and did not grow further until late in the third millennium B.C. Third, there seemed to be a regular pattern of smaller centers around the towns, suggesting placement for transport efficiency. Thus, though there was little evidence of interregional exchange until after state emergence, there was perhaps a transformation of local exchange coincident with state emergence. Clearly a complete rethinking of my position was needed. I spent the autumn of 1969 evaluating my concept of explanation, my definition of the state, and the possible ways of explaining state development. I circulated several papers embodying these thoughts to various colleagues, and I profited immensely from their copious and often deservedly harsh comments.

In the autumn of 1970 I returned to southwestern Iran with a relatively large staff. We planned (1) a resurvey of the settlements on the large and centrally located Susiana Plain, (2) a program of geological soundings around a sample of settlements of the fourth millennium

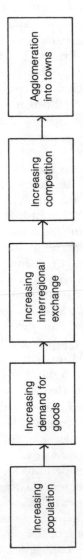

FIGURE 6

The Working Model of 1969

Increasing population → Increasing demand for goods → Increasing interregional exchange → Increasing competition → Agglomeration into towns

B.C., and (3) an excavation on a small rural site of about 3400 B.C., the period of state emergence. The completely restructured working models could be diagrammed as in Figure 7. This model expresses a situation similar to what Sanders (1956) has termed "economic symbiosis" in Mesoamerica. The separation of "administrative" from "political" problems results from the realization that internal competition could have been as important as information processing in the development of specialized administration. During the fieldwork we hoped to check the population estimates based on earlier surveys and to test the specific hypotheses about local exchange derived from settlement spacing by comparing samples of craft manufactured goods from various sites. However, our primary objective was to elucidate the organization of rural agriculture production. The specific proposition which structured this aspect of the season's research was that if estimated grain production on the plain could be demonstrated to increasingly exceed rather than balance the estimated demand of the settled population, then the excess grain must be moving in intra-regional or interregional exchange networks, probably to fully transhumant herders, who in this region cannot survive without external sources of grain and craft goods. Furthermore the animals raised by such transhumants would be moving into lowland settlements. Such interaction would require the increasing specialization of administrative organizations for several reasons. For example, the assembly of grain and the redistribution of animals would require administration. Also the inevitable trespass of nomads on cultivated fields would lead to conflicts which would have to be either adjudicated or fought out.

Even at the present stage of analysis it is still not certain that useful direct estimates of grain production can be made. Such estimation will require more knowledge of the present habits of the flora and microfauna whose remains were found in our sampling units and more samples of seeds from rural village sites of the fourth millennium B.C. Thus the working proposition cannot be either accepted or rejected at the present time. However, the results of the detailed settlement survey conducted and analyzed by Gregory Johnson have far exceeded our expectations. Utilizing a specially developed ceramic chronology, Johnson has been able to demonstrate changes in settlement size and density over relatively short periods of time. By studying minor stylistic variations on pottery vessels, he has been able to isolate what are probably the products of a single workshop or closely related group of workshops. By mapping the distribution of these varieties, he has been able to test specific hypotheses, generated with settlement spacing data, about the relations between specific towns, small centers, and villages (Johnson 1973).

FIGURE 7

The Working Model of 1970

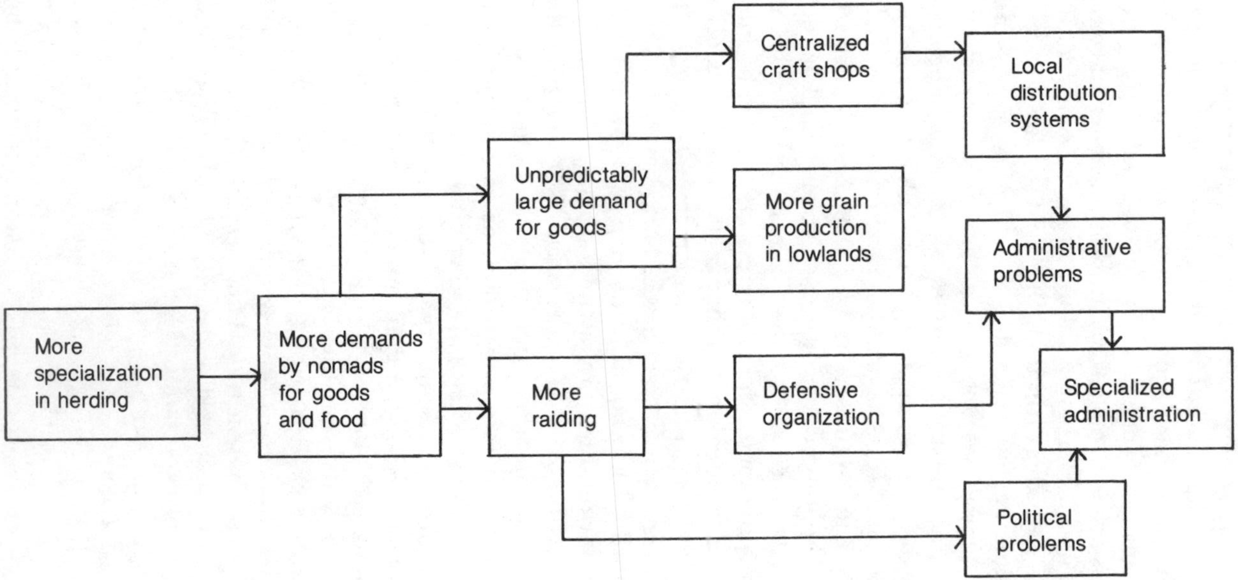

The results of the 1969 season were considerably amplified, and our knowledge of the mechanics of population change and local exchange was vastly improved. An unexpected but welcome result of Johnson's analysis was the identification of settlement spacing changes both around 3800 B.C. and around 3200 B.C. that can best be explained as resulting from military competition. Johnson has suggested some specific hypotheses about the causes of this competition and has pointed to the actual sites where these hypotheses might best be tested (Johnson 1973).

In the next field effort, I plan a general survey of certain upland valleys in an effort to elucidate the development of fully transhumant herders. The working model will be only slightly modified. Some further work on small rural settlements and on towns may be needed to round out the first stage of research. In preparation for the second stage, first versions of computer simulations of interregional exchange and of agricultural production have been prepared. However, the presentation of a comprehensive regional simulation model of southwestern Iran in the fourth millennium B.C. is several years in the future.

Even though research is not far advanced, some concept of the type of explanatory theory that will emerge is possible. The specific processes that are important in the models built for each case will probably not be important in the general theory. But the type of interaction between these processes will be important. For instance, population growth and competition over land or water might be crucial in one case, while the interaction of economically specialized groups might be more critical in another. Both sets of specific processes would create similar problems of information processing and competition. It seems possible that the problems generated by a single process would not lead to the emergence of specialized administration, since the ranking decision makers could accommodate by shifting their administrative resources around. Only when problems were generated in several areas would the decision-making apparatus be forced to change.

Summary

This chapter has briefly presented one archaeologist's approach to the development of a theory of the origin of states, one of the most complex transitions in the record of cultural evolution. I have discussed some recent attempts at explanation, all of which I have attempted to rework and synthesize in the context of my understanding of the scientific process and my own field experience. From these attempts has come the flexible research strategy I am using in southwestern Iran.

Several points merit emphasis.

1. Research strategy depends upon what one wishes to explain. For instance, had I been interested in "urbanism" rather than "states" when I turned from questions of trade and population in 1970, I probably would have focused on craft organization in towns rather than on rural production and local exchange.

2. Research strategy depends upon one's criteria of explanation. In the first place, if I had felt that to specify a prime mover was an adequate explanation, I would have begun my work with a study of population rather than a study of interregional exchange and competition. To have held such a view of explanation, and to have demonstrated the complex variation in population in 1968 rather than almost two years later, would presumably have led me to an immediate questioning of my basic assumptions. However, since I felt that the demonstration of many links in a system of variables was necessary to adequate explanation, the question of which links to begin with was a matter of practical, not theoretical, importance. In the second place, if I had felt that to show general correlations between variables sufficed to demonstrate linkage, I would not have been concerned with such quantitative measures as numbers of people, or quantities of goods exchanged, or areas of land used for different purposes. As a result, my survey and excavation methods might have been quite different.

3. In planning and field research, formally phrased hypotheses, rather than a general problem or working model alone, are valuable. On the one hand, they force one to try a variety of methods to produce satisfactory test data rather than to reapply blindly a traditional set of methods designed for other types of problems. On the other hand, they force one to think carefully before diverting all one's resources into the interesting but unexpected phenomena that always appear in the midst of excavation or survey.

4. Any field project requires a number of such hypotheses, since field conditions usually prevent the measuring of one or more critical variables and thus the testing of one or more of these hypotheses.

5. Models and simulations are best viewed as means for the construction of testable hypotheses about specific systems. They are not ends in themselves.

I hope that this essay will provide others with useful insights into the practical problems of building explanatory theories. It should at least convey an understanding of the amounts of time and effort required. I myself am convinced that this investment has been, and will continue to be, worthwhile and that in the foreseeable future we shall have extensively tested predictive theories of state development.

Acknowledgments

The research discussed in this paper was supported by grants GSO1936, GS-2194, and GS-3147 from the National Science Foundation, as well as by grants from the Horace Rackham School of Graduate Studies and the Ford Foundation Archaeological Traineeship Program.

References

Adams, R. McC.
   1962   Agriculture and Urban Development in Early Southwestern Iran.
          Science 136: 109-122.
   1966   *The Evolution of Urban Society: Early Mesopotamia and Pre-
          hispanic Mexico*. Chicago: Aldine.
Carneiro, R.
   1970   A Theory of the Origin of the State. *Science* 169: 733-738.
Diakonoff, I. M. (ed.)
   1969   *Ancient Mesopotamia*. Moscow: Nauka Press.
Engels, K. F.
   1891   *The Origin of the Family, Private Property, and the State*. Re-
          print edition, E. B. Leacock, ed., 1972. New York: International
          Publishers.
Hole, F., K. V. Flannery, J. A. Neely, and H. Helbaek
   1969   *Prehistoric Human Ecology of the Deh Luran Plain*. Memoirs
          of the Museum of Anthropology No. 1. Ann Arbor: University of
          Michigan.
Johnson, G. A.
   1973   *Local Exchange and Early State Development in Southwestern Iran*.
          Anthropological Paper No. 51. Ann Arbor: Museum of Anthropol-
          ogy, University of Michigan.
Le Breton, L.
   1967   The Early Periods at Susa. *Iraq* 19: 79-114.
Quastler, H. C.
   1955   Studies in Human Channel Capacity. In C. Cherry (ed.), *Informa-
          tion Theory: Third London Symposium*.
Sanders, W. T.
   1956   The Central Mexican Symbiotic Region. In G. R. Willey (ed.), *Settle-
          ment Patterns in the New World*. Viking Fund Publication in
          Anthropology No. 23. New York.
Sanders, W. T., and B. J. Price
   1968   *Mesoamerica: The Evolution of a Civilization*. New York: Random
          House.
Von Bertalanffy, L.
   1968   *General Systems Theory*. New York: George Braziller.
Wittfogel, K. A.
   1963   *Oriental Despotism: A Comparative Study of Total Power*. New
          Haven: Yale University Press.

Wright, H. T.
    1969   *The Administration of Rural Production in an Early Mesopotamian
            Town.* Anthropological Paper No. 38. Ann Arbor: Museum of
            Anthropology, University of Michigan.
    1972   A Consideration of Interregional Exchange in Greater Mesopo-
            tamia: 4000-3000 B.C. In E. Wilmsen (ed.), *Social Exchange and
            Interaction.* Anthropological Paper No. 46. Ann Arbor: Museum of
            Anthropology, University of Michigan.

Irrigation, Conflict, and Politics: A Mexican Case

EVA HUNT AND ROBERT C. HUNT

One of the most controversial sets of functional hypotheses about relationships between human social institutions has to do with the nature and consequences of irrigated agriculture. Now primarily associated with the name of Wittfogel (and the society type he called "Oriental Despotism"), this particular mine has been worked by several other scholars of note (cf. Steward 1955; Wittfogel 1957; Millon 1962). Price (1971) has stated very clearly and succinctly the hypothesized relationships between social and technological systems that deal with water control. She quite properly separates them into two parts. The first is a set of statements about the cause and effect relationship between the invention of irrigated agriculture and the origin of the state. As she clearly and effectively argues, this problem is diachronic, and there are only a half dozen or so cases which are clearly relevant to the discussion. We shall not be concerned with this part of the problem here.

The other half of this endeavor concerns statements about the synchronic functional relationship between irrigation, on the one hand, and various parts of the sociocultural system, on the other. Mainly, these propositions have to do with the domain of the social system we usually call *political institutions* or *political structure*. It is to this nexus of functional statements that we wish to address ourselves.

There is a single major model in the literature of the relation between the two systems. Wittfogel and his followers, using Marx's ideas about Asiatic society, have characterized the prototypic irrigated society on the basis of their model of China and southeast Asia. In such societies, the political life is controlled by an elitist bureaucracy of full-time specialists with both secular and religious (theocratic) powers. This bureaucracy also has a monopoly of many other social institutions, such as entrepreneurial activities and military organizations and action. It also has close to total control of the economic system, appropriating for itself all privileges derived from the control of the economic surplus created by the masses of producers. The ruling elite is not simply powerful, but is also highly centralized, small in numbers, physically concentrated, and despotic. Wittfogel argues that such despotic governments emerge in preindustrial societies which have an agricultural base supported by irrigation. The basic need to control water, administer the construction and maintenance of massive water works (by corvée labor), and allocate capital expenditures and resources, as well as to schedule the distribution to keep the system going efficiently, gives those persons in the irrigated society who occupy crucial role synapses in the irrigation system expansive powers in other domains of social life. In a sense, the ruling elites are supported in their increasing political control by the inherent inter- and intra-societal competition for the artificial control of water, which leads to a further need to enforce peace from above. On the other hand, high centralization and concentration of power facilitates the cooperation of larger masses of people for the common goals of the irrigation society, which frequently require large labor inputs. The ruling bureaucracy builds and reinforces its power because it can effectively undertake the functions and roles necessary in management which the masses cannot efficiently muster on the basis of consensus. The bureaucracy's monopoly, thus, is self-reinforcing, since the bureaucrats can use water to control the society, sanction revolt against their power, and build power in other realms of social life, which then again becomes self-reinforcing and self-serving.

This set of propositions deals with (a) the nature of total political power which a society practicing irrigation can generate; (b) the degree of cohesiveness the political elites can command; (c) the degree of concentration of political power that can be vested in a few privileged personnel (a bureaucracy, a limited set of governmental roles, etc.); (d) the degree to which political power generated in irrigation can be generalized or transferred to other domains of the society; and (e) the degree to which irrigation generates both cooperation and competition within a society and between societies.

Wittfogel has modified his prototype hydraulic society by indicating that some of the conditions of his ideal model are not likely to be met when the scale of the society, the scale of the irrigation system, or other historical conditions are not met. However, part of his major theory (i.e., the despotic quality of the state) applies only to a special case, that of oriental despotism, the major type being Chinese hydraulic society. The core elements of this special case are a "single" physical irrigation system, massive in scale, managed by a highly centralized despotic regime. Wittfogel has left himself open to very serious criticism, however, because he has been less than clear in operationalizing the variable of scale and defining the ethnographic limits to which the core theory of depotism applies. Even in a recent statement (1972) Wittfogel appears to consider that a vast range of societies which practice irrigation fit his model, although it is obviously absurd to conceive of them as despotic political systems (e.g., the Hopi). The domain of societies which manage water for agricultural purposes ranges from primitive acephalous cultivators (e.g., the Nuer), to chiefdoms (e.g., Hawaii), to agrarian states (some of which had and others of which didn't have despotic regimes historically), to industrial states. Such variants take only one dimension (type of political system).

There is as yet no general model presented in the literature that can deal with all societies practicing irrigation. Nor is there a model that deals exclusively with some operationalized sample of small-scale systems and their attributes as opposed to those of large scale (whatever one may clearly define by small or large scale). Moreover, there has been in the literature an apparent confusion between political power and despotic political power.

Criticisms of Wittfogel's *model*, as opposed to evaluations of the accuracy of his assessment of particular empirical cases, must stay within the domain that Wittfogel has defined. Many such criticisms have been focused *not* on the possible relationship of irrigation, the economy, stratification, and politics but on the supposed nexus of irrigation (usually conceived generally, rather than with the specific limitations demanded by Wittfogel's theory), centralization, and despotism. This distinction must be kept in mind as one reads the irrigation literature, for a major effort has taken place to discredit the despotism part of the theory. In order to accomplish this goal, the relationship between irrigation and the political structure has been obscured, which is a case of throwing away the grain to rid oneself of the chaff.

Robert Adams, in the context of discussing the origin of the state, has been careful to separate other major effects of irrigation as a social force from the variable of despotism of a managerial class per se. Adam's argument is clearly stated in the following quote (1966: 72-74):

> Our special concern here, however, is not with the importance of irrigation as one of the vital, interacting factors increasing agricultural productivity and hence surpluses, or even with its possible contribution to the growth of social stratification through its encouragement of differential yields. If perhaps not quite to the same degree, these effects of irrigation almost certainly were present in central Mexico just as they were in Mesopotamia. But it is Wittfogel's contention that the primary significance of irrigation arose not from its encouragement of new economic resources and social complexity but rather from the impetus given to the formation of coercive political institutions by the managerial requirements of large-scale canal systems. And in this respect the available evidence, closely paralleling that for early Mesopotamia, fails to support him.

Both Adams and Glick (1970) have investigated irrigation systems in a diachronic framework. They both reject the theory of a managerial, bureaucratic despotism but find plenty of evidence for interrelationships of the irrigation system, production, role complexity, stratification, and the political system. Although Adams fundamentally disagrees with the notion that irrigation gives impetus to the formation of cohesive political systems, he doesn't reject, as Millon (1962) appears to have done, the implicit relation between irrigation and political processes leading to changes of social structure or, more specifically, he does not reflect the notion that irrigation system processes affect the sociopolitical structure of population aggregates under a single political hierarchy. Price (1971) apparently misses the subtlety of this position.

Glick's material doesn't support the view of the existence of a despotic system in medieval Valencia. It presents good historical evidence, however, that in a large territory the social consequences of irrigation were many and far-reaching, in terms of proliferation of political roles dealing with water control, adjudication, etc., and in terms of the generation and resolution of social conflict, harvest yields, and the historical buildup of a complex political code of norms, laws, and traditions dealing with irrigation. Our own historical evidence for the sixteenth-century Cuicatec (briefly outlined here, but dealt with in great detail in E. Hunt [1972b]) supports the view that there is no simple relation between despotism and irrigation (at least for small size, closed, physical systems) but there is a clear relation between water control and the sources of power of the ruling elites of the irrigated society.

There have been many responses to Wittfogel's work; these responses have varied greatly in degree of objectivity, strength of evidence, and nature and kind of ideological commitment. The basic set of diachronic propositions, however, has not basically been expanded from Wittfogel's original statement.[1]

There is as yet no general synchronic model of the kinds of functional relationships between irrigation and other sociocultural phenomena. Various studies have argued bits and pieces of the relationships. Leach (1961), for example, in his study of a village in Ceylon, argues that social relationships in the village are strongly determined by control of property, which is in turn determined by the water distribution system. Gray (1963), Fernea (1970), and Sahlins (1962) have all presented information on both the water management system and the system of political roles, paying some attention to the relationships between them.

Millon (1962) has provided the only even partially systematic comparative attempt in print to investigate the synchronic relationship between the degree of centralization and the size of the irrigation system. He states that he is not concerned with Wittfogel's "hypotheses," and he uses what he calls "small-scale" systems. However, his variables are the same as those proposed by Wittfogel, and the major problem is the same: Millon concludes that in small-scale systems not only is there no necessary causal relationship between irrigation and centralization but in fact there appears to be no relationship at all! We have argued elsewhere (E. Hunt 1972a) that Millon's results are suspect because of the biases in the sample and the ambiguities of concept definition. However, what is important here is that the literature presents us with two extreme, opposed positions and a number of case studies in the middle, the results of which are extremely ambiguous insofar as they support either set of positive or negative hypotheses.

As a consequence of our symposium meeting at the 1972 Annual Meeting of the Southwestern Anthropological Association at Long Beach in April, it became clear that there are a series of unsolved methodological problems which have produced, in part, the inconclusive and contradictory results we are faced with. First, it appears that there is no such thing as an irrigation society. There are many varieties of society practicing irrigation, and many forms of irrigation. Specification of variables and the conditions under which they function has not been systematic. Large waterworks to control major floods may differ greatly in their effect on society from flimsy waterworks on small streams or from the building of one isolated qanat. A situation in which upstream irrigators can control water flow has to be quite different from one in which they cannot. Paddy rice irrigation water moving through fields in countries with sufficient rain probably cannot affect social relations in the same manner in which maize irrigation water absorbed by a plot in an arid environment can. Moreover, we have all been remiss in specifying the meaning of our concepts. Such terms as *centralization, traditional practices, functional efficiency, small-* and *large-scale*, which are the cornerstones of the literature, have been left ambiguously defined at best and at worst are only privately intuitive in meaning.

We are faced, therefore, with at least three major tasks. First, we must define our terms. Second, we must specify the range of subtypes of irrigated societies, in each case specifying the relevant range of variation of each major theoretically significant variable. (The theoretically significant variables must be specified in terms of a particular theory.) Third, we should test the propositions about relationships between variables in the only valid way, with a large-sample comparative study. We could ideally control for the range of variation of all variables involved and the range of types of irrigation societies which will eventually emerge. Cross-cultural comparisons, however, require the existence of prior meticulous historical as well as synchronic analysis of specific cases. Such cases, which can be limited in number to cover each major irrigation system type (e.g., tanks, canals, and chain wells of differing size and specified range), will provide the empirical basis for the necessary comparisons leading to less flimsy generalizations than we have had up to the present time.

The successful application of the comparative method assumes the existence of a theoretical model which will cover most, if not all, of the variation found in the total population. This in turn implies a sophisticated knowledge of *each* of the types. These conditions can hardly be said to exist today with respect to the study of the social impact of irrigated agriculture. In summary, we need both good detailed case studies and comparative statements.

In this essay we propose to present a case study in depth, not a comparative study. We will present hypotheses and propositions which are restricted in application to a subtype of irrigated society. This subtype, the Cuicatec of Mexico, will be specified in detail in terms of its conditions, both ecological and sociocultural. As such, this essay will first present relevant ethnographic data on the social impact of irrigation in one society. Second, it will attempt to clarify in part a few methodological muddles of conceptual definition. Third, it will attempt to specify in detail the nature of the variables. Specifically we feel that, for any system studied, the following variables require unambiguous treatment.

1. The natural conditions in which the system functions (e.g., climate, water balance, soil, topography, nature of water sources).

2. The physical irrigation system, including how water is extracted, moved, and stored. This description includes the scale of water works and the technology of irrigation from a mechanical point of view. Considerable attention should be paid to the maintenance needs of the physical system. This variable of maintenance has two dimensions. One refers to regular upkeep of a working system which is in balance (e.g., monthly cleanings and repairs); the other refers to major maintenance to cope with environmental degradation (e.g., increased levels of soil salinity, significant changes in the level of the water table). The Cuicatec case discussed here deals only with maintenance in the first meaning of the concept. The reason is simple: there is no evidence of basic environmental degradation for at least the four-hundred-year period dealt with here. However, in adjacent areas north of the Cuicatec (the Tehuacán valley), maintenance in the second meaning is of major importance, since high levels of salt and travertine are present in the water, and a marked lowering of the water table has occurred in the last one hundred years. This lowering is partially related to enormous population growth and concomitant water demands in the valley.

3. The cultivation system. What crops are planted, their water demands, crucial watering periods, ecological balance, and competition between crops and between crops and wild plants; in other words, the general structure of the ecosystem within which domestic cultigens are produced.

4. The general characteristics of the cultural system, including the folk view of the environment and resources and the religious or ritually symbolic aspects which affect irrigation practices (usually including the calendar and round of sacred feasts and holidays dealing with water gods).

5. The general characteristics of the social system, particularly a description of the social structure and system of stratification as they affect the social aspects of irrigation and of the institutions which deal with the management of public goals, conflict resolution, and allocation of resources; that is, the specific system of institutions which deal with politics, particularly "water" politics, and such other relevant aspects in a given situation as the impact of ethnicity on access to economic privileges.

6. A complete description of the system of roles and groups in the society which are directly linked and concerned with irrigation. Such a

description should entail a discussion of to what degree and how such roles and/or groups are embedded in other parts of the social and cultural systems or meshed with roles or groups which have other primary functions.

In what follows, we have not been equally successful in dealing with each of these variables. Notably absent from this essay is an account of the cultivation system and the general cultural system. We have attempted, however, to utilize our data for all of these categories.[2]

In summary, we are operating in the context of a single synchronic case study, attempting to specify the conditions under which a particular system operates, and focusing on functional relationships which have already been proposed in the diachronic, historical literature with inconclusive results. Our purposes are to isolate parameters, specify a possible subtype of irrigation society, and generate hypotheses for future comparative testing.

The Concept of Centralization

Before we proceed any further, we must clarify the meaning of the concept of *centralization*, which, though it has been a crucial variable in the anthropological study of irrigation, has been left defined at a level of ambiguity which makes it, at times, unusable. In our view, centralization of authority should be understood within two different contexts. One refers exclusively to authority in terms of the irrigation system. The other refers to generalized political authority, which may involve other functions of control outside or above simple water control. In one case, authority is exercised over different decision-making rights in terms, exclusively, of the social or technological needs of the irrigation system per se. In the other case, authority is exercised over water as one aspect of the decision-making rights of a complex political role or of a large, multifunctional political machine.

It is usually the case in chiefdoms and state systems that there is at least an incipient (if not well-developed) system of organic integration of the political community which involves multidimensional functions. These functions are allocated to territorial units (and the social groups they contain), which are hierarchically nested within each other. In this case, the degree of centralization could be measured by the extent to which a particular total function, such as water control, is located at the top level of the hierarchy or at lower levels. In fact, however, it is most likely that different aspects of water control will be allocated at different levels of the total political structure. Higher levels may delegate some functions to local authorities, but with centralization *sovereignty* lies at the top levels of the political structure.

Homologous (same size or same function) groupings do not make decisions about each other (for example, two villages of the same political status using the same stream), particularly if there is any question of competition, but decisions are likely to be made at the next higher level of the authority ladder or power hierarchy. Then decisions at the lower levels (e.g., decisions usually left to village officers) which appear as local in their power base are not truly autonomous, because they are linked to a functioning central government structure which contains higher levels of decision making. These strata have the potential power to override lower-level decisions and introduce external controls if it appears necessary.

If we consider centralization of authority purely in the context of irrigation systems, the concept may refer to several different kinds of unified social control—that is, to several separate, different variables. These variables can be located at different levels of the social structure. In addition to responsibility for construction and maintenance of a canal system (or dams, or water tanks), we must also include the rights to allocate water (one of Millon's major variables), the control and management of services connected with conflict resolution between water users, the duties connected with the legal or military defense of water sources and improved irrigated lands, the administration of labor resources to maintain the physical system, the responsibility for the proper performance of rituals insuring water supplies, and so on. These functions may involve a single role or a set of specialized roles, which may or may not be ranked vis-a-vis other political roles in the society. The functions may also involve a specialized institution or simply be a set of functions embedded in other sociopolitical institutions expected to perform other functions.

Water control is linked to other social controls in more or less direct ways but always in terms of the viability of the water-control mechanisms within a particular social structure. Societies which irrigate by canals have some clearly established networks of control in which differences in authority and differential power over water exist among persons, roles, and institutionally recognized social groups. Power differences concerning water, moreover, do not occur purely in isolation; water rights usually dovetail with the social allocation of other superordinate rights. Thus, wealth, social class, hereditary descent group membership in aristocratic lineages, and ascription to political roles which imply control of other resources may correlate with rights within the irrigation system. If centralization of authority is understood in these terms, allowing for the variations of (a) degree of unification of decisions about several separate variables in a single role, set of roles, or institution, and (b) intensity of embeddedness of the decision-making machinery about water in the larger political institutions, we have to talk about differences in the degree of centralization rather than its simple presence or absence. Moreover, measures of the degree of centralization should involve several independent variables.

A good analysis will also focus on the real versus the ideal degree of local autonomy which exists in different systems. This focus is important. Some systems, such as the one described in this essay and that of Pul Eliya (cf. Leach 1961; E. Hunt 1972b), appear at first glance to be decentralized because of the smoothness of operation at the local level. Decisions appear to be made at this level when in fact, for major variables, these are not autonomous systems at all. Upon occasion the actors of the system may appear autonomous and believe themselves to be so. In fact, roles are nested in a hierarchy of state-supported and legitimized water-control institutions and are articulated in their actions into an elaborate system of linked activities. If roles and institutional activities are out of phase with each other, the harmonic workings of the traditional social arrangements concerning water are very likely to become disrupted.

Rather than an institutional form, "centralized authority" may refer to a set of roles which specialize in controlling, at the public domain level, water allocation, labor management, defensive warfare over water, internal conflict resolution for a particular irrigation system, and so on. For examples of roles centralizing arbitration and conflict resolution, one could mention the role of water judges in medieval Spain (Glick 1970).

In summary, the degree of total political centralization at the state level (i.e., far above the limits of the irrigation system as a physical unit) in such cases as Iraq and Mexico cannot be treated as equivalent to the degree of centralization at the level of a village in a tribal society or a district in a feudal one. We have asked: Can centralized authority be treated as an equivalent phenomenon in all these cases? Can the autonomous villages of the tribal Sonjo, a subtribe or a segment of a society dominated by a foreign metropolitan colonial power such as the British Empire, and a federalized national state such as Mexico be conceptualized as equivalent societies or even as having equivalent degrees of centralized authority? And if the answer is positive, what definition of centralization could make it possible? We believe that all societies cannot be so regarded and that levels of political integration and articulation need to be clearly differentiated (cf. Richard Adams 1971 for an illuminating theoretical discussion of this issue). We also have to distinguish the anthropologist's and the native's views of the system. Irrigators may not be aware of the total system in which they participate, especially when a system is highly traditionalized. The natives may also not be aware of the social consequences of their system. Hence, the irrigators may see the system as egalitarian when in fact it makes for differential access to control of water supplies, or as decentralized when in fact it is not, simply because the potential of force inherent in the state safeguards the maintenance of order without constant supervision.

It would appear that the crucial factors in considering the issue of centralization are the degree to which roles are embedded, the number of roles that have control functions, and the degree to which the roles are connected with the apex of the political system. When roles are embedded, small in number, and connected with the apex, the system is highly centralized. By *embeddedness* we mean that the roles directly connected with irrigation are usually combined in a person or persons who control a number of other powerful roles integral to other parts of the economic and political institutions. By *number of roles* we refer to whether or not a small number of roles are involved in directing or controlling the activities of a large number of persons. By *connectedness with the apex* we mean the degree to which decisions made at any level of a system contribute to actual or potential decisions made at the apex of the largest political system, including the social territory in question.

As we shall see in this essay, a major problem in understanding a state with irrigation is to determine how the local activities and structures are related to activities and structures in wider domains. For our purposes here, we shall refer to these two domains as local and national. A major point this essay makes concerns the articulation of the local and national decision-making agencies concerned, in one way or another, with irrigation.

A full understanding of this articulation demands a distinction between two types of task: frequent day-to-day decisions, mostly concentrated on maintenance and allocation; and infrequent decisions, usually linked with major construction, defense, and adjudication. The day-to-day decisions are manifestly under local control, sometimes involving specialized agencies with roles that are little embedded. The number of roles can be large or small, and there is little if any communication between these local agencies or role systems and those in wider domains (for these specific tasks). These decisions and subsequent activities are the most visible to the observer in terms of everyday accessibility in the field and therefore are the ones easiest to gather data on. It would be easy to decide that the irrigation system in San Juan is decentralized, if only these activities were taken into account.

It is when the infrequent but crucial decisions in terms of long-range existence of the system arise that centralization becomes most manifest, for it is on these occasions, at least for the contemporary period, that the state becomes most plainly visible. It is in this context that the social embeddedness of irrigation system roles (the social organization of the irrigation system) is most crucial. Another significant point we are making is that in this case study the conflict resolution (and defense) functions are of major importance to the personnel in the system in terms of maintaining status inequalities but also in terms of keeping the system functioning smoothly, and these functions are the most centralized. This centralization solves the problem of articulating local and national social systems through the double membership of the local elites in the local and national role systems. These elites are not merely passive in their relationship to either system. Rather, they generate power both locally and nationally and use the power generated in each domain to strengthen their position in the other.[3] Moreover, decisions based on perception of economic or political needs at the local level may contradict decisions based on perceptions of economic or political needs at the national level. This situation was clearly present in our case study, specifically in the context of the building of a new dam by the Papaloapan Commission. Thus, it is also of importance to show the role of local and national elites in mediating, fostering, or slowing down processes based on decisions made at different levels of the system.

The Physical System

In the literature on societies which practice irrigation, one frequently finds statements which refer to "the irrigation system." What some authors mean by this term is the entirety of phenomena concerned with irrigation; some mean the society itself which practices irrigation; others, such as Fernea (1970), usually mean what we are here calling the *physical system*. This ambiguity in a key concept has led to some confusion. In our view, it is important to distinguish the physical system from the social system. By the *physical system* we mean the relevant physical environment (e.g., amount of water available) plus the artifacts in and on the ground (dams, canals, sluices, etc.). By *social system* we mean the social organization connected with the control of the physical system(s). The size and other attributes of these two systems can vary independently of one another. The physical system can be as small as a single Ceylonese tank or as big as the systems in the Mesopotamian valley, where the canals are often river size, covering scores of kilometers. Three possibilities exist concerning the relation of size of physical and social systems. First, the social system may cover all, and only, a single physical system. It is conceivable that a single physical system could support two or more separate and distinct social systems. (On a logical basis, it appears to be unlikely that this condition would be stable or enduring. Competition and conflict would probably be too extreme to permit two alien societies to share a physical system. However, two subsystems [i.e., two communities of the same politically defined society] often share a physical system.) The third possibility is a single social system which deals with several different physical systems. This case exists where the politically defined society is a state and the physical irrigation systems are small: e.g., systems based on small streams, wells, qanats and/or systems in which tanks are the major form of bulking of water.

In this latter case, anthropologists have tended to focus upon the scale of the physical system to the detriment of a full understanding of the total scale of the social system and the relationship between physical and social systems. For example, Price's criticism (1971) of Robert McC. Adams (1966) can be traced in part to the fact that "the size of the irrigation system" may mean the size of the canal network (the physical system) or the scale of the centralized polity. This ambiguity results from the term "irrigation system." If the term refers only to the size of the physical system, then clearly Pul Eliya, for example, does not conform to a limiting condition in Wittfogel's model, the large irrigation system, but is, as Millon (1962) indicates, a small-scale system. But if "irrigation system" refers to the social system (i.e., the state of Ceylon, of which Pul Eliya is only a small cog), it is large in scale. A state may, and frequently does, contain a large social system concerned with irrigation, which has direct and indirect control of many small physical systems. Failure to attend to this distinction is a source of confusion in attempts to assess the relationship between irrigation and political centralization by the comparative method (cf. E. Hunt 1972).

THE LANDSCAPE OF THE CUICATEC REGION

The Cuicatec region is one of differentiated ecological characteristics. From the canyons of the Río Santo Domingo and Río Grande (La Cañada de Cuicatlán or Tomellín) at 500 to 600 meters above sea level, the terrain slopes up to the uninhabited Llano Español plateau at an elevation of about 3,200 meters.

Basically, there are two ecologically different agricultural zones, the semi-arid Cañada del Río Grande and the high temperate mountains to the east. The canyon, or Cañada of the Río Grande, supports a

xerophytic vegetation consisting of such plants as mesquite, thorny
bushes (*cardoneras*), *cuajilote, palo mantecoso*, hard grasses, and
organo cactus. It is characterized by low rainfall, high evaporation
rates, and a large permanent river, the Río Grande. The affluents of the
Río Grande are shallow, narrow mountain rivers with steep gradients
which have deposited rich soil at their confluence with the main river.

These relatively flat alluvial flood plains are intensively cultivated with irrigation. Their fields produce 800 to 1,500 kilograms of
maize per hectare per planting. Plums (*obos*) are raised, as well as
chicozapote, mango, chile, tomatoes, some rice, and fodder. Sugar cane
is grown commercially and processed locally. Habitation in the
Cañada is found only in association with these alluvial fans, in loca-
tions where the canyon opens out into a relatively wide valley floor.
Elsewhere the terrain is rough and nonirrigable. Of the towns and villages located in the fertile localities, all but one, Valerior Trujano, had
pre-Hispanic antecedents.

Above the Cañada region, the lower ranges of the hilly flanks are
unusable for agriculture. This area contains small animals and edible
varieties of wild plants. Various wild seedpods and cactus fruits are
still gathered here by the very poor. In prehistoric days this area was
inhabited by hunters and gatherers living in rock shelters (E. Hunt
1972b). The thin vegetation is a mixture of the forest and plants found
in the richer areas above and below.

The mountain towns at altitudes between 1,500 and 2,000 meters
are located on small, flat areas or plateaus or on spurs alongside the
streams. Here is found the bulk of the highland population; lands
above and around the towns are used for seasonal rainfall crops. The
land is cultivated by an outfield-infield system, which produces maize
at the rate of 400 to 600 kilograms per hectare. The size of the areas
irrigated is very small; sometimes only two or three parcels of land
support an equal number of households. Irrigation is thus a very
minor component of the agricultural highland complex, playing a
supplementary role in terms of yields. This situation is unlike that in
the canyon, where irrigation is basic for survival of the agricultural
system.

The upper slopes are covered with a sparse primary forest of
deciduous trees and secondary grasses. Above 2,000 meters are some
high-altitude agave plantations. Otherwise, a mixed forest provides
firewood and lumber for house construction. Several species of pine
are the source of cellulose used by the Tuxtepec Paper Company. The
country is cold, sometimes touched with frost and snow.

In the remainder of this essay we shall concentrate primarily on
the Cañada itself, at first summarizing the significant ecological

contrasts. The Cañada climate is semidesertic and extremely dry for agriculture. As Tables 1 through 3 show, the Cañada is an arid system where there is a high net water loss to the atmosphere during every month of the year. For six months of the year there is literally no rain at all, and the maximum number of months of drought (*meses con sequías* ≥ 28 *días*) in a year is ten and eleven respectively for each of the two reporting stations. For six months of the year, therefore, there can be no agriculture dependent upon an atmospheric supply of water. Furthermore, as the precipitation minima show, there are often whole years in which no agriculture based on atmospheric supply of moisture is possible.

The total supply of atmospheric water to the Cañada is in general quite low—the lowest of the entire Papaloapan Basin. Of even more importance, however, is the measure of usable rain. In the Cañada there are in effect seven months with no usable rain, and of the remaining five, only three, on the average, have more than 24 mm. It should be stressed that these figures are means and that in the case of minimal total rainfall, no usable rain over 24 mm. will fall, if indeed any falls at all. Therefore, agriculture without irrigation in the Cañada has such a high risk potential that it can be said to be culturally nonviable. The people in the canyon say that agriculture without irrigation is impossible. In San Juan one man tried to grow plum trees above the highest canal, watering them by bucket, and everybody thought he was crazy. He was an outsider from the valley of Oaxaca, where well irrigation is traditional, and when his venture failed, he left town. In fact, all agriculture since the sixteenth century has been based on canal irrigation.

A comparison of the Cañada with the slope and peak areas of the mountains to the east shows dramatic differences (Table 3). In general, the higher slopes get twice as much rain, three times as much useful rain, nearly twice as many months of useful rain, and fewer drought months in a year. The highlands are cooler, cloudier, and more moist. These highlands support a sizable population based largely, though not entirely, on what is called temporal agriculture— that is, agriculture based on seasonal rainfall.

While the atmosphere rarely bestows significant moisture, the Cañada contains a large permanent stream, the Grande River, which is one of the sources of the Papaloapan. The Grande runs, for most of its length, through a narrow canyon. Smaller streams and brooks flow down the mountains. Although some of these streams are permanent, they vary greatly in flow between the dry and the rainy season. The gradients of these streams, especially the small ones, are quite steep. The principal one for this essay, the Río Chiquito, which flows through the town of San Juan, drops 2400 meters in 23 kilometers.

Source: Data summarized from Comisión del Papaloapan 1956.

Table 1 Relationship of Evapotranspiration to Mean Precipitation, in mm., for San Juan

	Jan.	Feb.	Mar.	Apr.	May	June	July	Aug.	Sept.	Oct.	Nov.	Dec.
Evapotranspiration	80	85	145	160	180	175	160	160	130	100	80	65
Precipitation	0	0	5	5	35	115	120	60	100	55	0	0
P — E	—80	—85	—140	—155	—145	—60	—40	—100	—30	—45	—80	—65

Source: Data summarized from Comisión del Papaloapan 1956.

Table 2 Useful Rain (Rainfall ≥ 24 mm. with 80% Probability) per Month, Quiotepec Reporting Station

Jan.	Feb.	Mar.	Apr.	May	June	July	Aug.	Sept.	Oct.	Nov.	Dec.
0	0	Trace	Trace	Trace	30	35	20	35	20	0	0

Source: Data summarized from Comisión del Papaloapan 1956.

Table 3 Comparison of Cañada, Slope, and Mountain, on Various Climate Variables

	Cañada	Low Slope	Mountain Towns	Plateau
1. Temperature: Jan. mean	22°C	17°	13.9°	13°
2. Temperature: July mean	27°	20°	17°	17°
3. Insolation: January	> 70%	?	?	40-60%
4. Insolation: July	40-50%	?	?	40-50%
5. Annual evaporation	2,750 mm.	2,000-2,500 mm.	2,000-2,500 mm.	<2,000 mm.
6. Number of months with ≥ 28 days of no rain	11, *10*[a]	8	7	?
7. Mean annual precipitation	570 mm.	800 mm.	1,000 mm.	1,500 mm.
8. Total annual useful rain[b]	135, *146* mm.[a]	200 mm.	500 mm.	500-1,000 mm.
9. Number of months with useful rain ≥ 24 mm.	3, *4*[a]	5	5	6

Source: Data summarized from Comisión del Papaloapan 1956.

[a] In the Cañada, there are two reporting stations, thus the double response. The San Juan response is in italics.

[b] Useful rain is defined as 75% of precipitation over 5 mm., for each time it rains. 24 mm. were chosen as base line, for the Commission used this figure of necessary water for corn, derived from figures for the State of California.

These streams are young geologically, and have narrow rocky beds for most of their length. The streams frequently cross aquifers, whose seepage accounts for a large percentage of the total flow of each stream (personal communication from a Papaloapan engineer, 1964).

The Cañada valley system soils and terrain are for the most part unusable for irrigation. As we mentioned earlier, the loci of cultivation and human settlement in the Cañada are the alluvial fans of the mountain streams, which represent a small percentage of the valley floor and are separated from one another by stretches of narrow, uninhabitable canyon. Within the whole length of the Cañada, including the Vueltas River, there is a string of eleven settlements, beginning with Atlatlauca in the south and ending with Quiotepec in the north. The major settlement is San Juan, which we will discuss in detail.

The agricultural lands in the Cañada are irrigated by small, closed canal systems, which service every settlement. For a system of irrigation of this type, three different characteristics should be considered: first, how the water is extracted from its natural source; second, how it is transported to the fields; and third, how it is made available to the plants that utilize it. In the San Juan area, the conditions are among the simplest. The major sources of supply of water are the fast-running, steep-gradient streams; a secondary source is the Grande River itself. Diversion occurs far above the fields; water is transported by gravity flow down small, unlined ditches. This system simply continues into the fields in small subsidiary ditches: there is no bulk storage of water for irrigation.

These environmental conditions have some significant human consequences. The diversion dams must be strong enough to withstand, for a reasonable amount of time (several months), a fairly rapid stream flow. The distributory canals are by and large short (the longest is 10 kilometers, most are less than 5), and collect relatively little silt when compared with nearby systems such as those of the Tehuacán Valley or with other systems such as those in Iraq, in which silting is a major problem. Flow in the canals is good, as it is into the fields if the canals are cleaned regularly. There is therefore relatively little demand for an input of complex technical knowledge and esoteric skills; however, the labor input of such a system is not low.

Since each settlement has, typically, sole and undisputed access to its stream and alluvial soils, each community tends to depend on a physical system independent of other communities. That is, there is a very strong tendency for a physical system to be community specific, which means that the take-off or diversion dam and the transport system are entirely within community boundaries and, further, that all the water in the system is utilized by the community. Given the abundance of aquifers, there is little if any opportunity to deprive a downstream community of water. It is also possible for some communities to have two or more independent physical systems operating simultaneously, due to a plethora of very small sources.

However, a major problem is created by low water supplies, given the demands of the population. During the hot, dry season from December to the beginning of April, water for irrigation is scarce.[4] Several factors besides lack of rain increase scarcity. Sizable amounts of water are lost by evaporation and absorption. Parts of the stream beds are porous sand and loose stone, and in some cases 40 percent of the running water is lost. As might be expected, water in this area is and was extremely valuable; the need to control water supplies is a powerful influence on the social structure (E. Hunt 1972b).

IRRIGATION IN SAN JUAN

In the Municipio of San Juan, the major area of agricultural fields in the Cañada, the physical irrigation systems function without any impressive or major permanent physical superstructure attached to them. Two types of permanent waterworks exist which are of marginal utility. Within the town of San Juan, there is a stone-faced (and partially covered) network of street ditches, which is utilized to provide household water; part of this water is used to irrigate fruit trees in house yards. This arrangement, of colonial origin, exists only within the few central blocks of the contemporary town and is left in a state of disrepair. Each household keeps up its own branch of the ditch as it sees fit. Outside this miniscule system (servicing approximately ten blocks), the colonial government built several small aqueducts in the typical Spanish arch design to service a few towns in the Canyon area (Martinez Gracida 1883). These aqueducts have either been allowed to collapse or are used in a near-total state of decay with loss of water and inefficiency of distribution.

The bulk of the agricultural lands today are irrigated by extremely simple techniques. Several major feeder canals (*apantles,* from the Nahuatl word *apantli*) serve the fields and orchards which surround the town of San Juan itself. Minor irrigation ditches spread over the irrigated land in the *municipio* like a spider web. These ditches are open and shallow, with mudpacked walls. The deepest is one meter, but most are between 30 and 40 centimeters. Where topographically necessary, a simple rock or brick buttress against a cliff face supports them; here and there a metal pipe or a hollow log (called a *canoa*) takes the canal over a break in the terrain. Gates and sluices are temporarily built of piled-up, uncut stones, mud, and branches. *Tomas de Agua,* the main diversion openings or "dams" from the stream, are built of mud and branches. Larger ones are built of chains of small pyramids made of piled-up branches stuck in a semivertical position. These "dams" are locally called *chalchihuites*, a Nahuatl word which means "green stones," or "necklace of precious green stones," and is a pre-Hispanic poetic symbol associated with surface water and its Goddess Chalchiuhuitlicue, companion of Tlaloc, the rain god (Florentine Codex 1953: Vol. I:6-7; Caso 1953; Piña Chan 1960: 80-81, 84, 115). *Chalchihuites* are easily washed away by freshets or strong currents, particularly in the rainy season, so that constant servicing is necessary. Cleaning the canals and opening or barricading sections of ditches and the primitively built *chalchihuites* are simple but tiresome and frequent tasks. The number of man-hours involved in those services varies from one case to another, depending on the size of the canals and the form of canal "tenure."

To maintain minimum standards of efficiency, decisions on when and how well to repair the system, especially in the rainy season, require skilled decision making. Waiting too long to repair a dam may result in discovering that it has been totally destroyed by the strong current. If repairs are made too soon, the labor costs are often higher than necessary, thus deflecting scarce resources from more productive pursuits.

In San Juan, two town canals using water from the small permanent stream, the Chiquito River, cross the residential area above the central part of the town. One services the house orchards and land around and below town; the other services lands north of the town, in a section called "The Grassland," where most small landowners have their parcels. The southern canal is again divided into two major branches; one of these crosses the town southward, the other in a western direction.

Within the municipal boundaries there are two major areas of agricultural fields which are not irrigated by publicly controlled canals. The best land of San Juan, adjacent to the Grande River, is located outside the range of irrigation of the town-controlled ditches. This area, called "Spanishland," is an extremely fertile flat shelf which edges the alluvial fan of the Chiquito River, parallel to the Canyon's lower spurs below the railroad line. One major feeder canal drawing water from the Grande River services all the Spanishland to the north through a complex network of ditches arranged in a perpendicular and parallel rectangular pattern. This pattern is quite unlike that of the town canals, which, being located in poorer, rougher terrain, follow natural features of the landscape, fanning outward from the major canals in a branching pattern. The southern section of the Río Grande shelf is irrigated by another canal (San Pedrito) which originates in a small stream "owned" by an Indian barrio which is a municipal dependency of San

Juan. This canal bed was built in a previous generation and is kept in working order by one of the elite families of San Juan, primarily to service the family's own lands.

Another main canal drawing water from the Grande services the small *ejido*-controlled lands further north of the town. These *ejidos* are cooperatively held lands, owned by the federal government, in which household heads hold usufruct rights.

The Social Organization of Irrigation

THE SOCIAL STRUCTURE OF SAN JUAN

In this section, we will be primarily discussing the relevant aspects of the social structure of San Juan as a semiautonomous community, but we will have occasion to refer to the national-level system, of which a brief description follows. Mexico as a nation is a federal entity, composed of states (*estados*). These states are sometimes divided into districts, and always subdivided into semiautonomous territories called *municipios*. The political institutions of Mexico are strong and highly centralized in a single party system and a unified federation controlled from the capital of the nation (cf. Gonzalez Casanova 1965; Padgett 1966). Of primary importance in this context is the government itself with its various bureaucracies, which reach down to the local district and municipal levels with varying degrees of effectiveness. In addition to the courts and tax-collecting systems, which may affect water usage, there are agencies directly concerned with the administration and management of water resources. One is an agency of the Federal Ministry of Agriculture and Livestock, the other a Ministry in its own right, called Recursos Hidráulicos (Hydraulic Resources). The watershed of which San Juan is a part has been centrally organized and developed since 1946 by a National Federal Commission (Comisión del Papaloapan), which has had responsibility for planning, construction, and management of a large series of water works including the major Alemán dam and, at the local level, small diversion dams, other irrigation works, and tanks for potable water. This commission has its own federal budget and works with state and local government in coordination. It has sponsored research (Attolini 1949, 1950), published various kinds of data relevant to irrigation works (e.g., Comisión del Papaloapan 1956), and even had a history written on it (Poleman 1964).

The other central political institution which is of major importance for this essay is the political party in power, the Partido Revolucionario Institucional (the PRI). This party is a more or less unified, enormous bureaucracy, which parallels the government but is not identical to it (O. Paz 1972).

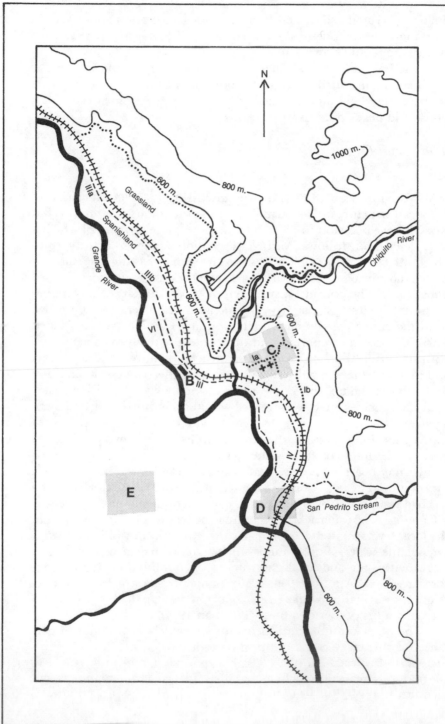

FIGURE 1

Main Geographical Features of the San Juan Irrigation System

KEY

A = Airfield
B = Sugar Mill ▬
C = San Juan (town)
D = San Pedrito (barrio)
E = Valerior Trujano
+ + = Town Cemetery
······· I = Main Branch of Town Canal (Water Commission control)
········ Ia, Ib = Main Subdivisions of Town Canal
········ II = Town, Grassland Branch Canal (Water Commission control)
– – – – III = Spanishland and Mill Canal (mill, private control)
– – – – IIIa, IIIb = Main Subdivisions of Spanishland and Mill Canal
–··–· IV = Private Canal off San Pedrito Water (private control)
–··–· V = San Pedrito Barrio Main Canal (barrio control)
–·– VI = One of the *Ejido* Land Canals (*ejido* control)
╫╫╫╫ Railroad
∿∿∿ 600 m. = Elevation

Graphic Scale in Kilometers

The major local unit of government and political organization in San Juan is the *municipio,* which is incorporated with all other Cuicatec settlements into a judicial and electoral district. The Federal Constitution of 1917 and the state law codes guarantee its local sovereignty in internal affairs of the community such as elections of officers. Local political agencies and institutions are therefore legally under the control of local citizens, who make many everyday decisions for the locality. San Juan also has a Court of First Instance, which gives it a local judge who also heads the judicial district. There is, therefore, something of a disjunction between the central federal and state governments on the one hand and the government of the *municipio* on the other. At the same time, however, the PRI has a local branch committee at the *municipio* level. Its leaders, following a pattern which is repeated all over Mexico, are the locally powerful people, powerful both in wealth and in access to outside sources of support in politics. Part of the political redistribution system in Mexico operates by local committeemen of the PRI funneling substantial campaign contributions and personal support of their clients up the PRI channels. In return, members of the local elite receive support for their candidates in nominations for elected and appointed positions in the government, and other kinds of special considerations. The PRI itself, then, provides the one way in which local social systems are articulated with the national ones at the political level, but outside the government apparatus itself.

The national landscape, as we will see below, is relevant in a discussion of the social effects of irrigation. But before we turn to a discussion of the specific role systems and other social phenomena directly connected with irrigation, we must present some important features of the social structure of San Juan. Primarily, the following pages focus on the differences between the social classes of San Juan, differences which are directly related to the uneven access to water of the town's social groups.

The town of San Juan is the capital of a *municipio* and the capital of an *ex-Distrito.* During the days of the Porfiriato, before the Mexican Revolution, the state of Oaxaca was divided into a score of districts, each of which was administered by a political chief (*jefe político*) appointed by the central government. With the reforms of the Revolution, the *municipios* were granted a degree of political autonomy, including the absence of centrally appointed district administrators. Today the districts do not officially exist as territorial units, but a unit called the *ex-Distrito,* which functions for judicial purposes, census taking, taxation, and so on, is still extant. Its functions are much attenuated from the past, but it has continued to be a socially significant unit. The major importance of the district, from our point of view here, is that the capital of the district contains many federal offices, such as tax, postal service, and court. These offices provide a listening post for local elites, opportunities for patronage appointments, and easy access to this level of the federal and state bureaucracy.

As we mentioned, San Juan is also the administrative center (*cabecera*) of its own *municipio*. The state of Oaxaca has by far the largest number of *municipios* in all Mexico. As a consequence they are generally much smaller in area and population than in the rest of Mexico, especially in the Cuicatec Indian area, where most *municipios* have fewer than 5,000 people, and are rather heavily nucleated and small in area. The Municipio of San Juan is unusual in that it contains most of the population of the Canyon in several settlements spread out over a distance of more than 30 kilometers. Moreover, the Canyon *municipios*, unlike the highlands, have been populated by mestizos (Spanish-speaking people of mixed Spanish and Indian ancestry) since at least the late seventeenth century. The civil-religious hierarchy which controls much of the political life in homogeneous Indian *municipios* does not exist in the Canyon towns. This circumstance has direct effects on the social organization of irrigation (cf. Lees 1970).

As the *cabecera* of the *municipio*, San Juan contains considerably more division of labor at the official level than do other, smaller dependent settlements. The town is governed by elected municipal officers who remain in service for three years. In addition to being a center of intensive irrigated agriculture, San Juan is also a commercial, banking, transportation, and service center for the district. One of the two priests in the district is located here, as well as the only doctors, a dentist, the only medical facility (run by Social Security, a federal agency), and the major wholesale establishments of the district. Most San Juaneros are involved in agricultural tasks primarily for the production of irrigated cash crops for the national market and in business activities involving import and export trade with the Indian hinterland and the larger urban centers of Mexico.

San Juan contains three distinct social classes, which have different positions vis-à-vis control of land and water. There is a small elite class (*la gente de categoría, la clase alta*) comprising approximately 10 percent of a population of 2,500 inhabitants, a small middle class (*la clase media*) of approximately the same size, and a majority of the lower class (*los peones, los de menos*).

The members of the elite in town are the major owners of land and commercial establishments. They control the bulk of the best irrigated land, in which they plant sugar, rice, and fruit trees; they own all the major stores and market stalls. The elite is organized in terms of corporate kindred, which are homogenous with respect to class and political faction. These kindred are intermarried across town boundaries; such kinship networks form the basis of cooperating economic groups and political support and spread, territorially, into other irrigated towns in the district and wider region and into major metropolitan centers (cf. E. Hunt 1969; E. and R. Hunt 1969; R. Hunt 1965, 1971, for more extensive discussion of these issues).

The middle class derives income primarily from (white collar) service jobs and to a degree from retail commercial activities and minor cash cropping, primarily of fruits and sugar. The local doctors, druggist, and dentist are a part of this class, as are the full-time bureaucrats. Relatively well-paid full-time clerks and assistants in the stores and the owners of small retail stores are also in this category. There is some ownership of irrigated property, but it is not of major importance to the income of the middle-class family compared with that of the upper-class family. The members of this class disdain manual work and tend to devalue agricultural pursuits, unlike the elite class, which is intimately involved in agricultural and water management.

The lower class includes a roster of low income San Juaneros, from the owners of small parcels of irrigated land sufficient to produce cash to provision their family to completely propertyless individuals who must work at agricultural tasks for wages. Individuals in this class own some minor cash-producing property, such as a very small field, or an inherited share in the profits of the harvest of a fruit tree. It is rarely the case, however, that low-class families can live solely on the proceeds of their property. Their major source of income is peon work, manual labor connected either with the soil (work in fields or on the irrigation works), with construction, or with the carrying of burdens (moving goods from a store to the house of customers, moving items in a warehouse, helping to load or unload a train boxcar, etc.).

Many other social features correlate with these three Weberian classes. Education beyond the sixth-grade level is limited to the two upper classes. Only the elite and the top of the middle class have access to university levels of education. Life-style correlates directly with income and education, as does the kind of knowledge and experience the person has of the outside world. Critically, the members of the elite and middle class are the only San Juaneros who, on a regular basis, cope with the metropolitan world, including the higher levels of the government machinery.

San Juan also contains two political factions. These factions are essentially struggling for control of the basic wealth of the community, which is composed about equally of the irrigated fields and their products and of extensive commerce with the Indian hinterland. The division between factions is very strong among the elite, less strong among the middle class, and weak enough to be an opportunity for manipulation of clientship "privileges" (including access to water) among the lower class. There are virtually no occasions on which the elite cooperate across factional lines. The two exceptions involve control of irrigation and taxes, as we shall see below.

The stranger is struck by the number of government jobs in San Juan. Many persons in town are full-time government employees, from the *mozo* (field hand) who sweeps out the jail to the district judge. Many others, it turns out, work in an official capacity on a part-time basis. The municipal president is usually a member of the upper or middle class, and such posts as *jefe político* or now congressman have seldom left the hands of the upper class. Of even more importance, however, is the fact that the vast majority of persons occupying government offices do so to some extent at the pleasure of the local elite, either as a consequence of decisions made within the local PRI committee or as a consequence of powerful patron-client and *compadrazgo* relationships that local elites have outside the town with powerful persons in central bureaucracies.

We must turn now to some formal aspects of water control, and its connection with the class structure. An important feature of states, frequently ignored by anthropologists engaged in community studies, is the relation between local norms and regulations and the codification of rules of access and alienation of property and resources by a literate central bureaucracy. This relation is eminently important in this case study.

In Mexico, water is owned by the nation and in theory is available to all potential users in an egalitarian fashion, which involves taking regular turns at being served and paying identical rates of taxation. But the ideal picture of an egalitarian system of water distribution, maintained by an egalitarian system of duties with respect to the physical maintenance of canal networks, is distorted by a complex system of water or canal and land tenure and different actual water demands of the crops planted by the different canal users. Land in San Juan is owned privately by individuals, by family trusts, by private corporations (a mill), cooperatively by the local *ejido* members, and by the town corporation to grant in usufruct. Some land can be rented, leased by long term contracts, or mortgaged. An additional complication is that permanent standing crops such as fruit trees can be sold, rented, or leased independent of the land on which they stand (the origin of this practice is pre-Hispanic [Millon 1955]).

To complicate this normative picture, irregular and illegal aspects of the social organization of the irrigation system are omnipresent. The way in which the physical systems are actually administered is an extraordinary example of the divergence between normative structure and actual practice frequently observed in other aspects of mestizo Mexican village life. It is important that this point be stressed, for accurate field data are crucial and easy to miss on account of this divergence.

Whenever asked about conflict or bribery in regard to water, which is endemic in San Juan, most informants who are not well acquainted with the anthropologists act as if they were blind and deaf. Admitting knowledge of the illegalities occurring in the system is tantamount to admitting that one has engaged in them oneself. Thus, getting lists of irrigators, of true water schedules, of payments, or accounts of specific resolutions of conflict is difficult in the extreme at the beginning of fieldwork. It was only by living in the town for a sufficiently long time and acquiring access to intimate, private information that we discovered how the social organization of irrigation in fact works, rather than how it is supposed to work. The wife of one of our informants put it quite graphically when she said that her "husband will not talk about water business, not even to himself when he is asleep." This point is an important one, because a picture of water control in Mexico based on interviews during brief stays in communities (for example, using information obtained in surveys) will give only a formal, ideal picture of how water-control systems are expected to work if legal, normative arrangements are followed. The actual picture of water control is very different from normative expectations.

At present several different social agencies control the physical irrigation systems. There are "private" canals, a public, town-controlled canal network, an *ejido* canal system, and a drinking water system.

THE CANALS OF THE TOWN

The two town-controlled canals service the majority of users of irrigation water.[5] Theoretically every town resident who desires can have access to town water for irrigation purposes. In fact, only those who have lands located in the path of the canals and cannot afford any other water source pay the town for its water. The town-controlled canals and water are administered by a specialized agency whose officers have no other authority; that is, their roles are exclusively defined in terms of water control and formally isolated from other political roles in the community. Their agency is called the Water Commission (La Junta de Aguas). Officially, it is a branch of the federal government, which owns all national water sources.

The present Water Commission is administered by a governing body whose officers are elected annually. The officers receive payments from water users. The income of the Water Commission (approximately $500 monthly) is used to defray the costs of the town-controlled sections of the irrigation system, including the salaries of the commission employees. The Water Commission also decides the price of water according to the degree of scarcity during different seasons, adjudicates conflict cases between water users within the village, keeps schedules and general bookkeeping of irrigation turns, and decides when to ration water by the hour in times of scarcity.

Nobody in town wants the administrative jobs in the water commission except the *fontanero* position (see below) because they give no advantage in water control for the men in charge. Officers are constantly suffering from pressure by different water users to favor their lands. The poor serving in office find that they cannot resist the pressure of the larger landlords (who are usually their patrons and creditors). The rich find no advantage in taking officerships on the committee, because they can control decisions by delegating their power to their clients who serve as officers, and/or because they can irrigate from other water sources not controlled by the Water Commission. Thus, no one wants to monopolize these positions. One informant said that he found the service unprofitable because it involved innumerable headaches: three or four hours of daily evening meetings, hearing constant complaints, and "not even the possibility of getting more water for oneself."

Basically, the Water Commission's authority is derived from the strength of the community as a whole, indirectly backed by the centralized federal state. The officers of the commission hold this authority by maintaining consensus among the small landowners who use town water and by not antagonizing the large landowners.

The commission's governing body has a president, a secretary, a treasurer, five committeemen (*vocales*), and two water policemen or distributors (*fontaneros*). The president is responsible for reports to the membership and for decisions on cooperative labor for canal cleaning and repair; he also acts as liaison with the federal offices of the commission. The secretary acts as scribe and record-keeper, copying irrigation schedules, bills, and records of decisions made by the membership in open meetings. The treasurer keeps the money and the

accounts of cash transactions. The *vocales* act as representatives of
the body of town water users during regular meetings.

The water policemen are officially in charge of the two town
canals. They open and close sluices. They make everyday decisions
about where and how long to irrigate specific parcels by determining
how dry they are and whose turn is coming up. They police the sections of land being irrigated, guarding the canal sluices with guns.
They are expected to arrest those they find stealing water and to take
them to the local jail. Each of the water policemen is supposedly in
charge of one of the canal branches, taking turns at work as water is
diverted from branch to branch. In fact, however, they work together to
protect each other from attacks by irate water users who find themselves in disagreement with their water allocation policies.

The work of the *fontanero* officers is thus the most dangerous but
it is also the only profitable kind. If skillful, they can make a substantial income from bribes, mostly during the dry season, when everyone
tries to gain an advantage over his neighbor in irrigation turns. Moreover, they are major adjudicators on a day-to-day basis of conflict
between parcel owners and are thus called water judges (*jueces de
aguas*). Hence, although their regular monthly salary is only 40 pesos,
it is said that they in fact get enough money from illegal payments on
water to live on their income.

Because water in the town canals is legally cheap, salaries for the
water officers are low. But water from the town canals is illegally
expensive; because of their low salaries, water policemen are expected
to overcharge, particularly during the periods of water shortage. Even
after payment, a man has to wait near the ditch when his turn comes
up, to make sure he will not be bypassed. Many do so armed with guns
or machetes for insurance. Official payments for water are made as
fields are irrigated, according to the prearranged costs on a *pro rata*
basis. Water can be paid for by the hour. The most common agreement,
however, is payment by amount of seed measured in *arrobas* or
maquilas, a standard calculation being that an *arroba* is equivalent to
one quarter of 2 hectares. The price per *arroba* is modified by the crop
planted, which San Juaneros feel is just, since some crops require
more water than others. Corn, the cheapest crop, runs about 1.50 to
3 pesos per *arroba*.[6] Tomatoes, which require about three times more
water and are a popular crop, cost at least 4.50 pesos per *arroba*. A cul-
tivator calculates how many *arrobas* he plans to plant, and makes an
agreement with the Water Commission officers beforehand, ascertain-
ing that he will be able to get sufficient water for his crop and agreeing
on a minimum annual payment for it. Most of the land irrigated by the
town canals, however, is in household orchards inside the town. Fruit

trees are irrigated about every twenty days by paying for a certain number of hours per watering. Fruit has been one of the most important town export crops from pre-Hispanic times. These payments are permanent costs for orchard owners, since mangoes and *chicozapotes* produce annual fruit for longer than a human lifetime. Everyone in San Juan, irrespective of class, tries to own fruit trees.

Receiving water also implies an agreement to contribute laborers or one's own effort to canal maintenance and cleaning, though as we indicated, these payments are separate from payments made for specific waterings. Prices of labor also vary with the crop planted. Sugar cane requires twice as many man-hours of labor as corn (3 to 6 laborers per hectare). Thus a man drawing water from a public canal is expected to provide maintenance service proportional to his consumption of water. The actual work of cleaning, however, is done by the lower class. Large wealthy landowners, when drawing water from public canals, hire men to perform their share of the cleaning. Small landowners and renters do the work themselves, sometimes with the help of kinsmen. During the planting and growing season, crews of *mozos* (field hands) are regularly at work under the supervision of canal owners, foremen employed by them, or officers of the town Water Commission, who are sometimes aided by the municipal authorities. Such work crews are primarily concerned with the maintenance of the system—that is, cleaning and repair of canals and sluices.

We have not attempted to calculate the total number of man-hours necessary to maintain the whole of the canal network of the town because, early in the fieldwork, which was focused on other problems of research, it became obvious that we would not have the time to collect all the necessary data. However, various figures are available. Canal cleaning, digging, and repair, where controlled by the local town water authorities (i.e., the Town Water Commission), take up the larger part of the total communal town labor. One single cleaning of the Grassland branch canal required two full days of work for 115 men, which at the local average of 6.5 hours per day amounts to about 746 man-hours. For maintenance of the few large, privately controlled canals, one or two *mozos* are permanently hired for continuous work. Extra crews of five to ten men are routinely hired for major cleaning and repair; they may also be hired for various periods of time to take care of emergencies. Several permanent crews are in charge of opening and closing sluice gates which divert water to different fields. When water is being allocated, these crews are constantly present to prevent farmers from stealing it. In seasons when water is in short supply, stealing water is very commonly engaged in by owners of neighboring parcels of irrigated land, especially at night. Therefore, most townsmen prefer to irrigate during the daytime, even though the volume of water per hour is greater at night because of a much lower evaporation rate.[7]

Individuals' claims to rights to irrigation water are validated by residence and town membership, and by paying the dues or taxes for services of the Water Commission. But payments to the Water Commission are not made unless one cultivates land irrigated by town-controlled canals. Thus, although in theory the town as a whole controls the Water Commission, in fact only users of town canal water actually have any indirect control over distribution and allocation of this water. Users include both landowners and renters or share-croppers, the last two acquiring water rights indirectly from the landowner's potential rights and directly by payment to the Water Commission.

Water users have to add to regular payments and taxation a certain amount of labor on their own to keep clean the subsidiary ditches which reach their parcels; the town does not assume this responsibility. Usually, water users controlling a smaller ditch in common clean sections in cooperation or by agreeing to provide a certain number of man-hours (themselves or peons) for upkeep of their ditch.

Although the Water Commission does not keep up subsidiary canals, it has the power to enforce upkeep by a ditch user. If a man refuses to cooperate with the neighboring parcel owners and keep up with his share of labor, the other irrigators can complain to the Water Commission and insist that water be refused to him until he complies with his proportion of work.

All these agreements made in or through the control of the Water Commission do not represent the bulk of the irrigated land. The major area of parcels of the Grassland has a total surface of less than a third of the cultivated land of the town, although all but a handful of cultivators plant there. (There are over 200 water users in the commission.) Parcels are very small; except for the center of the area, most parcels cannot be irrigated in the dry season because of water scarcity. This problem is one of the major sources of internal strife over water.

THE ELITE CANALS

The Spanishland and San Pedrito canals irrigate the bulk of the best lands of San Juan. Spanishland includes about one hundred and ninety hectares of the best alluvial land. The private canals of San Pedrito control a minimum of sixty hectares of alluvium, but errors and omissions in our data (as compared to the map of irrigated land) suggest that perhaps the real figure is above one hundred hectares for both cane and fruit trees. All these lands are controlled by the major landowners in cooperation with the owner and administrator of the local sugar mill. The Spanishland canals and ditches are regulated by a separate Water Commission, administered by the sugar mill for the large landowners, who plant sugarcane they sell to the mill. Priority rights on buying the sugarcane harvest are given in exchange for credit on labor, equipment, and water. The mill administrator himself makes decisions on both repair work and water allocations. The second canal, San Pedrito, is controlled by a family of descendants of the original builder. The water is paid for by this family in the form of local taxes to the Indian barrio officers.

Payments in the Spanishland private canals are measured in *tareas*: a person pays according to the number of *tareas* his land requires. A *tarea* is the number of hours which it takes to plant or weed a piece of land approximately 10 meters by 10 meters, or the equivalent time in canal work (i.e., it is a measure of labor in time).

These "privately" owned and "privately" controlled major canals and their subsidiary ditches irrigate the best land and are all held by a small handful of major elite landowners. Approximately 190 hectares of these lands are irrigated by the mill canal. Of these, 150 are owned by five extended families of major landowners, four of which belong to the political faction which at present controls town politics. There are, however, twenty different landowners in this section. The Indian Village canal, which irrigates over sixty hectares, is also controlled by one of these four families but serves more than ten different water users. Cultivators who do not belong to the town Water Commission membership because their lands are marginally located with respect to the town canals do not get water and thus do not pay taxes to the town for water. Since they are small cultivators and cannot afford to maintain their own canals, they buy the water (an illegal practice) from the private canal owners. The owner pays for canal maintenance and policing, schedules and keeps books on the distribution himself, and hires salaried policemen to watch night water turns. Thus, officially, water is not sold (which is illegal since waters are federally owned). What is sold by the mill and private canal owners are services in canal repair, policing, construction, and bookkeeping, as well as credit. These activities are a direct source of political power. All water users in private canals are political and business clients of the men who control these canals. Usually these users contract to sell their crops to the mill or the private canal owner (under a system called *refacciona-miento*). If a particular user does not "pay his share" in bribing costs, or does not support a political candidate, or refuses to sell his harvest to the man who gives him credit and water, he can easily be punished by cutting off his water supply. A man joining the opposition is sure to find sooner or later that he has been discovered, which means the ruin of his crop or the sizable reduction of his basic income (cf. Simpson 1937: 370-71 for a comparable case). In fact, one water client who joined the opposition was discovered when we were in the field.

Water selling in itself is a quite profitable enterprise. Private canal owners at times prefer to sell water and leave part of their own land fallow if they do not have sufficient water for both their water clients and themselves. In the case of the mill, the administrator is definite about the necessity of the mill for unified water control. If the mill doesn't manage the canals, he claims, fights between landowners cut down the sugar harvest. It is thus to the advantage of the mill owners to ensure that there is a just distribution of water among the large sugarcane planters. Only by maintaining the support of the growers can the mill function at a profit. With the exception of the present administrator (who is a professional), all mill administrators since the middle of the nineteenth century have been senior men of the San Juan landowning elite. As one of my landless informants phrased it: "They keep the water and the jobs among themselves."

But water selling can be made profitable only for those with a secure source of capital, because initial investments and canal upkeep can be quite expensive. A single day of repair of the diversion dam for a branch of a private canal cost its owner 500 pesos (40 dollars) just in labor costs. Another repair of a branch dam cost 350 pesos, including the labor of seven men for five days. The cost of operating one private ditch was calculated to be 8,000 pesos per year.

The Papaloapan Commission (cf. Poleman 1964) has tried to solve the problem of water storage (which greatly affects production levels for the district) by proposing a diversion dam and a new canal from the Rio Grande which will increase the amount of water available for irrigation and increase the area of land which can be regularly irrigated by a maximum of two thirds of the present area in Cuicatlán. This project has been looked upon with jaundiced eyes by the local upper class, which perceives that it will cut into an important source of income and power. At the time that we were in the field, the upper class (unified on this issue despite otherwise irreconcilable political differences) was exercising a coordinated effort to interrupt the building of the dam, both openly in town meetings and sub rosa by secret lobbying and meetings.

THE EJIDO CANALS

A third, separate canal irrigates *ejido* lands further north. The *ejido* canal irrigates from Rio Grande waters and is controlled by a separate set of officers elected by the *ejido* members. Officially there are twenty *ejidatarios* (those who hold usufruct rights to an *ejido* parcel); unofficially there are thirty-seven separate parcels, amounting to 113 hectares, or approximately 3 hectares per *ejidatario*. This canal is administered in a third, and different, arrangement. The officers in charge of water allocations, conflict resolution, and ditch cleaning are not separated from other roles connected with the *ejido*. Water-control functions are assigned to *ejido* officers as part of their general functions. *Ejidatarios* are primarily members of the lowest class. Their economic links with the elite are not based on water—which, uniquely, is independent of the elite—but on a dependence upon the elite for credit and sale of their products. *Ejidatarios* are also the regular skilled laborers at the sugar mill, near which many have their homes. This small handful of members of the lower class is disproportionately powerful politically since they are doubly protected by the federal government, both as members of the mill union and as the only members of the lower class with independent (*ejido*) access to water.

THE TOWN TANK

The town also controls the potable water tank, which services the central part of town through modern metal piping. Again, this water service is not universally utilized. To receive water into the house, the occupants must pay special taxes, initially to extend the pipes and annually for water received. This service has been introduced by the federal government through the Papaloapan Commission. Since it serves only the central, most urbanized part of the town, it is basically a service provided by the town for the richest households, all of which are located in this town section below the canals. The poor live in wattle-and-daub houses on the dusty, hilly slopes of the town above the canals and without direct access to household water. This inequality of access to "potable" water had no social importance in terms of class conflict because, as everyone in town was aware, the tank water was not any better than ditch water: the builders had forgotten to install the appropriate filters. In fact, the tank, with its coat of thick green slime and mosquito colony, looked mighty unsalubrious.

Thus in San Juan several separate arrangements of water allocation, related to separate loci of power, exist simultaneously. One set of loci is the control of each single physical system, one is at the level of the minimum autonomous political unit (the village, the *municipio*), and a third is at the level of the total society. In terms of official arrangements, the system is unified under the Water Commission, representative of the town of San Juan as a whole but not of the *municipio*, which should be formally the unit (the *municipio* contains other settlements and physical systems). The Water Commission is responsible directly to the federal government. In terms of actual arrangements of water-controlling roles and agencies, three separate canal groups operate: the Water Commission, the Mill Commission with the private canal owners, and the *ejidatarios*. Over these lords the town's municipal government, which can bring water cases to court in time of conflict—into its own municipal court or into the district court also located in the village. Above the *municipio* is the Mexican federal government, which, through two of its separate ministries and other government institutions (e.g., the Ejido Commission), can reverse local decisions, arbitrate water disagreements between villages or within village factions, and introduce changes by building major water works.

Hence, water control is located in a set of institutions which are territorially localized and hierarchically nested in a vertical ladder of increasing power. This power ladder is isomorphic with the political and economic power ladder of the region and of the national state, and thus is ultimately centralized in a normative pyramidal arrangement but simultaneously decentralized and semiautonomous at the local level in terms of control of each physical system.

The Historical Evidence

The picture of water control in tribal societies, or post-English colonial Iraq, or in modern rural sectors of complex states such as Japan, cannot be directly used to explain the original evolutionary conditions under which water control did or did not become a significant social factor. It is obvious, however, that we can make some inferences about the universal requirements of irrigation under specified conditions by utilizing cross-cultural comparative materials and diachronic information in historically well-documented cases. Such materials may enable us to interpret cases which appear to be affected by the same distribution of variables. It is in this context that we wish to present historical information from the Cuicatec. We believe that our analysis of this ethnographic example suggests hypotheses of value to a clarification of some issues connected with more general problems of the analysis of the impact of irrigation on society. The following comments, therefore, are only hypotheses; generalizations would be premature, for these hypotheses have yet to be adequately tested.

Evidence from ethnohistorical materials indicates that the Cuicatec states were already developed at the time of the fall of Tula (ca. A.D. 1200). Our only evidence of pre-Hispanic canals, however, comes from the post-Classic period, when the town of Cuicatlán was already a major semi-urban center, with a probable population of 5,000 inhabitants (Hopkins 1970; E. Hunt 1972b).[8] Thus the Cuicatec evidence at present cannot add anything to the question of the origin of Canyon states in relation to irrigation. We have extensive evidence, however, on the role that the Cuicatec ruling elites had in the sociopolitical life of their communities during the sixteenth century and the period just before the Conquest. This evidence firmly supports the view that the provincial rural elites of Mesoamerica, such as the Cuicatec, were actively engaged in providing leadership for the management of the agricultural affairs of the polities they ruled.

At the time of the Spanish Conquest, the Cuicatec were a loosely integrated ethnic and political unit, composed of several autonomous town and city-states of Cuicatec-speaking peoples, each ruled by a native elite. It was a small provincial society, part of Mesoamerican civilization but geographically isolated from expanding culture centers. Its economic cornerstone was intensive, irrigated agriculture, adapted to this harsh, inhospitable ecological niche.

The two different habitation zones which exist today existed in the sixteenth century. Territories of the communities in each, with few marginal exceptions, have been continuously occupied until the present, both in the semi-desertic Grande Canyon and the piedmont. Hardly anything that the Mesoamerican native planted can grow without irrigation in the Canyon. But with irrigation the Canyon is much more productive than the mountain hinterlands. In pre-Hispanic times, population pressure led to warfare and attempted invasion of the Cuicatec-improved irrigated fields. In the Canyon, the several pre-Hispanic city-states grew in the center of their permanent orchards and agricultural fields, and their wealth attracted unsuccessful attempts at conquest until the last Aztec king took the major city-states under the empire for tax tribute.

The Cuicatec masses were primarily farmers, cultivating most of the known Mesoamerican subsistence crops but also specializing, in the Canyon area, in the cultivation of fruit trees in extensive irrigated orchards (cf., for example, Paso y Troncoso 1914). Agricultural activities were carried on in communally held lands cultivated by a free peasantry. Village cultivators were controlled by stewards who were responsible to local aristocratic magistrates, and minor rulers who themselves were dependent on the major rulers of the several Cuicatec city-states. These government officers were directly involved in the administration of agriculture.

Rulers did not control agriculture by monopolizing privately held land; the village communities were repositories of such rights.

Rulers, however, were in charge of annual land redistribution among the peasantry. They directed corvée labor and controlled the processing of raw materials such as salt. The rulers supervised the redistribution of agricultural tribute for themselves and, in the period immediately prior to the Conquest, for the Aztec overlords who had conquered the region. They regulated the scheduling of religious festivities associated with the temples dedicated to water and fertility gods and goddesses. The rulers also controlled the sources of water for irrigation and the canals attached to individual towns and hamlets, and they exacted tribute (later taxation) from adjacent settlements which bought surplus water from their canal system. Such water tribute was collected on a seasonal basis. The Cuicatec ruling elite was not only a depository of the administration rights in land and water. It was also primarily responsible for directing defensive warfare against encroaching groups, which in several cases attempted to obtain, by force, access to the water sources and improved irrigated lands (cf. example in Burgoa 1934). The ruling elite also relocated or founded communities to protect water sources. Moreover, in the sixteenth century, as their contemporary counterparts do today, caciques manipulated water control as a source of power to obtain political following. For example, in a lengthy court case (1562), an illegitimate heir to the cacique post in the Cuicatec Estancia of Yepaltepec obtained public support of the Mazatec neighbors in an adjacent community by promising them that, if appointed cacique, he would grant them Yepaltepec waters free. Up to this time, these villagers had paid for the scarce water, because they had lost a war several centuries before the Spanish Conquest over the rights to the water spring which fed their lands.

Caciques had a complex set of rights and duties vis-à-vis their subjects. There was a clear distinction between classes in terms of the division of labor and different usufruct rights over the means of production and surplus. Each class was also integrated into a social system which was clearly and markedly rank stratified and which involved, among other power domains, differential control over water.

The maximum level of permanent political integration, however, did not occur at the level of the macroethnic group (defined by language), which formed only a loose polity integrated by symbiotic trade and intermarriage of ruling-class members. We have discussed extensively in another work the possible causes of Cuicatec political fission above the city-state level (E. Hunt 172b). Each city-state, controlling its own independent water sources, was the maximum extension of the centralized political community. The separateness and isolation of scarce, small water sources gave the Cuicatec the characteristic Mesoamerican cantonalistic tendencies mentioned by

Armillas (1949). But within each city-state, clear unification of authority existed, with marked differences in rights of water control and other political privileges between social classes. The functions of the elite were a monopoly, and acquisition of rights was primarily determined by ascription, by proof of aristocratic birth and rights of succession. Such rights were jealously guarded until the beginning of the seventeenth century, when the Cuicatec native elite gave way to pressure from the Spanish colonists in the Canyon area.

Hence it is possible to argue that the native elites of the city-states controlled water because they had centralized political power in their hands, and at the same time that water control was one of the sources of their political power. However, the system of irrigation as it exists today in the Canyon and as it existed at the time of the Conquest has clearly discernible requirements related to the social need for technical and managerial skills and for unification of decision making to avoid conflict. Without effective control of the technological aspects, the irrigation network can physically collapse in a very short time. Without effective control of the sociological aspects, the irrigation system can fall into anomic internal conflict, which disrupts the normal flow of production and peaceful neighborly coexistence.

The Spanish Conquest produced just such a disruption of the normal Cuicatec political process and was accompanied by a steady lowering of production, reflected in the increased number of desperate petitions to reduce tribute on agricultural products. During the early period, many native irrigation works were abandoned, primarily perhaps because of the decimation of the population by epidemics but also because the social upheavals introduced by the Conquest disrupted the normal process of water control. Fights over water and irrigated lands erupted in the Canyon as well as the piedmont between villages sharing water sources. These were taken to Spanish courts in lengthy legal hassles. In the Canyon, Spaniards soon found it profitable to displace the Indian peasantry and dedicate themselves to cultivating sugarcane and other irrigated products of interest to the Spanish entrepreneurs. Soon several major landed estates were formed (e.g., Tecomaxtlahuaca, Guendulain), some originally granted as *encomiendas* (temporary royal land grants), some as private mills. These estates encroached on the best Indian lands and waters. The Spaniards built new irrigation networks to service the haciendas and mills. They granted rights on water to themselves at the expense of the Indian towns (this process is extremely well documented in the Ramo de Tierras of the Archivo General de la Nacion for the area north of the Cuicatec, in the lower Tehuacán Valley).

Masonry and stone aqueducts soon dotted the Canyon countryside. During the seventeenth and eighteenth centuries these aqueducts were controlled either by the local Spanish *corregidores* (governors nominated by the Spanish Crown) of the towns or directly by the *hacendados* themselves, with support of the Spanish courts and colonial government. The small population size, a consequence of earlier disastrous epidemics, reduced land and water pressure in spite of extensive Spanish invasions. The drop in population density led to an "abundance of water" (Paso y Troncoso 1914: 187) for cultivation. This circumstance prevented major conflicts of access over water, judging by the absence of court cases.

The colonial water works have been abandoned totally or are in a state of extreme disrepair, being either partially utilized in combination with open ditches or left waterless as a monument to a bygone era when organized, major building activities of civil improvement were still possible.

In the nineteenth century, after independence, the colonial arrangements were hardly disrupted. Municipal officers controlled water for the whole Municipio of San Juan and throughout the district. But municipal authorities were often appointed and always were political dependents of the landed upper class. District chiefs (*jefes políticos de distrito*), the major local officials appointed by and directly responsible to state governors, were in San Juan always appointed from the families of major landowners. (Their grandchildren control San Juan today.) Some of the major haciendas in the Canyon were treated by the colonial and later by the independent government as separate political entities (*municipalidades*) and thus controlled their own water sources. Two small haciendas, however, were totally within the San Juan municipal boundaries and could secure most of the water from the town's municipal system. One *hacendado* owned his own aqueduct within the *municipio*. There was thus a single official decision-making source for all of the users of any one municipal system. The members of the *hacendado* class controlled district politics, including water politics, and used this control for their own benefit irrespective of normative municipal regulations.

During the last period of the hacienda boom, in the late nineteenth and early twentieth centuries, population pressure on the Cañada led to expansion of hacienda control into the highland *municipios* and to increasing unrest and conflict in the Canyon lands themselves. But the strong Porfirian government of the district maintained the elite control of water unchallenged. Changes in the social organization of irrigation occurred only after the upheaval of the Revolution. Bribery, uneven allocation of water, excessive water taxation of the poor, water theft, and other injustices in access to irrigation are in San Juan complaints which are no different today than they were in the late nineteenth century. However, the system functions fairly smoothly in spite of constant petty conflict, and there is no evidence to indicate that it may collapse. For half of the year (the rainy season), all fields receive sufficient water. In the dry season, the small cultivators either do not plant a second crop, plant a crop with low water requirements, or grow a stunted crop with insufficient water. They do not like it, but they cannot, at present, change the structure without another major revolution. The official monopolization of power over water by the states through the Water Commission, united with other sources of political strength on the part of the local ruling class, prevents both the reform of the irrigation system, and conflict running rampant.

Even with the changes over a four hundred year period in the Cuicatec, water control has been, as far as our historical record shows, an important aspect of elite and local government prerogatives. The theoretical implications of this historical picture are discussed in the following sections.

Conflict in Irrigation

CONTEMPORARY INTERNAL CONFLICT IN SAN JUAN

One result of the complex situation described above is that some conflict is generated by the contemporary contradiction between the normative expectations of the majority of water users and the actual distribution practices. The officially accepted egalitarian ideology with respect to access to irrigation water, which has been written into federal law, has been locally applied to the formation of bureaucratic mechanisms for water distribution. But the actual situation in San Juan reveals highly varied and competitive alternatives for control of land and water resources. The private control of land, water scarcity, the differential water demands of the various crops planted, the great differences in size and quality of fields, as well as the differences in wealth and power of the landowners involved, affect water allocations. The resulting uneven distribution of actual access to water, in contrast to the potential or ideal, results in constant petty conflict. This conflict in the past has occasionally developed into physical aggression and even homicide when the local government lost its grip on the reins of water control. Until about thirty years ago, the personnel in charge of water control were part of the municipal government staff. The water users had been, increasingly since the late nineteenth century, highly exasperated by the municipal handling of the town canal waters. The officers were arbitrary in their allocation of irrigation turns and the evaluation of water costs. They favored themselves and the town's largest and wealthiest landowners, demanding bribes and other unofficial costs. This control became more disruptive with the great increase in population size after 1900 and with the demands upon the water system for newly introduced, water-hungry cash crops such as rice.

Prior to the Mexican Revolution this situation was accepted because the landed elite, in conjunction with its appointed local officers, had the recurrent support of the state in its monopoly of both land and water. Then, however, because of favorable state attitudes, the town poor, who had had little voice over water control prior to the Revolution, found themselves supported by outside institutions which were hierarchically superior in official power to the local authorities.

During the immediate postrevolutionary period, conflict became rampant. The power of the local landed elite over water was openly challenged. *Usuarios* (water users) refused to pay water costs or participate in canal cleaning. Water stealing became a common practice, and several violent fights and murders occurred in a period of a few years.

Once the traditional unified authority of the *hacendado* class and local rural elite was partially broken by land expropriation and other external events, conflict increased greatly. Many small cultivators who usually planted tomatoes in the Grassland section discontinued the crop. Because tomatoes are a high water-demand crop, the uncertainties of obtaining water made their cultivation unprofitable. One informant said he completely stopped cultivating for several years, simply because there were too many dangers of becoming involved in fights over water or losing the whole crop because of water mismanagement.

To reestablish order, which was affecting small as well as large landowners to everyone's disadvantage, the community sought help by looking for external restraints in the shape of intervention by the federal government. A committee of water users petitioned the government to have a branch of the Federal Water Commission (Junta de Aguas) formed in town, to reduce the disorder. Many members of the local elite (who controlled ditches for their private use) were opposed, but the majority won, and the Junta was created with the state's blessings. Its creation was an attempt to remove undue influences and resolve some of the past conflicts and alleged corruptions which interfered with an equal and just distribution of irrigation water. Decision-making power over water was therefore officially unified in a single agency but also separated from other decision-making bodies which affected the whole community (especially the municipal government). In theory, control of water thus became unified, insulated from other political controls, and located above the municipal level. This agency was supposed to prevent interference of the locally influential power groups (the rural landed elite) in matters of water control and to vest power in the small water users, who elected representatives from among themselves.

What in fact has happened, however, is that the local elite now controls the Water Commission when necessary for its purposes, through its political clients who are the officeholders in that agency. This control is analogous to their control of the other formal government bodies in town. Many of the poor in San Juan now believe that the solution to the present problems of water allocation is to bring men in from the outside to manage the water system. Others believe that they should go back to the old system of municipal control, "without its corrupt elements." No one suggests, however, that the San Juaneros can do without some sort of unified control, nor can anyone suggest how to eliminate corruption or conflict except by increasing water supplies to meet current demands. One of our informants summarized their problem by stating flatly that "water makes people dishonest and peaceful men fight. If there is not enough, even the most honest man will be tempted to get an unfair share for himself and his friends . . . if he can find the way."[9]

INTER-COMMUNITY CONFLICT

In a previous work we have extensively discussed the ecological, sociological, and political factors which hindered centralization of the Cuicatec above the level of the small city-states and their subject hamlets (E. Hunt 1972b). Many of these factors are not directly related to the economy of irrigated agriculture. However, the nature of the irrigation system may have been related, in part, to the schismogenetic tendencies of the communities of the district. First, the irrigation niches are small. Second, they served communities in which there was little if any colonial land pressure and water was abundant, given the size of the population of cultivators. Third, in most cases, a single city-state controlled a single major water source and its length. When the water source was formed by several minor affluent streams, a subject hamlet of the city-state was located in each headwater to protect it from enemy takeover or intrusion. If two subject hamlets shared a water source (e.g., San Lorenzo and San Francisco of Papalo), the ruler of the city-state administered the water and controlled the diversion canals and water allocation for both segments of the political community. Settlements of peoples who were not subject to the same city-state, located downstream (e.g., Quiotepec vs. Papalo), paid for the water in tribute. Legitimate rights to control of the length of a water course were reinforced by control of the spring from which a river emerged within the territory of the state and by a history of military defeat of the downstream communities. Local, short-lived wars of defense of water sources which continued sporadically into the colonial period (under the name of *tumultos* or *montoneras*) reinforced traditional rights and reaffirmed the legitimate power of the city-state rulers to control their water sources. However, when a downstream community was superior in political might, population size, etc., to the upstream community which shared its waters, it appears that peaceful agreements about land and water were necessary between rulers. These agreements sometimes involved intermarriage of the rulers' successors.

The nature of the Cuicatec streams makes the relation between upstream and downstream communities quite unusual. The Cuicatec streams are fed throughout their length by subterranean aquifers and cut the piedmont into deep, narrow canyons which traverse uninhabitable territory, making it impossible to use their waters for irrigation purposes in the middle section of their length. Thus, upstream communities cannot cut off downstream communities completely from access to water (although they have a marginal control over some water surplus). The communities of Cuicatlan and Papalo, which have shared a stream until the present, exemplify this relationship. We do not know, however, how conflict over water during the dry season (if it existed) was handled between communities in the pre-Hispanic period.

We have argued that the evidence strongly suggests that soon after the Conquest there was no population pressure on the land, since chroniclers report that there was abundant water for city-states. Thus, conflict did not arise in terms of water competition between Cuicatec centers, and pressures to centralize to avoid conflict were not present.

At present, several towns and municipalities engage every year in lengthy negotiations arbitrated by state officials over the quotas of water which they may share from common sources. The community of Quiotepec, which since remote times has shared a water source with Papalo, since these same times has been engaged in recurrent conflict with Papalo over water. In pre-Hispanic times they were controlled by different ethnic units (Mazatec vs. Cuicatec) and fought a war over the water rights. At the time of the Conquest, they were in constant open conflict about tributary rights which Papalo claimed over Quiotepec in exchange for water. This same conflict has been flaring up over and over again during the last 400 years, particularly in markedly dry years. The conflict does not reach armed attacks, however, because it is now handled through the state and federal courts, with regular state intervention and arbitration. When we were in the field, the male author of this paper was thoroughly welcomed and feasted by the villagers of Quiotepec, because they were under the erroneous impression that he was a secret agent of the government (an engineer) who was investi-

energy in distracting conflict and anomic decision making. In San Juan, construction, but especially maintenance and policing, became concentrated in institutionalized political roles which include in function water control and differential access to power. In a system of this type, the maintenance of the major or core physical system is a labor-consuming undertaking. Normal repairs are a constant chore, and decisions have to be made every day about how much work is needed where. Then the work has to be supervised so that it is done properly and without damage. There are emergencies which require the ability to mobilize a substantial number of workers on short notice and to get them to do the work effectively.

In this arid land, with population pressure creating a water shortage, policing the system is a serious consideration, both in scheduling water allocations and protecting the receivers of the water; it is also necessary to detect theft of water and, most seriously, to resolve satisfactorily the conflict which arises over competition for a life-giving scarce resource. For a physical system such as San Juan, involving scores of domestic groups, routine administration even when thoroughly traditionalized and free of conflict as in Pul Eliya is complex and vital to the survival of the system. Bookkeeping for the system is of some importance also. The work has to be exchanged for money or other privileges, or the individual workers must be persuaded or coerced to carry out the work. The individual clients have to receive the amount of water which is regarded as their due and for which they may exchange either labor, tax, or tribute. Marked mismanagement of the administrative duties provokes open antagonisms. Lack of consensus has led to temporary anarchy, while recurrent injustices of distribution steadily build tension and conflict, to the point of social collapse. Coordination of decision making may function, however, to prevent such extreme developments.

If the system is large enough, it may encourage, if not require, that several functions be centralized by being allocated to specialized roles within the government apparatus: some of these roles require relatively scarce skills when compared with other roles in the same social system. Today, even with the simple technological aspects of irrigation in San Juan, there is a differential distribution of knowledge, especially engineering knowledge, of ability to organize and supervise, and of access to information. It is perhaps not logically necessary that all of these skills co-occur in the same role-syndromes, but all have to be available. It would appear that in San Juan skill at and responsibility for performing the critical functions of the irrigation system (maintenance, allocation, conflict resolution) are not homogeneously distributed in the population. At the lowest skill level, all farm hands can perform the work of directing water into fields and cleaning the irrigation ditches. The more critical functions are those of deciding when to apply maintenance procedures, how to manage the maintenance crews, as well as how to handle allocation and the conflict it engenders in such a way that the system can continue to operate at some moderate level of productivity. These skills are far less widely manifested than the others, and tend to co-occur in the same role-syndromes monopolized by the upper classes. While these skills are by no means restricted to one or very few people in the social system (as witness the existence of four separate management and allocation agencies, two of which rotate persons through leadership roles for a small population), they are not widely distributed either.

Virtually all persons who occupy roles having to do with management of the irrigation system also occupy other political and non-political roles of control. That is, the roles which deal directly with irrigation are, for this system, thoroughly embedded in other political and economic networks. There are complex ways in which one activity system affects another. Skill in managing relations with the cash crop and money market are important in generating capital to manage and maintain the physical system. Maintaining a canal system is important for keeping political clients satisfied, and for keeping a profitable cash crop in production. All these interactions affect and are affected by skill in coping with outside bureaucracies, bribing, etc. Some of these interactions deal with water, but others, such as dealings with taxation officials, do not.

The fact that the middle- and lower-class people could theoretically run the physical systems as well as the elite would seem to argue that the concentration of all functions in closed clusters of roles, and the linkage of these roles with other power roles in the social system, is not necessary from the point of view of agriculture. It is not so clear, however, that this degree of concentration of power is not necessary from the point of view of conflict resolution. The members of the elite, who have a double function of control of the social aspect of the irrigation system and the local governmental apparatus, frequently involve themselves in internal matters of irrigation. It may well be, therefore, that the conflict resolution services of the elite are the most crucial to a situation of population pressure, which in part explains why the roles are so concentrated and monopolized in the very few persons at the top of the social structure.

While it is true that not all managers of water are members of the elite, it is true that all politically powerful members of the elite are or have been managers of irrigation. This fact suggests that irrigation is a vital part of the elite's power. It is not hard to see why it is so in San

Juan. Irrigated agriculture yields cash crops, which generate cash. Cash is necessary for successful participation in the PRI, in private management of a canal system, and for the urban life-style which the elite partakes of. Irrigation also yields several opportunities for extensive patron-client ties. The more people who are dependent upon individual members of the elite, with their self-appointed management power, the more voters these individuals have to support their faction in the local political contests. Also, their cash is crucial for the supply of credit to the local poor, a vital link in maintaining patron-client ties. In San Juan, therefore, water managers do not have to be members of the elite, but members of the elite have to be effective water-managers. The elite of San Juan needs control of the irrigation system.

It is our hypothesis that the power elites are crucial for the resolution of conflict over water. The persons occupying water-control roles are intimately connected to the distribution of power in the society. (This connection is even true for the Sonjo, which is a simple, stateless society [Gray 1963].) It is certainly true for San Juan, in the sixteenth as well as the twentieth century, that water-control activities are intimately connected with power roles, which are built into the government apparatus in some way or other. These leadership roles are connected to land and to the higher levels of authority, have differential power with respect to water, and are stabilized in the local and national systems of stratification. It is clear, therefore, that power over water can be, and in this case is, linked with differentially distributed economic power, which in turn permits greater differential control over labor and capital for the construction and maintenance of the physical irrigation system. It is not theoretically imperative that such events occur, but our data suggest the hypothesis that this situation has a high adaptive potential.

We have, following Millon, advanced the thesis that a major issue in the consideration of irrigation systems is the degree of centralization of the conflict-control system. In this instance, the question is how the San Juan social system copes with recurrent conflict between irrigators. At first glance the system seems to be centralized because of the existence of a single Water Commission. At second glance, it would appear to be locally decentralized, for there is not a single official, unified decision-making body but at least three such (the Water Commission, the Municipal Government, and the Ejido Commission), and in addition the mill owners and wealthier landowners who are also private canal owners exert pressures of their own. But if we look behind the scenes, control of conflict at least is hierarchically centralized. Conflict is kept under control (and this is the natives' belief as well as our observation) by the effective use of legitimate force employed by several local government agencies which are coordinated in their actions (e.g., the Water Commission and the local municipal police) and by the combined pressure of the cooperating wealthier landowners. Essentially, a few families which make up the San Juan upper class have unified ultimate decision making at the local level in their own hands by effectively controlling all dimensions of the body politic. This situation has existed since the sixteenth century, in spite of radical changes in population size, crops planted, and governmental organization at the local level, and in spite of periods of great political change and reform at higher levels of the state structure.

The majór question to which we addressed ourselves in this essay is the relationship between generalized political centralization and levels of conflict in a society based on canal irrigation. In more general terms, this question focuses on the problem of the evolutionary adaptive value of centralization in societies with irrigated agriculture. The hypothesis which emerges from our case study is that one condition under which centralization of authority is adaptive in reducing conflict is under conditions of water scarcity (i.e., when there is population pressure on land and water resources) and that this adaptive response might be particularly effective in a system of food production which is totally dependent upon canal irrigation agriculture.

We suggest that without unified decision making, high levels of social disruption and conflict will tend to paralyze the socioeconomic system. Over long periods of time, the threat of anarchic conflict will generate further pressure to centralize the system, if it is to survive. However, stating that a variable is logically or functionally adaptive, or that it has evolutionary potential, is not necessarily to imply that it will always be adopted. Secondly, centralization of decision making over water is probably not adaptive under all conditions, and it is most likely adaptive only up to the maximum territorial extension of the particular irrigation system. We suggest, hence, that when water becomes a socially scarce resource, control of canal irrigation—e.g., the control of springs, water allocation, etc.—can be manipulated to diminish or increase conflict for political purposes within the political system in which the irrigation system is embedded.

Centralization of the political system facilitates higher levels of productivity by reducing social conflict at the local levels. It also may allow the formation of an institutional frame and specialized roles which could be potential springboards to other realms of local power or control, if the social structure allows for a stratified control of resources. However, in all probability there is a feedback loop involved here, because sustained power in other realms of the society will probably increase the likelihood of particular persons either assuming themselves, or being regularly recruited to fill, the decision-making roles connected with irrigation. At this time, we see nothing in the data which permits us to decide to make irrigation either the independent or the dependent variable when considered with other kinds of politically controlled systems within the same society. But neither can we suggest from the empirical evidence that the irrigation system is epiphenomenal to the political process or to the degrees of centralization of authority which may be most adaptive to maintain social conflict at low levels. On the contrary, irrigation appears to be, for the system considered here, one of the major foci of the political field.

Acknowledgments

The fieldwork and archival research on which this paper is based was generously supported by NSF Grant GS87; the major writing was produced when the senior author was freed from teaching duties by NSF Grant GS3000. We wish to thank Professors Gibson and Downing for first suggesting the participation of E. Hunt in the Long Beach symposium. The senior author also wishes to thank the faculty and student body of the Department of Anthropology of the University of Arizona, who gave her the opportunity to present a preliminary version of this paper and who generously offered useful comments. Robert McC. Adams, Robert Betteral, George Cowgill, Jeremy Sobloff, and Alex Weingrod read a draft and offered suggestions. We alone of course are responsible for its final form. The ethnographic present refers to the years 1963 to 1966. The bulk of the data was gathered in 1964.

Notes

1. A partial exception is the trend among archaeologists to probe into the evolutionary potential of irrigation vis-à-vis the state, which was not a part of Wittfogel's original conception.

2. This method will lead, at times, to what might appear to be a surfeit of ethnographic minutiae, but we prefer to differ from past accounts by swinging to the side of over-documentation.

3. The nature of the latent existence of national, centralized power and its infrequent manifestation has important implications for field research strategies. It is a difficult topic to gather data on. The events which are manifestations of institutional centralization are infrequent and are easy to assign to other institutions such as stores, land transfer, and political parties. Several years may go by without a case becoming public. Moreover, it is a subject on which informants are reluctant to talk at all. At one point during fieldwork, we were prompted to conclude that the elite of San Juan showed as much willingness to talk about water as large American businesses show about discussing price fixing and monopolies. The

first responses of most informants in San Juan, even those who had little if any personal concern with water, were "that never happens here," "we never fight about water," "here everything is pacific." It takes further probing to uncover the fear of retaliation by the local elite (if they are caught speaking) or of "getting into trouble with the authorities." This phenomenon is not common only to San Juan. Lees (1970), who was able to administer a formal survey schedule on irrigation in Oaxaca, found great difficulty in gaining access to information which dealt with actual practices, such as lists of irrigators and watering schedules.

We suggest that archives, especially the court archives, are excellent sources of particular cases and should be looked into. Diligent inspection of a few cases should be enough to establish promising hypotheses about the patterns for resolving such disputes, which can then be investigated with informants.

4. Figures for volume of water for the minor streams is lacking. Only the major rivers (such as the Grande) have been investigated by Mexican hydrologists and geographers. The text here is based on the strong impressions, sporadic knowledge, and educated guesses of the local head of the district watershed, who is a hydraulic engineer specializing in the construction of diversion dams. We are grateful for his patient assistance in answering our naive questions on the topic of water.

5. The total land under irrigation controlled by San Juan is a little more than one thousand hectares. Our figures are incomplete. We have both official and unofficial figures for Spanishland, the privately controlled canals, and the *ejido*. These come from the Ministry of Hacienda, canal owners, mill administration, and other informants. Figures for the Grassland were obtained in *maquilas* (a measure of seed used in planting) and transformed into hectares. However, different fields require different amounts of seed. The average is between 1.5 and 2 *maquilas* per hectare. Unfortunately, we were not able to obtain official figures for the Grassland because at the time of fieldwork the office of the tax inspector dealing with registered lands was involved in a complicated tax dispute with the town's elite (particularly the faction in power at the time), and we found that our attempts to obtain information were in danger of being misinterpreted as interference with the conflict.

6. Prices are presented in the ethnographic present of 1964.

7. Other factors are the disruption of sleep and work schedules and the supernatural dangers associated with the night.

8. An extensive treatment of these materials can be found in E. Hunt 1972b. All relevant published and unpublished evidence is presented there, accompanied by an annotated bibliography. Reasons of space preclude repetition here.

9. "El agua hace a la gente deshonesta y un peleador al hombre tranquilo. Si no hay bastante, hasta el mas honesto trata de agarrar más de lo que le toca para él y sus amigos . . . si encuentra el modo."

10. Examples are the Netzahualcoyotl dike in the Tenochtitlán Lake and such contemporary works as the Alemán dam in Vera Cruz.

References

Adams, R. N.
  1971   *Crucifixion by Power.* New York: Random House.
Adams, R. McC.
  1966   *The Evolution of Urban Society: Early Mesopotamia and Prehispanic Mexico.* Chicago: Aldine.
Armillas, P.
  1949   Notas sabre sistemas de cultivo en Mesoamérica: cultivos de riego y humedad en la Cuenca del Río de las Balsas. INAH, *Anales* 3: 83-113.
Attolini, J.
  1949   *Economía de la cuenca del Papaloapan: agricultura.* Mexico City: Instituto de Investigaciones Económicas.
  1950   *Economía de la cuenca del Papaloapan: bosques, fauna, pesca, ganadería e industria.* Mexico City: Instituto de Investigaciones Económicas.
Burgoa, Fra. F. de
  1934   Geografica descripción. . . . *Publicaciones del Archivo General de la Nación,* XXV. Mexico City.
Caso, A.
  1953   *El Pueblo del Sol.* Mexico City: Fondo de Cultura Económica.
Comisión del Papaloapan
  1956   Atlas climatológico e hidrológico de la cuenca del Papaloapan. *Estudios y Proyectos.* A.C. Mexico.
Fernea, R.
  1970   *Shaykh and Effendi: Changing Patterns of Authority among the El Shakana of Southern Iraq.* Cambridge, Mass.: Harvard University Press.
Florentine Codex
  1950-
  1956   Bernadino de Sahagún. *General History of the Things of New Spain.* Anderson and Dibble (trans. and eds.). School of American Research Monograph No. 14. Santa Fe.
Gallego, J.
  1914   Relación de Cuicatlán. In F. Paso y Troncoso (ed.), *Papeles de la Nueva España.* Segunda Serie, vol. 4.
Glick, T.
  1970   *Irrigation and Society in Medieval Valencia.* Cambridge, Mass.: Harvard University Press.
González Casanova, P.
  1965   *La democracia en México.* Mexico City: Ediciones Era.
Gray, R.
  1963   *The Sonjo of Tanganyika: An Anthropological Study of an Irrigation-Based Society.* International African Institute. London: Oxford University Press.
Hopkins, J.
  1970   *Report of an Archaeological Survey to the Instituto de Antropología.* Mexico City.

Hunt, E.
  1969   The Meaning of Kinship in San Juan: Genealogical and Social
          Models. *Ethnology* 8: 37-53.
  1972a   Irrigation and Centralization: A Critique of Millon's Argument.
          Paper read at the Annual Meeting of the SWAA.
  1972b   Irrigation and the Socio-Political Organization of the Cuicatec
          Cacicazgos. In F. Johnson and R. MacNeish (eds.), *The Prehistory
          of the Tehuacán Valley*, vol. 4. Austin: University of Texas Press.
Hunt, E., and R. Hunt
  1969   The Role of Courts in Central Mexico. In Bock (ed.), *Peasants in the
          Modern World*. Albuquerque: University of New Mexico Press.
Hunt, R.
  1965   The Development Cycle of the Family Business in Rural Mexico. In
          J. Helm (ed.), *Essays in Economic Anthropology*, Proc. 1965 Ann.
          Spr. Meeting, AES. Seattle: University of Washington Press.
  1971   Components of Relationships in the Family: A Mexican Village. In
          F. L. Hsu (ed.), *Kinship and Culture*. Chicago: Aldine.
Leach, E.
  1961   *Pul Eliya*. Cambridge: Cambridge University Press.
Lees, S.
  1970   Socio-Political Aspects of Canal Irrigation in the Valley of Oaxaca,
          Mexico. Ph.D. dissertation, University of Michigan.
Martínez Gracida, M.
  1883   *Cuadros sinópticos . . . de Oaxaca*. Anexo 50 a la Memoria Adminis-
          trativa Presentada al Congreso del Mismo el 17 de Diciembre de
          1883. Oaxaca: Imprenta del Estado.
Millon, R.
  1955   Trade Tree Cultivation and the Development of Private Property in
          Land. *American Anthropologist* 57: 698-712.
  1962   Variations in Social Responses to the Practice of Irrigation Agricul-
          ture. In R. Woodbury (ed.), *Civilizations in Desert Lands*. Anthro-
          pological Paper No. 62. Department of Anthropology, University of
          Utah.
Padgett, L. V.
  1966   *The Mexican Political System*. Boston: Houghton Mifflin.
Paso y Troncoso, F. (ed.)
  1914   *Papeles de la Neuva España: relaciones geográficas del siglo
          dieciséis*. Segunda Serie, vol. 4.
Paz, O.
  1972   Three Faces of Mexico. Paper read at a Meeting of the Brandeis
          University Latin American Committee.
Piña Chan, R.
  1960   *Mesoamérica*. INAH, Memorias No. 6. Mexico City.
Poleman, T. T.
  1964   *The Papaloapan Project: Agricultural Development in the Mexican
          Tropics*. Stanford: Stanford University Press.
Price, B.
  1971   Prehispanic Irrigation Agriculture in Nuclear America. *Latin Amer-
          ican Research Review* 6: 3-60.
Sahlins, M.
  1962   *Moala*. Ann Arbor: University of Michigan Press.

Simpson, L. B.
1937   *The Ejido: Mexico's Way Out.* Chapel Hill: University of North
        Carolina Press.
Steward, J. (ed.)
1955   *Irrigation Civilizations: A Comparative Study.* Pan American Union
        Social Science Monograph No. 1. Washington, D.C.
Wittfogel, K.
1957   *Oriental Despotism: A Comparative Study of Total Power.* New
        Haven: Yale University Press.
1972   The Hydraulic Approach to Pre-Hispanic Mesoamerica. In John-
        son and MacNeish (eds.), *The Prehistory of the Tehuacán Valley,*
        vol. 4. Austin: University of Texas Press.

The Proto-State
in Iranian Baluchistan

PHILIP CARL SALZMAN

At the turn of this century, the *hakom* (ruler) of Kuhak was the aging Ghulam Mahmud Nusherwani. He owned half of the twenty-four-hour cycle of irrigation water upon which the date palm and grain cultivation depended. The ownership of the other twelve hours was divided among the several hundred Nakibi *shahri* (cultivators). Hakom Ghulam Mahmud was a good man, and showed consideration for the Nakibi. Because he had daughters but no sons, and thus no male heirs, he decided that the water and land which he controlled should go to the Nakibi when he died. After Ghulam Mahmud's death, the Nakibi expected to take over the deceased *hakom*'s property. But things worked out quite differently. Another Nusherwani, not from Ghulam Mahmud's family, came to Kuhak to replace the deceased *hakom* and take over his property, claiming that he was *kom*, a kinsman, of Ghulam Mahmud. The Nakibi refused to accept this other Nusherwani and his claims; they denied that he had a right to what had been promised them. But Kadrabaksh Han Nusherwani, for such was the name of the pretender, called upon the Gambarzai and Malukzai *baluch* (nomads) from the countryside, who came to Kuhak and supported the pretender with force of arms. It was thus that Kadrabaksh Nusherwani imposed his control on Kuhak, and became the new *hakom*. Kadrabaksh took half of the water, twelve hours, and gave the other twelve hours to his *baluchi* supporters, leaving no water or land for the Nakibi, who had to work for a one-quarter share of the produce of their labor.

This is a recent (1972) account, given by a Nakibi living in Kuhak. It is not fully consistent with other versions of the same set of events. Mahmud Han Nusherwani, the son of Kadrabaksh, says that his father did come to Kuhak from Isfandak (an oasis some twenty-five miles to the west), but that he was accepted as *hakom* by the Nakibi.

125

Adapted from Figure 1, Spooner 1964: 56.

Furthermore, the genealogy given by the Nusherwani indicates that Kadrabaksh Han was a close patrikinsman of Ghulam Mahmud, who was Kadrabaksh's father's brother's son's son. Perhaps even more to the point, Kadrabaksh was Ghulam Mahmud's son-in-law, having married his daughter. This was also the case with Kadrabaksh's brother, Mirab Han, who married Ghulam Mahmud's other daughter, and who remained at Isfandak as the *hakom*.

How contradictory are these two accounts? Perhaps they are closer than they seem at first glance. The facts of kin ties among the Nusherwanis can be accepted without denying the Nakibi assertion that Kadrabaksh was not a member of Ghulam Mahmud's family in a restricted sense. The differing significance given to the kin ties among the Nusherwani by the Nakibi and the Nusherwani need not contradict the fact of the ties. And the initial resistance by the Nakibi and their ultimate capitulation to Kadrabaksh, if such is indeed what happened, encompass both accounts of the succession, there being only differences of emphasis in the two accounts. The primary thing that remains unresolved is the issue of legitimacy, of consent.

There are serious differences in the two accounts, and these cannot be ignored in order to fabricate a neat reconstruction. Indeed, the safest way to deal with these different accounts is to view them as ideological statements rather than historical ones. In this sense, the two accounts can be understood as statements about social conditions in Kuhak today, as told by actors in the contemporary Kuhak scene. As Leach points out in regard to a similar set of "historical" assertions,

> . . . the truth or untruth of the tale or any particular part of it is quite irrelevant; the tale exists and is preserved in order to justify present-day attitudes and actions. . . . [It is] "a language in which to maintain social controversy" [1954: 85].

Present circumstances in Kuhak, especially demographic and economic facts, fit with many of the assertions made in the "historical" accounts. (The political situation has changed significantly since the incorporation of Kuhak in the Iranian state in 1928.) Table 1 sets out (an estimate of) these basic facts. As the table shows, there were a very few members of the ruling group, with control over much of the productive base; a larger group identifying itself as supporters of the ruler, with some control of the productive base; a majority, with no control of the productive base; which received a share of the produce in exchange for its labor; and a very small group of menials. The status ranking implied in this distribution of resources, and explicitly stated in the culture, was reflected in various aspects of social life. For example, the Nusherwani would take women from the *baluch*, but

would not give women to them, and they would not take women from
the Nakibi or the Chakari; the *baluch* would take women from the
Nakibi but would not give them, and they would not give women to or
take women from the Chakari; the Nakibi would neither give women to
nor take women from the Chakari.

Certainly the present situation leaves much to be desired from the
point of view of a Nakibi. An "historical" account which asserts that
the present distribution of resources, which is highly disadvanta-
geous to the Nakibi, is illegitimate, and the rightful control of the
resources in Kuhak was wrested from the Nakibi through the use of
force, could certainly be considered a commentary on contemporary
circumstances and a language with which to instigate and carry on a
social controversy. And no doubt it is such an ideological statement.
But it is something more. For the differing details of the two accounts,
the contradictory statements about particular events and relationships, depend for meaning, and thus for their use in controversy, upon
a common set of understandings about the realities, if not moralities,
of social and political life. This point is made by Leach about his case:

> Argument of this kind rests on the assumption that the hearer of the
> story will be familiar with the general range of Kachin ideas about land
> tenure, rank, affinal relationship, and so on [1954: 99].

If one cannot be certain about the processes of Kadrabaksh Han's
succession to the position of *hakom* of Kuhak from the conflicting
accounts, one is able, with some confidence, to abstract a model of the
social and political relations that lie behind the events. This model, of
a small number of property-owning rulers, supported by a group of
"agents of the rulers," extracting labor from a large, majority population, is corroborated by other ethnographic evidence.

The *baluch* of Kuhak hold the same general model of social and
political relations as do the Nakibi, although they tend to regard the
arrangements as acceptable and desirable rather than taking the more
negative Nakibi view. How is it that the *baluch* are in their relatively
advantageous position, and how did they become *wakil-i hakom*,
agents of the ruler? One answer given by *baluch* is that they have a
large *kom*, kin group, and (by implication) that this large group has
solidarity and will act together. And yet there are twice as many Nakibi
in Kuhak as *baluch*, so in what sense are the *baluch* a large *kom*? In
two senses: First, the *baluch* are organized in patrilineages of some
depth, and thus are tied together into fairly large groups, whereas the
Nakibi *shahri* are socially fragmented into a large number of small,
shallow groups of a bilateral nature. Second, and perhaps more impor-

TABLE 1 Socio-economic Profile of the Population of Kuhak

Name	Status	Role	Number	Hours of Water Owned
Nusherwani	*sardar* (the term used to replace *hakom* since pacification)	rulers, landowners	5	12 (until recently, when 4 were sold)
Gambarzai, Malukzai	*baluch*	landowners, *wakil-i sardar*, (agents of the ruler)	300	12
Nakibi	*shahri*	*sharik*, agricultural laborers	700	0
Chakari	*ghulamzai*, descendents of slaves	household servants, agricultural laborers	10	0

tant, the *baluch* in Kuhak are only an arm of the body of tribesmen living in the surrounding region. Indeed, there is something anomalous about landowners and cultivators living in Kuhak being called *baluch*, for the term primarily designates nomadic, tent-dwelling herders of the countryside. This anomaly is skirted by reference to the origin of the Kuhaki *baluch* in the countryside, by the continuing ties that are maintained with the *baluch* in the countryside, and by the maintenance of the customary role of the *baluch* as *wakil-i hakom*, agents of the ruler, vis-à-vis the Nakibi *shahri*. That this is a customary role of all the *baluch* adds a new spatial and social dimension to the picture.

The *hakom* of Kuhak had his seat of authority in Kuhak; he resided in the large mud fort situated by the river bed close to the cultivation. (The remains of the *kalat-i Kuhak*, destroyed by Persian army artillery in 1928 during the siege in which Kadrabaksh Han was killed, are massive and impressive still.) But the seat of the *hakom* was not coterminous with the realm of the *hakom*, for the *hakom* was the ruler (and the current *sardar* is the leader) of a larger region, including the *shahri* of any small settlements other than the *hakom*'s seat and the *baluch* tent-dwellers of the countryside. The territory of the cooperating *hakom* of Kuhak and of Isfandak has traditionally included the area to the north, up to and including the Siah Kuh, or Black Mountains, and the area to the south, the eastern portion of the region called Bampusht. The *baluch* of the region look to the *hakom*—and the current *sardar* of Kuhak, Kadrabaksh Han's son Mahmud Han, and his cousin, brother-in-law, and collaborator, Sardar Mehim Han Nusherwani of Isfandak, are still referred to as *hakom* by *baluch*, especially the older men—as the highest authority (aside from agents of the Iranian government). The Siahani, *baluch* of the Siah Kuh, for example, have no tribal leader, no chief. The *hakom* previously filled, and the *sardar* today fills, this role. Should there be conflicts among the Siahani that cannot be resolved through tribal forms of mediation, the tribesmen go to the *hakom* for a settlement. The *hakom*, for his part, frequently travels through the countryside, staying with the *baluch*, mediating disputes, presiding over ceremonies, and in general maintaining contact with his followers. The agricultural center, and traditionally the fort, may be the seat of the *hakom*, but the region is his arena, and the wise *hakom* will not be found sitting too long, lest others move into his arena and ultimately pull his seat out from under him.

The greater part of the *baluch* lived and still live scattered through the countryside in small herding groups, depending for their livelihood primarily upon their herds of goats and secondarily upon cultivation of a few date palms and minute plots of grain and vegetables in run-off channels. However, one of their staples, often their primary staple, is bread. Bread is supplemented with milk in various forms, with dates, and with vegetables, such as onions, peppers, and tomatoes, when available. Although pastoralism is the main form of production among the *baluch*, the products of cultivation are important for them.

The *shahri*, the primary agricultural cultivators of the area, are tied to the settlements, which are situated to make use of the rare water sources for irrigation.

Now in a hypothetical decentralized, acephalous, "anarchical" situation, the relations between groups such as the *baluch* and the *shahri* would most likely be unstable. While the differences in adaptation of the *baluch* and *shahri* present a potential for cooperative exchange, there are two major destabilizing factors. First, there is an imbalance of power. The *baluch* are mobile, and can band together into large groups when necessary and later disperse. The *shahri*, in contrast, are tied to immobile resources which must be tended constantly and are difficult to protect. And there is no way for *shahri* of different settlements to band together. Second, there are differential consequences of the frequently recurring droughts. The *baluch*, directly dependent upon pasturage for the welfare of their animals, suffer the consequences of drought more heavily than the *shahri*, who depend upon the relatively reliable irrigation water. This means that during a drought the *baluch* will be deprived relative to the *shahri*, and in some instances means that the *baluch* will have great capital losses while the productive resources of the *shahri* remain intact. These two factors, existing in the context of an "anarchical" situation, would result in a serious threat to the *shahri* by the *baluch*, who would have need of the resources and products of the *shahri* and who would have a military advantage. At the same time, it would not be to the advantage of the *baluch* to destroy *shahri* settlements, or to inhibit cultivation by the *shahri;* this would remove the source of the needed products—unless, of course, the *baluch* wished to become cultivators themselves, which they definitely do not wish (although they would not be averse to being landowners with cultivators working for them). There would likely be a very ambivalent relationship between the *baluch* and the *shahri* under these circumstances. The *baluch* would benefit from peaceful exchange during good years, as would the *shahri*, but would tend to be predatory during bad years, a fact that would make the *shahri* quite wary if not completely uncooperative just about all of the time. It is difficult to see how the ambivalence in the relationship and the instability in the system could be avoided without some kind of mediating institution.

There is no evidence, however, of such an acephalous, "anarchi-

cal" situation in southern Baluchistan. What is found, rather, is a
regional system in which (prior to the arrival of the Iranian government) the *baluch* and the *shahri* were articulated through the ruling
hakom, who functioned as the head of each group (or, more exactly, as
the head of all of the groups within each of the two categories). The
baluch gained access to the areas of cultivation through the *hakom* and
received, directly or indirectly, agricultural products as patronage from
the *hakom.* The *shahri,* on their side, received protection from *baluchi*
predation.

Both the *baluch* and the *shahri* had customary obligations which
paid the *hakom* for his trouble (Spooner 1969: 141). First, the *hakom*
usually owned a master's share of the scarce and limited resources in
the areas of cultivation—i.e., water and land, and perennials such as
date palms—and when, as often was the case, his land was worked by
his own *ghulam,* slaves, he received virtually all of the produce, which
was not far from the case when *shahri muzar,* laborers, worked the
land. Second, the *hakom* received a tithe on the agricultural produce of
shahri who owed him allegiance. Third, there was a tax gathered from
both *shahri* and *baluch,* much from the latter being received in pastoral
products. Finally, there was service, *sren-bandi,* from *baluch* who
recognized him as their leader. This service was often military or
quasi-military. The *hakom* thus received different kinds of rewards
from the two kinds of people, the *baluch* and the *shahri,* under his
authority. As Spooner (1969: 142) puts it, "the *hakom* relied basically
on a subject peasant population for their income, and on allegiance
from nomadic pastoralists for their physical strength." What the
hakom got from the one allowed him to draw from the other, and vice
versa. It was this mediation between two disparate populations for
which he could provide different benefits that gave the *hakom* his
position in relation to each.

What the *hakom* received was more than goods and service; it was
status, power, and authority. Because he had military power at his
disposal, he was more than a *shahri.* Because he had agricultural
resources at his disposal, he was more than a *baluch.* Because he had
both, he was able to use positive and negative sanctions with the
baluch and *shahri,* which gave him power and authority, making him
more than either the *baluch* or the *shahri,* making him the *hakom,* the
ruler. The *hakomzat,* the family of the *hakom,* was consequently a distinct social class, superior to all others, and given to association and
intermarriage with *hakomzat* from other regions.

Spooner suggests that the origins of the system lie in a conquest
by outsiders:

> . . . a tribal, pastoral group of people invades a settled, agricultural

area. . . . The leading family of the invaders becomes the focus of power in the settled area, and therefore *de facto* rulers of both peoples: those that entered the area with it—the pastoralists—and those who were in the area when it came—the peasants. . . . And the leading family tends to become "dynastic." . . . In the new situation the settled people are a source of agricultural wealth and labor for the dynastic family, while the tribal following is a source of military strength and, secondarily, of pastoral products [1969: 147-149].

This is a plausible model, made more so by the fragmentary historical and linguistic evidence which suggests that *baluchi* tribes moved from northwestern Iran to southeastern Iran—i.e., the present-day Baluchistan—in the relatively recent past (Frye 1961). On the other hand, it is possible that the area was little populated prior to the *baluchi* immigration, or that the *baluchi* tribes drove everyone else out. In either of these cases, the system described here could have arisen from adaptational differentiation within the *baluchi* population and the attendant difficulties of the differentiated populations in dealing with each other.

It is obvious that it would be of great benefit to have a clear developmental picture of the *baluch-hakom-shahri* system based upon sound historical evidence. This, unfortunately, we do not have. The literature on the history of Baluchistan presents a very tentative and sketchy outline based upon highly fragmentary evidence and heavy doses of speculation (Frye 1961; Spooner 1969, 1971). In lieu of an established history beyond scattered facts, the primary contribution of a study of Baluchistan toward an understanding of the origins of the state will have to be structural and functional, based upon comparative analysis. An attempt will be made here to suggest some of the structural and functional circumstances which, where they are present, seem to be associated with what can be considered proto-state institutions.

But what exactly are state and proto-state institutions? Or is it necessary, for present purposes, to know "exactly" what they are? Even if one could construct an ideal type of "the state," ways of conceptualizing earlier developmental stages might remain elusive. And there is always the danger that the ideal type would oversimplify by emphasizing a small number of factors and by implicitly suggesting that all of the defining factors vary together. For these reasons, a set of dimensions will be set out here to be used in place of an ideal type or definitional construct. These dimensions bear on various attributes of leadership institutions: (1) geographical range, from local (placed on the left end of the continuum) to increasing degrees of supra-local (placed on the right end of the continuum); (2) obligation of obedience by public, from low to high; (3) role of leader, from elicitation of consensus and mediation to determination of policy and adjudication; (4) sanctions available to leader, from disapproval to physical coercion; (5) institutionalization of leadership role, from those roles based upon personal attributes to those based upon incumbency of office; (6) areas of intervention, from few areas in social life open to intervention to many areas open to intervention. It would probably not be controversial to argue that the farther to the "left" (in the graphic, spatial sense only) on these dimensions, the less like a state, and the farther to the "right," the closer to a state. These dimensions thus facilitate depiction of differences, and allow discussion of developmental stages and "proto-states" more than a state/non-state distinction. Several other factors might be included as dimensions of "stateness" or might be kept separate as (tentative) empirical correlates: (a) institutionalization, proliferation, and specialization of subordinate "agent of the leader" roles; (b) control of the means of coercion; (c) control of the means of production; (d) control of the products.

Keeping these considerations in mind, we may turn to a comparison between the *baluch-hakom-shahri* system and the independent *baluchi* tribes. The details of this comparison have been presented elsewhere (Salzman 1971), and so a summary of the findings should suffice here. The *baluchi* tribes of the Sarhad Plateau of northern Baluchistan, the Yarahmadzai (Shah Nawazi), Gamshadzai, and Ismailzai (Shah Baksh), and the Bameri of the Jaz Murian basin in western Baluchistan, were independent of any *hakom*. The members of each tribe thought of themselves as descended from a common ancestor, and they were organized in patrilineages with responsibility for blood vengeance and the welfare of their members. They were each led by a chief, a *sardar*, who was the leader in extratribal relations and who was responsible for maintaining internal peace through mediation. The *sardar* was a *baluch* like the other tribesmen; no qualitative distinction of social rank existed between the *sardar*, his family, his lineage, and his fellow tribesmen. The life-style of the chief was not qualitatively different from that of his fellow tribesmen, and his economic resources were not substantially greater. The *sardar* did not play much of a part in the daily lives of his tribesmen. They migrated according to their own lights, carried on the various productive activities—pastoralism, date palm cultivation, a bit of grain cultivation, raiding, some hunting and gathering—as they chose, and had equal access to the tribal resources of pasturage, natural water sources, and unaltered land. The chief had no special sources of physical coercion available to him, and did not have the right to apply capital or corporal punishment to his tribesmen. His influence depended largely upon his personal stature, which was related to his success, both diplomatic and military, in dealing with outsiders, and his success at settling disputes within the tribe, as well as to his deportment as a *baluch* and as a Muslim.

The *baluchi* tribal leadership institution, substantially farther to the "left" than the *baluch-hakom-shahri* on the dimensions of obligation of obedience, role of leader, sanctions available, and areas of intervention (with perhaps not much difference in geographical range and institutionalization), is largely a function of adaptational and economic arrangements among the *baluch*. These *baluch*, like those in the *baluch-hakom-shahri* system, were nomadic in the course of their multiresource extractions, but they had additional resources available, especially the date groves at Mashkel Basin (cultivated without irrigation, thanks to the high water table) and the prizes from raiding caravans and peasant villages in the north and west. On the other hand, there was little agriculture in their areas, because of a colder climate and a lack of water. Each *baluchi sardar*, therefore, led a population of nomadic tribesmen who controlled their own capital resources, the major part of which, the herds, was mobile. The *sardar* had virtually no economic patronage to dispense, and had little way of coercing mobile followers with independent resources. Even if a *sardar* had managed somehow to form a military arm loyal to him alone, the other tribesmen could have massed in opposition, or else could have loaded their camels and disappeared. The *sardar* had neither the economic base which agriculture provided the *hakom*, nor the two economically specialized, spatially separated, and socially differentiated populations, the *baluch* and the *shahri*, which were in need of articulation.

It was through the articulation of the two differentiated populations that the position of *hakom* was made possible. There was a rudimentary development of subordinate "agent of the leader" roles, with servants of the *hakom*'s household acting as his representatives and on occasion enforcing his orders. The *hakom* had control of a substantial section of the means of production in the agricultural sector, and likewise control of the products. But he did not have anything close to exclusive control of the means of coercion (tough men with military capability, arms, rapid transport), which were distributed widely among the *baluchi* population. The *hakom* was ultimately dependent upon the loyalty of the *baluch* for his coercive power, and was able to maintain that loyalty by articulating the *baluch* with the *shahri* according to terms advantageous to the *baluch*. The *shahri* seem to have had relatively little choice in the matter, but were relieved of unrestrained depredation and thus gained a certain security, while providing the economic base of the system.

The articulation of spatially separated, economically specialized populations of close to equal size in mutually exclusive niches is one basis for the development of proto-state institutions. If, however, the populations differ greatly in size, the political significance of articulation is reduced. The small population of agricultural serfs among the Sarhadi *baluch*, and their very limited production, had little impact upon the political structure of the *baluchi* tribes and their leadership institutions. Elsewhere, among the Pathans of the Swat Valley, the presence of a small number of Gujar nomadic herders and Kohistani transhumant herder-cultivators in the hills around the fertile river valley with its dense population of agriculturalists seems to have been insignificant in the political system of the area (Barth 1956).

If the populations occupy niches that are not exclusive, that can be combined, then articulation by an independent agency is less likely. The Yomut Turkmen tribes encompassed individuals whose adaptation emphasized cultivation, though they maintained a nomadic establishment and some animals, and also individuals whose adaptation emphasized pastoralism, usually supplemented with a bit of agriculture (Irons 1975). The habitat of the Turkman supported both pastoralism and cultivation in the same annual round. The gradation in adaptations among the Yomut did not generate distinct social categories, and nontribal mechanisms of articulation were not present. The resources—pasturage, water, and agricultural land—were available to any Yomut who needed them; this availability, combined with the feasibility of combining modes of production, removed the possibility of one population coveting the resources of another population. The relationship between the Yomut Turkmen and the Persian agricultural populations to the south reflected the limited impact of agricultural resources on the Turkmen's political structure (Irons 1971). Yomut tribes extracted tribute from these villages and provided "protection" from raids under arrangements made by a Yomut officeholder who was the official "protector" of the villages. This official had no great power or authority in internal tribal matters and was not socially distinct from his fellow tribesmen. The reason, it would seem, is that he was providing supplementary resources to tribesmen with similar sources of their own rather than very important resources to poor tribesmen who had no other sources.

The development of proto-state institutions through the articulation of differentiated populations is not, of course, limited to Baluchistan. A system in many respects similar to that of the *baluch-hakom-shahri* was found in the Hadramaut region of southern Arabia (now part of Yemen) prior to the establishment of the British protectorate (Bujra 1971). Hureidah was a town based economically upon irrigation agriculture. Most of the townsmen were agriculturalists, but there was a fairly rigid system of stratification based upon idioms of descent and religious status. Patterns of wealth distribution and marriage reinforced the stratification system. The rulers of the town were holy men with special claims to sacred status. The town was surrounded by desert, inhabited by nomadic or quasi-nomadic tribesmen. The tribesmen recognized the sacred status of the town leaders, and granted sanctuary status to the town. The town provided a neutral place for the meeting of tribesmen, for dispute settlement, and for economic exchange. The tribesmen could call upon the town leaders for mediation of tribal disputes, and would provide coercive sanctioning of the townsmen on instructions of the town leaders. The town leaders used their religious powers and neutral position on behalf of the tribesmen; the tribesmen recognized and supported the town leaders and used coercive power on their behalf. The agriculturalists and laborers of the town were consequently in a subordinate position, but benefited to some degree from the security and prosperity of the town as neutral sanctuary. In this case, both the town and the desert contained substantial populations, and the adaptations of the two populations were distinct and exclusive. Since the religious status of the town leaders is an element not present in Baluchistan, it is not a necessary component in a proto-state. Nor is it, where present, a sufficient cause for such organization, since religious status and mediation within a homogeneous population of tribesmen do not in themselves lead to the development of proto-state institutions, as is shown by the Cyrenaican and Atlas cases (Evans-Pritchard 1949; Gellner 1969).

A not infrequent variation on proto-state leadership institutions arising from the articulation of differentially specialized populations is that of dual elites, with one elite representing each of the populations, and with the two elites cooperating in the articulation of the two populations. In the Funj area of the Sudan, the peasants have their leaders, for the most part economically powerful merchants, and the nomadic tribesmen are represented by the traditionally leading family of the tribe (Ahmed 1973). These two elites cooperate in articulating the groups they represent, compete in extracting resources from the national government, and collude in maintaining their elite status. One way the elites collude is in the maintenance of boundaries between their two populations, which is done partly by the withholding of information and the restricting of interaction. The more isolated each population is from the other, and the less able each is to associate and communicate with the other, to gain access to desired resources, and to develop a sense of security in relation to the other, the more each will depend upon its elite and thus insure the elite's superordinate position.

Another example of dual elites is found in the well-known case of the "centralized chieftainship" of the Basseri of south Persia (Barth 1964). One of the main bases of the autocratic power of the Basseri chief lies in his function as middleman:

> The chief's role in mediating relations with the sedentary society, in pro-
> tecting the nomadic herders' interests *vis-à-vis* the often formidable and
> always confusing organizations that structure parts of their environment
> and encroach on their life, is correlated with a strong feeling of respect
> and dependence among the tribesmen [Barth 1964: 80].

The Basseri chief resides in the provincial capital, and there he is able to represent his tribesmen through his association with members of the sedentary elite:

> Where conflicts arise between tribesmen and villager, the chief can repre-
> sent the interests of his tribe, just as the landowner or local adminis-
> trator can represent that of the villagers. They can meet as equals before
> the Provincial Governor, or in court, or directly. . . . [The chief is] an equal
> of the local *élite* because he is like them—he shares their diacritical sym-
> bols and can participate in their activities [ibid.].

The institutionalization of dual elites seems to be related to the presence of an overarching higher elite, a stronger authority which provides a context of enforced peace. It may well be that in an autono-mous local context various political and military processes would tend to militate against the existence of dual elites and tend to generate a single elite (Salzman 1975). Nonetheless, these examples are sug-gestive for an autonomous situation. The Basseri chieftainship was much more autocratic than the traditional *baluchi* tribal chieftainship. The Basseri chief dictated policy, adjudicated, and applied corporal punishment; his tribesmen were strongly obliged to follow his orders. The chief had a life-style qualitatively different from that of his followers, and he controlled tribal resources, especially pasture, and had his own extraordinary economic resources, agricultural villages. None of this was true for the *baluchi* tribal *sardar*, who did not articulate his tribesmen with another differentiated population, for there was no such population. All of these characteristics were true of the *hakom*, who, like the Basseri chief, was deeply involved in articu-lating differentiated populations.

The general position implicit in the discussions of these various cases, which has been made explicit in the cases of the *baluchi* tribes and the *baluch-hakom-shahri* system, is that people do not get in-volved or stay involved in proto-states unless they believe that they are benefiting from the arrangement or unless they have little choice in the matter. There was little benefit for the nomads of the *baluchi* tribes in granting their chiefs autocratic power, and there was no way for the *baluchi sardar* to impose his will on his tribesmen. But the *baluch* of Kuhak-Isfandak and other areas received various benefits from supporting autocratic *hakom,* and the *shahri* had little choice in accepting the proto-state leadership institution imposed upon them.

That benefits for some and coercion for others result from the articulation of differentiated populations has been illustrated by a number of cases. This is not to say that all differentiated populations must be articulated. It is quite conceivable that differentiated populations could exist in the same region and yet remain more or less isolated from one another, each carrying on its own distinct life pattern without contacting the other. Differentiated populations need not require exchange and communication. What is suggested here is that *if* such differentiated populations become closely involved with one another, *then* elaborate social mechanisms are required, and that these mechanisms will most likely take the form of proto-states. The primary case presented here, the *baluch-hakom-shahri* system, is one in which there was particular need for one of the populations, the *baluch,* to be articulated with the other population, the *shahri,* which was particularly vulnerable to coercive sanctions. This situation was paralleled in the Hadramaut case. It would be imprudent to assert unconditionally that relationship patterns of all differentiated populations must mirror that of pastoral nomads and irrigation agriculturalists.

This somewhat meandering essay on the articulation of differentiated populations as a basis for the development of proto-states has obviously been exploratory. The data presented illustrate rather than demonstrate, and the argument is meant to be suggestive rather than definitive. Perhaps the author can be forgiven for the usual pious wish that this discussion will lead to further investigation of the patterns described. That these patterns are only one part of the general problem is obvious from the lively discussions elsewhere on the importance of other factors—population growth, circumscribed areas, trade—in the development of the state.

Acknowledgments

The data on Kuhak-Isfandak presented here was collected during a short trip to southern Baluchistan in 1972. During this trip, I was able to reside in Kuhak and among the Siahani *baluch* in the countryside, and to visit Isfandak and some of the smaller settlements where cultivation was carried on. Interviews were carried out with Siahani *baluch,* with Kuhaki *baluch* and *shahri,* and with Sardars Mahmud Han and Mehim Han Nusherwani. I am grateful to those of the area who graciously received and assisted me, to my wife and to Shams A'din Shah Nawazi who accompanied me, and to the Iranian government for permission to carry out this research and to its representatives who offered hospitality and otherwise cooperated in the course of the research. The research was supported by grants from The Canada Council and McGill University.

Professor Brian Spooner, who has done the most extensive work in the southern portion of Iranian Baluchistan, initially drew my attention to the area. I first gained understanding of the area from his work, and his writings continue to provide insights and information.

References

Ahmed, A. G. M.
    1973   Tribal and Sedentary Elites. In C. Nelson (ed.), *The Desert and the Sown*. Research Series No. 21. Berkeley: Institute of International Studies, University of California.
Barth, F.
    1956   Ecologic Relationships of Ethnic Groups in Swat, North Pakistan. *American Anthropologist* 58: 1079-1089.
    1964   *Nomads of South Persia*. New York: Humanities.
Bujra, A. S.
    1971   *The Politics of Stratification*. Oxford: Oxford University Press.
Evans-Pritchard, E. E.
    1949   *The Sanusi of Cyrenaica*. Oxford: Oxford University Press.
Frye, R. N.
    1961   Remarks on Baluchi History. *Central Asiatic Journal* 6: 44-50.
Gellner, E.
    1969   *Saints of the Atlas*. London: Weidenfeld and Nicolson.
Irons, W.
    1971   Variation in Political Stratification among the Yomut Turkmen. *Anthropological Quarterly* 44: 143-156.
    1975   *The Yomut Turkmen*. Anthropological Paper No. 58. Ann Arbor: Museum of Anthropology, University of Michigan.
Leach, E. R.
    1954   *Political Systems of Highland Burma*. Reprint edition, 1964. London: Bell.
Salzman, P. C.
    1971   Adaptation and Political Organization in Iranian Baluchistan. *Ethnology* 10: 433-444.
    1975   The Study of Complex Society in the Middle East. To be published in the *International Journal of Middle East Studies*.
Spooner, B.
    1964   Kūch U Balūch *and* Ichthyophagi. *Iran* 2: 53-67.
    1969   Politics, Kinship, and Ecology in Southeast Persia. *Ethnology* 8: 139-152.
    1971   Notes on the Toponymy of the Persian Makran. In C. E. Bosworth (ed.), *Iran and Islam*. Edinburgh: Edinburgh University Press.

State Foundations:
A Controlled Comparison

RONALD COHEN

Analysis of state formation is rather like a projective test. The process is so complex and the data so voluminous that the choice of theories often provides us with more insight into the theorist than into the reality itself. Materialists see inequities of power and access to resources as having important causal priorities in pre-state systems (Fried 1967; chapter in this volume). Those with a more macroscopic view look to demographic features such as population pressure or to circumscription that prevents geographic expansion (Carneiro 1970; Alland and McCay 1973). This latter idea has been used by field workers like Netting (1972) as a basis for inquiring into the organizational and cultural effects of increased population pressure. Another aspect of this same approach is the attempt to see state formation emerging from increased conflicts between differing ecologies competing for similar resources.

Service (1975) has examined these positions and concludes that organizational features of state formation are the basic qualities that require exploration. He finds stratification, conquest, and population pressures to be secondary or derivative features as against the mutual benefits to be derived from hierarchical organization (Service 1975: 272). Service is clearly most impressed by the benefits of statehood, while the materialists stress its cost and inequities. For them the fundamental point is clear: early states are tyrannical and exploitative, and it is to further the class interests of those in power that states come into being.

Leaving aside materialist and nonmaterialist interpretations, a growing body of literature has heaped support on a number of fac-

141

tors—stratification, population pressures and circumscription, theocratic rule, ecological competition, slavery and clientage, urbanism,
etc.—that are associated with early forms of state formation. What is
lacking is an agreed-upon model or explanatory paradigm that puts
these correlates together into the set of processes that produces states
from pre-states.

This essay is based on the proposition that there is no clear-cut or
simple set of causal statements that explains the phenomenon of state
formation (Cohen 1978). The formation of states is a funnel-like progression of interactions in which a variety of pre-state systems
responding to different determinants of change are forced by otherwise
unresolvable conflicts to choose additional and more complex levels
of. political hierarchy. Once this particular solution is hit upon, the
structural features of the adaptation and the benefits derived cause
these polities to converge culturally and socially into early states. As
Robert Carneiro points out in this volume, the convergence process
continues and accelerates through time as the number of states de-
creases and their size and power grow. It is in this convergent sense
that the progression from non-state to state is "funnel-like."

From a theoretical point of view, then, the disagreements concerning early state formation are to a large degree spurious and misleading. In a recent review of the literature (Cohen 1978) I have tried to
show how all theories presently in use fit some materials but not
others. Furthermore, as Wright and Johnson (1975) point out, single-
variable explanations such as long-distance trade, population pressure, and presumably warfare stand up very poorly as consistently
antecedent correlates to the origins of states. What seems to be called
for is a systemic approach in which changes in one factor trigger a
chain reation of changes in a set of related factors, culminating in the
emergence of a state.

In order to illustrate this approach, I wish to look briefly at data
from the Chad-Borno area of northeastern Nigeria. Over the centuries
this area and others along the southern rim of the Sahara have wit-
nessed an almost continuous rise and fall of centralized states. I shall
describe three of these. Though quite similar today, they represent two
separate evolutionary trajectories towards centralized government.
The three are Borno[1] and Biu, where I have carried out fieldwork, and
Fombina to the south of them, whose state-building period at the
beginning of the nineteenth century has recently been studied in detail
by a Nigerian social historian (Abubakar 1970; 1972). In two of the
cases, Borno and Fombina, the state emerged out of the relations
between in-migrant pastoral or semipastoral peoples and local agriculturalists. The two states were formed in different periods through

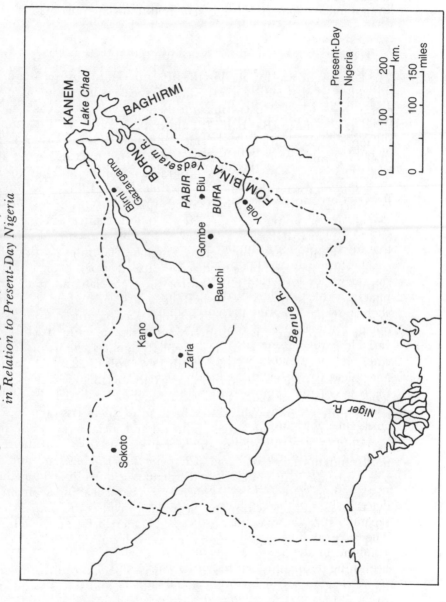

FIGURE 1

Map Showing Area of Borno, Pabir/Bura, and Fombina
in Relation to Present-Day Nigeria

relations between quite distinct ethnic groups, but similar state-building forces were at work in each. In the third case, that of Biu, a people—the Bura—with a common sociopolitical and cultural back-ground have differentiated into state and non-state portions.

Kanem-Borno

The Borno state was founded in the fifteenth century by the Magumi, a migrant clan of Islamic central-Saharan speakers from Kanem, north-east of Lake Chad. Most writers on the topic view Borno as a succes-sor state to Kanem (Barth 1857; Palmer 1936; Smith 1971). Although the topic is too complex to consider fully here, it is important to note that no permanent capital has been discovered for this earlier king-dom. The ninth-century Arabic geographer Yaqubi describes the area as having no towns, although later writers (e.g., Al Idrisi, twelfth cen-tury) mention Bilma and Njimi (Smith 1971: 170). Quite possibly some settlement was going on, especially at trading centers such as Bilma or at oases where dates and grain crops could be grown. The early con-trol over trading entrepôts such as Traghan, 800 miles north of Lake Chad, could very well have been accomplished as part of an attempt by warrior nomad chieftains to control the trans-Saharan trade at the southern ends of the route. Nevertheless, no firm evidence has turned up to indicate that the Kanem "kingdom" was organized from a stable seat of government. Instead, the record is replete with structural seg-mentary features such as the use of chiefly agnates (maina) as military and bureaucratic functionaries (Barth 1857, Vol. II: 583). All this leads me to believe that Kanem (circa A.D. 500 to A.D. 1500) was the seat of a series of related nomadic and seminomadic clan-based chieftaincies which differed from true states because of their fissionable socio-political structure. The Kanem political and social structure seems to have been not unlike that of the present-day occupants of the region north and northeast of Chad (Chapelle 1957). These are and were large nomadic, seminomadic, and sedentary groups linked together in classic segmentary fashion. Within each clan a leading segment and the leading lineage within the segment provided the mai, or chief. Heads of lineages were also called mai. Later in Borno the term was used for the monarch, although even today it can refer to anyone who heads a large political organization.

Heads of subgroups formed a council (nokena) of titled men and the clan chief also used close agnates, clients, and slaves as function-aries in his "administration." Normal lineage proliferation and a nomadic-to-seminomadic ecology provided for a continuous hiving-off of segments that could ultimately become rival clan groups. Nonetheless, Magumi traditions indicate that their Sefawa Mai was the Mai Maibe, or chief-of-chiefs, when clans came together for meetings or military expeditions. The picture that emerges, from admittedly scattered and not totally clear-cut evidence, is one of a set of nomadic and seminomadic chieftaincies, sharing a common culture, with a sense of ranking among them that allowed for common action and for adjudication when necessary, for clear ideas of permanent leadership, and for advisory councils of hereditary leader-nobles.

Slavery and clientage were well-developed means of adding to household size and to political followings, with the status or entry point into the society, of the master, determining slave and client status in the society as a whole (cf. Meirs and Kopytoff 1977). Trade and other contact with the wider Islamic world were common. Islam provided a foreknowledge of more complex governmental forms of law and of the relations and rights of rulers and their subjects; once it was needed such Islamic tradition could be applied and developed in this African setting.

In the mid-thirteenth to early fourteenth centuries the Magumi lost their ascendancy in Kanem. Rival clans, especially the Bulala, battled them for dominance. At the same time internal problems weakened the unity of the group. Debilitating struggles for succession caused a rapid turnover of Mais,[2] and according to tradition, normal fission processes separated the sons of the ruler into different regions (Smith 1971: 177). Finally, well into the fourteenth century, the Magumi leaders decided to leave Kanem and enter Borno, where the Magumi have remained to this day.

What followed is unfortunately obscure. We do know that the instability of the chiefly role continued. There were still many rulers, a usurpation occurred, and there are reports of a town or place named Kaga, or Kogu,[3] that was wrested away from the indigenous peoples of Borno. The period was one of constant warfare against these indigenes and of internecine struggles for power among segments of the Sefawa lineage (Cohen 1966; Smith 1971: 181). It is my interpretation that during this period the Magumi moved northwards and began setting up walled towns to protect themselves from both Saharan desert raiders and the indigenous agriculturalists of Bornu.[4] Segments of the Magumi vied for the position of most influence while the constriction of their new way of life forced ecological, social, and political changes in the society as a whole.

In the last decades of the fifteenth century one of these segments came under the leadership of a great leader, Ali Gaji, or Ali-the-Youngest-Son (of Dunama), who is said to have founded the great Kanuri capital of Gazargamo some 100 miles to the west and south of the earlier walled towns along the southern bank of the Yo River. This site protected the city from desert raiders and conquerors from the north and allowed for transhumant pasturage to the south as well as the establishment of a great state ruled from the citadel center of Gazargamo.

The data available to us at present lead to the conclusion that it is from this incursion and sedentarization and the development of walled towns that the Magumi under their Sefawa leaders created the great Borno empire. Now known as Kanuri, they slowly incorporated the Chadic-speaking plainsmen into this emergent, state-based, multi-ethnic national culture.[5] They developed a flexible set of center-periphery relations in which nobles at the capital were given or earned control over scattered, previously independent towns and villages of the plain. Local nomad groups with similar or different ethnic backgrounds were linked, annual tributes were collected, and militias were raised through this hierarchy. Occupational groups in the capital were organized residentially so that they too could be connected through their own leaders with the Kanuri court. Tributary relations with surrounding societies that maintained their independence were also developed, as was a complex system of trade, both internal and external, and foreign relations with other sectors of the Islamic world.

At the capital the nobles, royals, Islamic judges, and religious advisers formed an upper ruling class. They lived in large households or sets of households, with wives, concubines, slaves, clients, and their extended kin groups; they dressed resplendently and went about on horseback with slaves and retainers at their service. They had access to villages in the areas that they administered, and they were able to found slave villages whose inhabitants owed them foodstuffs to support their urban upper-class life. They were *kontuwa*, "important people."[6]

The common people were artisans, peasants, nomads, belonging to ethnic groups linked to the central government through these nobles. They paid taxes to their lords at the capital and a separate tax to the king *(mai)*, as well as market fees, adjudication fees, and fees for simply going into the presence of members of the political managerial class.

Although hints of this emergent system were present in the pre-state organization of Kanem, the data allow us to conclude that the Borno state was radically different from its Kanem precursor. Warfare with indigenous agriculturalists and creation of walled towns associated with sedentarization allowed the Kanuri to develop a centrally organized administrative system using non-kin officials and an authority structure linking conquered peoples on the Borno plain to the citadel, which itself emerged as a victorious segment among several, each of which vied with the others for leadership and dominance over the Magumi migrants from Kanem.

Pabir-Biu

Many of the peoples of the region came finally to be incorporated within the governmental system of the Borno state. Others ran away to mountains, hills, and forested areas to the south. Still others set up walled towns on its borders. To the south the Pabir kingdom of Biu was forced to evolve towards more centralized control and more hierarchy in reaction to the growth of the powerful, aggressive Kanuri state of Borno on its borders.

The Pabir are a Bura-speaking people who share most of their culture and social organization with the Bura, who live spread out over the southern portion of the area. The Bura live in locally autonomous villages separated into lineage-based dispersed wards. Early-ripening grains are planted closely around each compound so that as lineages proliferate down the generations, virilocal settlement expands topographically. Political organization is an aspect of descent and residential settlement patterning.

Founding lineages provide headmen both for wards and for the village as a whole. The village headman-descendant-of-the-founder adjudicates disputes, keeps the village shrine, announces village events, plants his crops first, organizes community work projects, and intercedes with his founding-lineage ancestors for the welfare of the village. Independent villages and semi-autonomous wards proliferate; fission occurs because of land shortages and internal disputes, especially disagreements over succession to village and ward headships.

The Pabir have religious beliefs similar to the Bura's with admixtures of Islam, especially at the top of the society. These beliefs center around the *haptu* or lineage shrines in each household. Worship at the shrines connects the living to the dead through the mediation of household heads and senior lineage members. Both Pabir and Bura also make offerings at village shrines to honor and request favors from the spirits of the place whose permission is needed in order for a village to be founded. On special occasions Pabir and Bura visit shrines at their own and in each other's villages. There are as well complex beliefs in witchcraft and sorcery that are virtually identical across both groups.

The Pabir, however, live in larger, more compact settlements, traditionally with high moated walls, and they have a monarch-chief who traces his ancestry back through twenty-seven predecessors to a folk hero who is said to have come from the capital of Borno. The monarch's compound in Biu is traditionally much larger than other peoples', and he has a court in which sit titled nobles in special patterns, as well as members of the royal family.[7]

As I have noted elsewhere (Cohen 1976), Pabir is a variant of Bura society that has differentiated from the original in response to its need to defend itself in reaction to early Borno raiding for slaves and booty. In the process, the people were forced to develop and build walls, gates, and moats around their settlements and live within them. Although overall density in the area quite possibly remained the same, the population of major settlements increased from a range of 50-200 to a range of 1000-3000. The practice of surrounding compounds with early-ripening grains was abandoned in favor of using nearby land just outside or inside the walls. The population then increased in size per settlement, in compactness, and decreased in its capacity to proliferate and expand across the landscape. In effect this meant that land use was intensified, and at the same time fission became a less attractive solution to intra-community shortages and conflicts. The adjudicative functions of the leaders were used more often as were their coordinating and managerial skills. The supernatural powers and priestly role of the headman of the settlement were now used for the welfare of a much larger group. His installation and burial became enormously elaborate ceremonies, and the royal burial grounds became the shrine for promulgating the national welfare. Heads of leading lineages of the town of Biu became, instead of a council of elders, a royal council or court in which former elders of segments were now titled nobles of the realm along with the *maina*, or princes, whose fathers had been kings.

Ultimately the nobles and their close kin formed a group of upper-class officials who carried out the governmental activities of the realm in Biu. To enhance their own solidarity, they abrogated or simply ignored traditional rules of Bura exogamy in order to marry one another's daughters. Preferential cross-cousin marriage evolved rapidly as a consequence, and the Pabir upper class borrowed the Kanuri kin terms for their cross cousins and the parents of these relatives (switching from generation-merging lineage terms to generational distinctions).[8]

The Pabir also developed (or borrowed) the widespread West African idea of the queen mother who is generally not the monarch's own mother but a father's sister or other close relative. She lived in a separate town, helped install the new monarch, and had as her close advisers and courtiers a group of royal relatives, her agnates, who had lost out in a royal succession struggle (Cohen 1977). Pabir say that the queen mother made a king: she had the sacred objects that an heir had to sit on to absorb kingliness, and only she could handle the objects with impunity. If a man had been in charge of such things, then (they say) he would have made himself a king. With a woman they were safe. Femaleness, queenship, in a separate unwalled town represented loyal opposition of a royal lineage segment that in pre-state times would have broken off. Queenship then symbolized continuity and subordination of the subgroups to the central government (Cohen 1977).

The king organized defense and public works on the walls, adjudicated cases, and carried out rituals at the nearby tombs of his ancestors (and elsewhere) for the welfare of the people. Although there was no regular revenue collection, he was always given some form of tribute at harvest time and from trading expeditions. The monarch received half of all goods taken in raids against other towns and villages. He sent trading expeditions headed by his own clients to Kanem for salt and natron (hydrated sodium carbonate) in return for cotton rolls, slaves, and primary products given to him as tributes. In his turn the king gave out local products and trade goods, especially the much prized salt and natron, to his nobles, clients, and through them (and in person as well) to the common people as gifts in return for their continued support of his authority. He also exchanged gifts with surrounding chiefs—e.g., the Jukun—on an annual basis. As noted elsewhere in Africa (Feierman 1974: 121), the proportion of productivity and tributes were often inversely related. When shortages were severe, people brought gifts to help the monarch offer sacrifices for the welfare of the land. The king sacrificed more bulls and performed more ceremonies during poorer, less productive times than when things went well. The meat and other foods were then distributed. In other words, "surpluses" were "created" when shortages were greatest, so that ceremonies could be performed and so that, as a by-product, the hungry could be fed. The authority system was supported by helping the society over economic hardship.

In the later stages of the kingdom, in the mid-nineteenth century, the Pabir of Biu united other Pabir towns to drive out Fulani who had fought their way in from Gombe (to the west of Biu) and tried to settle in the region. This produced the rough beginnings of a hierarchy of walled towns with Biu as the center and with the leaders of other towns, like Thlerima, subordinate chiefs under the chief-of-chiefs at Biu (Cohen 1976). Unfortunately this emergent multitown system was in its infancy (or atrophying?) when the British arrived, and I have only the barest outline of its workings. Basically, a series of towns came to look to Biu for leadership in massing fighting power for defensive operations against common enemies who intruded into the area. As far as I know, this enlarged militia was never used for aggression or expansion, but it is tantalizing to speculate whether the Pabir would have entered such an expansionist phase had history given them the chance.

During this entire period the Bura remained in independent small villages to the south of the Pabir.[9] Although similar in culture, language, and ecology, they were able to maintain autonomous small village polities while their Pabir cousins developed high-walled towns, social stratification, and inter-polity alliances bordering on a complex state system. In the southern area the terrain breaks up into hills, promontories, rivers, and thick forest groves. Raiding cavalry-led incursions from Borno or the western Fulani-held regions were spotted by scouts from hill-top outposts and the people fled to other hill-tops or into the forests. In contrast the Pabir area is on the southern edges of the Borno plains. There are hills and a few promontories but the vegetation is savanna and raiding by large forces is possible. As a result compacting into large settlements has never taken place among the Bura until very recent times when modern primary schools and markets on the main highway introduced a new stimulus. Significantly, this same north-south division between more complex walled towns possessing more developed political hierarchies on the one hand and smaller locally autonomous less politically developed villages on the other has occurred among other ethnic groups to the west of Pabir/Bura who live under essentially the same conditions of ecology, geography, and foreign relations.

Fombina-Yola

The next case is possibly the most useful since we have a full and detailed account of the founding of Fombina (Abubakar 1970; 1972). Prior to the nineteenth century the Benue Valley of Nigeria was occupied by Fulani peoples living as nomads, transhumant villager-herders, and fully sedentarized agriculturalists. Their traditional social and political system was based on patrilineal lineage groups under an *ardo* (lineage head) and elders of the constituent lineage segments. Segments under *ardos* were linked into nomad clan groups that had a strong sense of common identity and putative descent but no overall organization. An *ardo* officiated at ceremonies and was given a portion of all gift exchanges and bridewealth payments. He mediated disputes between segments with the elders and acted as a spokesman for his group to others. Decisions were made by the *ardo* and the elders, but each lineage and family segment was free to go out on its own if it felt the need for separate pasturage. Settled groups were also under *ardos,* but in this case the *ardo* of the founding lineage was a *jauro,* an *ardo* who had authority over all within the settlement. Through him the settled Fulani were subordinate to or linked to the owners of the land, the chiefs of the indigenous Benue Valley agriculturalists. Other *ardos* within the settlement, their slaves, clients, and any non-Fulanis who had come with them, were under the overall authority of the *jauro.* However, for most everyday purposes each Fulani subgroup was generally autonomous.

Fulani who migrated into the Benue region had to pay gifts of entry to local agriculturalist headmen or chiefs and extra and continuing gifts for grazing rights. They also had to provide animals for ceremonial feasts held by the owners of the land. Some Fulani were able to remain as full nomads, but others were forced to become partially agricultural in order to survive. Although pastoralism was the valued pursuit, many herds were too small to maintain domestic groups on surplus milk products and manuring of farm plots that were exchanged for grain and other requirements. Once herd size declined beyond a certain point, milk had to be reserved for calves and the use of the group itself. This forced some Fulani to take up semi-sedentary transhumance and become late-comers in a new land.[10]

The situation was complicated by geographical and associated economic and social factors. In these regions to the south of more usual Fulani migrations, there is better rainfall and soil than is generally the case where Fulani have developed patterns of symbiotic relations with local farmers. The result is that, even today, Fulani goods and services—milk products and manuring—are less needed or wanted by the host peoples than they are further to the north. This situation resulted in new terms of trade. Agriculturalists need meat, and the custom developed that all dead cattle belonged to the owner of the land on which the death took place. Nomads were forced to bring cattle for sacrifice to agricuturalists' ceremonies. The farmers were also attracted to Fulani women, whose beauty is widely agreed upon in this part of Africa. Chiefs demanded Fulani girls as wives, and throughout the upper Benue area it became customary for local non-Fulani headmen or their sons to have first-night sexual rights at Fulani weddings held within their territorial jurisdiction.

To make matters worse, by the beginning of the nineteenth century the upper Benue Valley was becoming a refuge for Fulani from farther north. A series of defeats in Borno and in the Baghirmi area south of Lake Chad brought two meandering streams of migrants—one from central Borno through Biu, another down the Yedseram Valley—towards the Benue. Competition for land and grazing rights, clashes with settled peoples and between Fulani clan groups, and the degrading first-night rights produced armed conflicts throughout the area. Fulani elders and *ardos* came together to mediate disputes and discuss their common plight in relation to the indigenous peoples. To the north the Kanuri and Baghirmi were Muslims and had centralized states. Here in the south the Fulani were among non-Muslims without complex governments, and they felt that the cultures and the demands of these peoples were therefore less legitimate. The period is referred to in Fulani traditions as *bone*—the times of hardship and oppression.

News of a Fulani-led jihad (holy war) uprising against indigenous agriculturalists in Bauchi, Gombe, and Damaturu spread southwards. One Fulani jihad leader, Buba Yero of Gombe, made a number of armed incursions into the Fombina area early in the nineteenth century. Finally, leading Fulani headmen of the Benue area met and decided to ask Modibba Adamu, one of their Koranic teachers, to go west to Sokoto to the center of the rising Fulani caliphate and ask for advice from Othman Dan Fodio, the central leader of the jihad. Adamu had no herds of his own to tend. He had been trained in Borno and travelled from one Fulani group to another, teaching and preaching the unity of all Muslims (which meant Fulani) of the Benue area. He took the 500-mile trip to Sokoto in 1809-1810 as the emissary of the *ardos* (Abubakar 1970: 207). There he was given a flag by Dan Fodio and told to return, start the jihad against the non-Muslims, and set up a centralized government with himself as emir. He was also to appoint Muslim judges, collect taxes, and protect women from illegal acts—i.e., first-night rights by the non-Muslims. By the time he returned, he had attracted numbers of warrior-Fulani along his route, who hoped for booty, glory, and position in his new state.

At first, the *ardos* at home were reluctant and dismayed. They had sent him for consultation and advice—he returned as their emir. Nevertheless, in the next two to three years he preached and rallied support over the entire region referred to as Fombina—the upper Benue-Yedseram river valleys. The density of the nomad population continued to increase; the former problems and conflicts intensified. Newer arrivals brought more horses, making for the beginnings of a cavalry capability. Other Fulani of Fombina going to Sokoto for advice were told to rally under Adamu's banner. By 1813-1815 Adamu had a number of widely acclaimed victories to his credit. Non-Muslim indigenes were told to accept Islam and Fulani overlordship or face death. If they accepted the terms, they were to send men for the jihad and annual tributes to Adamu, the new emir. Several sub-emirates were formed in areas where particular Fulani clan groups were aggregated. A number of non-Muslims sent messages suing for peace, offering military help and acceptance of subordination in return for non-aggression. Although the *ardos* and local Fulani segments always remained somewhat reluctant to subordinate themselves to Adamu, by the end of the 1820s a centrally organized state with its capital at Yola began to emerge from the upheaval of jihad.

At first, all the *ardos* and elders were linked to Adamu and his staff of advisers as officials and military commanders. The first step then was simply to proclaim a central authority over the previously autonomous lineage and clan segments and to preach unity by virtue of Islam, ethnicity, and shared oppression as a minority in a strange land.[11] By the late 1830s and early 1840s Adamu was organizing his government, using Kanuri titles for officials and offices of the realm. The government was divided into two functionally distinct sectors based roughly on peace and war or management and control. A set of officials was charged with governing, adjudicating, and carrying out government policy in the capital and connecting up, peacefully, to local populations outside the capital. Another set of officials was responsible for the armed defense of the capital, for putting down revolts, conquering recalcitrant non-Muslim groups in the region, and forcibly collecting revenues when local populations refused to send in annual tributes to the emir. Offices and titles soon began proliferating at the capital, slave settlements were set up in the area, and non-Fulani villages were given over to nobles as fiefs to use for personal support and to administer for the kingdom. Fulani villages delivered their revenues directly to the emir. Rebellious villages were put down ruthlessly. Abubakar (1970: 220) believes it was a state whose leaders quickly became dependent upon tributes and booty and whose officials replaced pastoralism and transhumant agriculture with centralized government, warfare, slave labor, taxation, and plunder.

After 1840 it became a full-time task to maintain the new state. Formerly autonomous Fulani *ardos* and *jauros* felt no need to accept costly subordination after the conditions oppressing them were corrected. Once the emirate was established in the mid-nineteenth century, Adamu and his supporters quickly initiated moves to achieve local autonomy outside the new Fombina state. There were plots to assassinate Adamu. Some tried to obtain their own flags and become emirs in their own right. Another claimed kinship to Dan Fodio at Sokoto and therefore superior status to Adamu. This particular leader actually succeeded in setting up an independent statelet for a while before being vanquished by Adamu's military forces. Still another (1842) sent large caravans of booty back to Sokoto, asking recognition for his own flag—that is for his emirate—in return. But Dan Fodio died at this time, and when Adamu threatened war, the rebel came to Yola and swore allegiance to Fombina. Nevertheless, the problem of rebellion remained, never to be fully settled until the colonial period brought the entire region under a more powerful regime.

Still, a state had formed. What had been a lineage-based nomadic and seminomadic minority of migrants in a strange land united under a religious soldier-leader who then created a central government bureaucracy and a hierarchy of administration and military control while propagating the faith and setting up a new elite way of life for the Fulani rulers of the region.

Analysis and Discussion

All three of these state-building episodes are in some sense "second-ary." In Borno the Magumi Sefawa leaders were Muslims who were aware of and had direct contacts with early states in other parts of the Islamic world. The Pabir of Biu were certainly aware of centralized institutions in Borno and quite consciously copied many titles and administrative procedures from them. Fombina under Adamu was in effect an outlying segment of the Fulani empire of Sokoto and was founded as part of that overall development. Knowledge of centralized government was certainly available to the Kanuri precursors, to the Fulani, and to the Pabir-Bura well before they actually founded states of their own.

On the other hand, many societies in these same regions also knew of centralized government and *did not* develop centralized govern-ments of their own. At the time these states emerged, locally autono-mous societies of the Borno plain remained uncentralized: the Bura did not centralize when their northern Pabir settlements developed more complex forms, nor did the indigenous agriculturalists of the Benue Valley centralize when the Fulani created the Emirate of Fombina. All these people *knew about* centralized government, but only some chose to adopt it.

Secondary states, like primary ones, do not just happen; they are the result of conflicts, struggles, and conditions of change that create a new overarching authority structure where none previously existed. In this sense, primary/secondary distinctions may be useful histori-cally, but for comparative and theoretical purposes it is more impor-tant to isolate the nature and conditions of change, using all cases of state formation as a pool of instances to create more general knowledge.

Borno and Fombina are cases of Islamic societies interacting with non-Islamic ones in which the former come to dominate the latter with an emergent state system. Contrarily, the Pabir are a non-Islamic people in interaction with Islamic ones. Clearly, Islam gave constitutional and judicial shape to both Borno and Fombina; the special place of the ulama, or learned men, as advisers, critics, and judicial officials in these states is quite clear in their history. However, the fact that the Pabir were able to form centralized government outside of Islam indicates that although this religion was of great importance in *shaping* state emergence in the Sudan, it was not the sole source of such tendencies nor even a necessary one in all cases.

The cases used in this analysis exemplify two separate pathways to statehood. Although the details of the Borno case are much less clear than those for Fombina-Yola, both states resulted from an original incursion or migration of nomadic peoples into the midst of locally autonomous agricultural villages. The Fombina data indicate that such nomad-agricultural relations are unstable. The structural-functional assumption of a balanced symbiosis between nomads and farmers turns out to be false when examined in historical perspective. Such relations change over time and in response to demands for nomad surpluses. Furthermore, herd sizes can vary with ecological conditions producing tendencies for nomads to take up agriculture even though they may maintain strong positive values for herding. This tendency to sedentarize is in turn associated with tendencies to acquire persons—slaves, serfs, clients, or women, who carry out many lower-status occupations for the now transhumant herdsmen. Nomads affected by these tendencies then shift towards more complex organization while maintaining some solidarity with their more nomadic cousins.

Local indigenous populations exact entry fees, tributes, and other forms of payments from the pastoralist newcomers. Given greater demands on the nomads, strong feelings by the nomads of cultural superiority, constant friction between the nomads and the indigenous peoples—any of these—outbreaks of violence will occur. If the inmigrants rally under a leader, and are able to bring superior weapons or superior numbers to the conflict, they will eventually coalesce in a citadel-town and develop bureaucratic and military means to maintain dominance under the monarch-descendant of the leader who first united them.

The other path to statehood is by way of defensive reactions by agriculturalists to raids and other aggression from newly formed nearby states. They, too, can coalesce in large, compact walled towns. Agriculture becomes more intensified as the population within the town increases. The former headmen and their advisers, descendants of the founders of the settlement, must spend ever greater amounts of time mediating disputes and coordinating larger-scaled activities. In time, this group forms an upper class of rulers and bureaucrats who marry within their class and who form the basic political factions of the state.

Both trajectories to statehood produce a central bureaucracy with control over military coercion. Both are associated with enhanced secular and sacred powers of the ruling class, and both eventually work out center-periphery relations. The nomad-initiated state is multiethnic from its beginnings; the defensive-reaction state has multiethnic capabilities. Pabir and Bura are semi-differentiated ethnic groups, and there are non-Muslim Fulani links to the Pabir throne, by marriage and because the monarch placed cattle with these non-Muslims for tending. In both cases fissioning of the state is resisted by institutional and military means. No matter how it evolves, once a centralized state starts to appear its more hierarchical organization of authority relations exerts strong selective pressure on whatever kinds of societies and polities have been forced into this position. The result is more convergence as time goes on. The different beginnings, often from very different courses, have then produced similar results.

About other well-known "causes of statehood" several statements can be made. There is no indication in any of these cases that long-distance trade preceded statehood or was related to its emergence. It is clear that rulers did develop such trade as part of their official duties as redistributors of valued goods and services. Population pressure, of sorts, can be said to exist in all the cases but only as part of, or in relation to, other factors, which shape and define it for the peoples concerned. Fombina history specifically mentions increased population pressure on pasture land as a pre-state problem. However in Fombina, and possibly in Borno, it was pastoralist-agriculturalist competition for control over the resources that created the conflicts leading to state emergence. Both Pabir and Borno built large towns compacting and reorganizing their populations, although overall densities may not have changed at all. In other words, population pressure is an over-generalized summary of complex interrelations among specific factors that operate differently to produce different results. Although Service (1975: 270-272) notes the nomad and agriculturalist routes to statehood, he rejects any validity to the notion of conquest (1975: 270). Certainly the Borno and Fombina nomad-originated states are clear cases of conquest, in which migrant nomads usurped control of the land from previous "owners" by means of military force.

Finally, what about stratification? Within-group stratification was of a low order before state founding in all these cases. Slavery in Africa, and most likely elsewhere among early pre-states as well, is not necessarily associated with class stratification (Cohen 1971; Meirs and Kopytoff 1977). On the other hand, if we look at Borno and Fombina as total ecosystems, ethnic distinctions were also stratified. Local owners of the land in Fombina had, in Fried's terms, unequal access to life-sustaining resources. Very likely this was true of Borno as well. The state was founded, however, *not* by the group with power over resources but by those denied access to the resources. In a sense, nomad-agricultural conflicts in Sudanic Africa produced revolutionary states in which the exploited turned the tables on their agricultural exploiters and became a despotic ruling class themselves. Once the new state became an organized reality, these new relations served as a basis for a highly stratified society whose ethnic relations placed the newly sedentarized nomads, or a group of them, on top (Spooner 1969; Salzman 1971).

The Pabir-Biu defensive state, however, had little if any pre-state stratification. Owners of the land were the village founders. Other lineage groups had somewhat lower status in the village, but this difference was minor. The village chief who later became king was not appreciably different from others. Pabir monarchs said they came from Borno. However, everyone in Buraland can trace his ancestry to somewhere else through lineage and clan affiliations.[12] Founders had very few if any privileges except a monopoly over the headship. Only later, when the state emerged, did clear-cut lines of social stratification appear. In such agricultural defensive states it is possible to have no conquest and no appreciable stratification before tendencies to statehood get under way. As pressures from outside continue, there is a constant tendency for unification of the walled towns and the stabilization of such a network into a larger state.

A final word about materialist, Marxian, anti-Marxian idealist, or any other quasi-political theology that guides our insights, hypotheses, and theories. The measurement devices for creating clear-cut tests of such viewpoints do not at present exist. We need therefore to look at well-documented historical cases, such as Fombina or those of early Europe and Asia, in order to obtain some appreciation of what specific factors have operated in any particular instance of state-building. Without these data, it is possible for everybody to illustrate, document, and support the particular viewpoint that most satisfies his or her own moral and political view of history and human evolution.

This may keep us all busy, but it will probably insure that we get nowhere—energetically.

Acknowledgments

Field research for this paper was carried out during 1972-1974 while the writer was on staff at Ahmadu Bello University, on leave from Northwestern University. Support for the work was granted by the National Science Foundation and the National Endowment for the Humanities. The writer is grateful to these agencies and to Northwestern and Ahmadu Bello Universities for granting him the support, the time, and the opportunity to carry out the research. I am also grateful for helpful comments from Raoul Naroll, R. McC. Netting, S. Reyna, and B. Trigger.

Notes

1. Borno is now the officially proclaimed and accepted spelling of what I have previously written of as Bornu.

2. The succession strife in Kanem is reflected in the very broad nature of the royal genealogy at this time, indicating many rulers in a short period (Cohen 1966). More interestingly, it is also signaled in the sacrilegious opening of a now defunct bundle (*mune*) of royal regalia. This act led supposedly to men intriguing unceasingly against one another. It is my hypothesis, based on Pabir comparative materials, that the *mune* was very likely of central importance in royal installation ceremonies. Succession rivalries led to fights over possession. In my view the legend is therefore an accurate rendition of the historical facts but simply reverses cause and effect—i.e., succession conflict led to fights over the *mune* because of its significance in creating a legitimated chief. Since it probably symbolized the welfare of the Magumi people, their loss of power was attributed to the conflict over its ownership.

3. *Kogu* is the Kanuri word for baobab tree, a shade tree associated with settled town life. *Kaga* may also be an early form of *kara*, meaning unsettled bushland. Attempts by some to link this fourteenth-century Kogu with the Pabir queen mother's much more recent town of Kogu are fruitless since Kogu is a common name for a village.

4. Bivar and Shinnie (1962) report on a number of burnt-brick sites in the area to the northwest of Lake Chad. These sites are either garrisons built after the founding of Gazargamo or are precursors to it. The latter interpretation, proposed by Smith (1971: 182) and accepted here, is consistent with a progressive sedentarization of the Magumi in the late fourteenth and early fifteenth centuries.

5. Even today Bornoans describe Magumi as the "true" or the "real" Kanuri because they were the people of Birni Gazargamo—i.e., of the citadel city when the nation was young.

6. This general picture emerges from oral history and my own research. Work being carried out at present by Mallam Kyari Tijani of Ahmadu Bello University will provide us with a much clearer picture of this pre-

nineteenth-century Borno administration than is now available.

7. The titles are Kanuri ones with the exception of the monarch's (*kuthli*), which seems indigenous.

8. The change is actually much more complex than this short statement implies. For example, relations among relatives at funerals, where the deceased's property, including wives, was redistributed, were also determined by exogamy rules. For the most part, these practices were retained but were changed by the inception of cousin marriage so that people who "joke" at one's funeral (potential in-laws) came to be much closer kin for the Pabir than for the Bura.

9. Although accurate this statement obscures the fact that a few Bura villages close to Biu were starting to build low stone walls by the end of the nineteenth century. Thus there were Pabir influences spreading to Buraland but these were arrested and deflected by the coming of colonialism.

10. Abubakar (1970) has not recorded any more detail than this. However, R. McC. Netting (personal communication) notes that this same process was occurring on the Jos plateau several hundred miles west of Fombina. Once Fulani nomad groups became sedentary or semi-sedentary in Jos the better water and pasture conditions caused their depleted herds to quickly multiply thereby producing further strains on the relations between the Fulani and their hosts.

11. This point is complex. Those not in the jihad were "habe." The term is sometimes translated as "non-Fulani," but this is not agreed to by many contemporary scholars in Northern Nigeria. Non-Muslim Fulani are said to be not fully Habe, yet bear some Habe features, while non-Fulani jihadi are Habe who have non-Habe features. I therefore see the jihad as partly ethnic, partly religious. On the other hand, Fulani/non-Fulani distinctions are so clear-cut in Fombina, and the inception of the jihad was so strongly associated with the Fulani of the area, that we are justified in using ethnicity per se as a factor in the rise of the Fombina state.

12. Horton (1971) notes that pre-state systems with disjunctive (Bohannan 1954) origins have an incipient stratificational difference between the owners or founders of the settlement and later-comers. However, except for the office of headman, other valued resources and positions are open to all members of the community.

References

Abubakar, S.
   1970   The Fombina Emirate 1809-1903. Ph.D. dissertation (History), Ahmadu Bello University.
   1972   The Establishment of Authority in the Upper Benue Basin 1809-1847. *Savanna* 1: 67-80.
Alland, A., Jr., and B. McCay
   1973   The Concept of Adaptation in Biological and Cultural Evolution. In J. J. Honigman (ed.), *Handbook of Social and Cultural Evolution*. Chicago: Rand McNally.
Barth, H.
   1857   *Travels and Discovery in North and Central Africa, 1849-1855*, vol. 2. London: Longman.

Bivar, A. D. H., and P. L. Shinnie
    1962   Old Kanuri Capitals. *Journal of African History* 3: 1-10.
Bohannan, P. J.
    1954   The Migration and Expansion of the Tiv. *Africa* 24: 2-16.
Carneiro, R. L.
    1970   A Theory of the Origin of the State. *Science* 169: 733-738.
Chapelle, J.
    1957   *Les nomads noir du Sahara*. Paris: Plon.
Cohen, R.
    1966   The Bornu King Lists. In J. Butler (ed.), *Boston Papers on Africa* 2:
            41-83.
    1971   Servility in Social Evolution. In *Migration and Anthropology*,
            Proceedings of the 1970 Meetings of American Ethnological Society.
            Seattle: University of Washington Press.
    1976   The Natural History of Hierarchy: A Case Study. In T. R. Burns and
            W. Buckley (eds.), *Power and Control: Social Structures and Their
            Transformation*. London: Sage.
    1977   Oedipus Rex and Regina: The Queen Mother in Africa. *Africa* 47:
            14-30.
    1978   State Origins: A Reformulation. In H. J. M. Claessen and P. Skalník
            (eds.), *The Early States*. The Hague: Mouton.
Feierman, S.
    1974   *The Shambaa Kingdom*. Madison: University of Wisconsin Press.
Fried, M. H.
    1967   *The Evolution of Political Society*. New York: Random House.
Horton, R.
    1971   Stateless Societies in the History of West Africa. In J. F. A. Ajayi
            and M. Crowder (eds.), *History of West Africa*, vol. 1. London:
            Longman.
Meirs, S., and I. Kopytoff (eds.)
    1977   *Slavery in Africa*. Madison: University of Wisconsin Press.
Netting, R. McC.
    1972   Sacred Power and Centralization: Aspects of Political Adaptation in
            Africa. In B. Spooner (ed.), *Population Growth: Anthropological
            Implications*. Cambridge, Mass.: MIT Press.
Palmer, H. R.
    1936   *Bornu, Sahara, and Sudan*. London: J. Murray.
Salzman, P. C.
    1971   Adaptation and Political Organization in Iranian Baluchistan.
            Ethnology 10: 433-444.
Service, E. R.
    1975   *Origin of the State and Civilization*. New York: Norton.
Smith, A.
    1971   The Early States of the Central Sudan. In J. F. A. Ajayi and
            M. Crowder (eds.), *History of West Africa*, vol. 1. London: Long-
            man.
Wright, H. T., and G. Johnson
    1975   Population, Exchange, and Early State Formation in Southwestern
            Iran. *American Anthropologist* 77: 267-289.

Secondary State Formation:
An Explanatory Model

BARBARA J. PRICE

It is paradoxical that there have been numerous studies of individual secondary states, including many which emphasize process and dynamics: all contemporary, all ethnographic-present, and the bulk of ethnohistorically documented states are secondary. Moreover, all direct, non-analogical, non-retrodictive knowledge of pristine states is in fact derived only from archaeology. Yet there has been almost no systematic theoretical treatment of the secondary state as a regular and lawful phenomenon. It is hoped that the present chapter might constitute a preliminary program for more detailed future investigation. Two quite distinct sequences, furthermore, are customarily lumped in the term "secondary state formation." The first is via historical succession from a preexisting state, itself either pristine or secondary; this will be of only tangential concern at present. In the second sequence an existing state, pristine or secondary, expands into areas inhabited by populations not heretofore state-organized. Two subtypes, which are more correctly regarded as poles of a continuum, may be distinguished: One involves direct pressure in the form of political incorporation or of massive economic takeover and control—a relatively overt colonialism. The other involves more indirect modification by irrevocable alteration of the socioeconomic environment, thereby creating conditions for the transformation of the infrastructure and institutional arrangements of the target area.

For two ultimately related reasons the problem of the secondary state is an important one. First, the spread and dispersal of the state as a level of organization are in evolutionary terms principal indices of its

161

adaptive success. An adaptive trait is one which increases the number of its carriers; state institutions expand at the expense of non-state ones via the process of secondary state formation. Second, it is evident that studies of secondary states are often uncritically, at least implicitly, retrodicted into pristine situations, thus raising questions of epistemological legitimacy. It is therefore essential that we distinguish what is generalizable in this fashion from what is not, that we establish some consistent basis to justify so obviously necessary an operation. Few isomorphisms between archaeological and other types of data have been established or made explicit. Nor have consistent procedures been developed to verify or falsify attempts to treat these diverse classes of data, derived by diverse methods from diverse sources, within a uniformitarian framework. This must be done for any evolutionary, and therefore diachronic, statement to be made at all. Development of these procedures must be based upon a nomothetic statement of the processes whereby secondary states are formed and the ways in which their institutions function. It may be noted in passing that this paper will raise questions it cannot yet pretend to answer.

What may generally be called adaptive models have had considerable impact throughout American anthropology, at least since the work of White and Steward. Such models are derived ultimately from the paradigm of Darwinian evolution; they are based upon the observed occurrence of random variations, the differential survival of which is nonrandom, governed by the principles of adaptation and selection. Since adaptive traits, or variants, are those which facilitate their own reproduction, it follows that the operational test of adaptation is in differential demography. Therefore the problem becomes the assessment of the extent to which the presence, or operation, of the element in question increases population numbers and densities or raises the carrying capacity of the environment exploited by that population. Such traits or elements may be morphological or behavioral: selection pressure may act upon any manifested variability. Thus all human behavior becomes analytically merely a special case of more general laws of living systems. As a special case, it will clearly require corollaries pertaining specifically to it; but these cannot contradict the more general statement insofar as they belong to the same universe.

While descended in large part from Marx, the materialist strategy (Harris 1968) clearly has Darwin as its other parent. Linkage of these two may seem unusual, in that these two positions are more often opposed than associated. The dichotomy appears in turn to be a function of the acceptance of the orthodox, dialectical Marxism, an intellectual position which does not generate the present chapter. Quite obviously the Hegelian dialectic and the Darwinian natural selection model are incompatible, in fact are epistemologically in direct competition: both are mechanisms which act to make a theory work, a theory of change. The present non-canonical interpretation of Marx emphasizes instead his substantive position, particularly his views on the determinative aspects of the mode of production upon social life. It is recognized that this is a classical "heresy," with an enormous literature, discussion of which is beyond the scope of this essay. A nondialectical substantive interpretation of Marx is not only consonant with an evolutionary model but can in fact be deduced from that model as a special case, a corollary which adapts general evolution to the specifics of human behavior. Such a model is capable of providing broader explanations, with greater parsimony, in the combined form than seems to be the case for either component taken separately.

Steward's (1955a) concept of the culture core, the expansion of this original definition by Sanders and Price (1968), and the further generalization that core features are determined operationally to be those most inexorably operated upon by natural selection, are all deduced from the higher-level paradigm. Core features regularly involve institutions responsible for the capture or harnessing, storage, distribution, and flow of energy within and between populations. In turn, this observation underlies the applicability to the entire range of human behavior of a single universal evaluative criterion, that of differential energy, once again deducible directly from the original paradigm. Even the traditional criterion of differential demographic growth is ultimately translatable into energy terms. Core features are those which can be described and compared in terms of energetic efficiency (secondary ones often cannot). It is in the sphere of the material conditions of life and in phenomena demonstrably linked to them— the infrastructure—that criteria of relative efficiency can be consistently measured, universally applied, and causally linked to questions of differential stability and change. This one parameter therefore permits, actually encourages, cross-cultural and diachronic comparison regardless of superficial differences of form, historical sequence, culture area, language, time period, level of integration, or other traditional anthropological classificatory categories.

Adaptive models differ in emphasis among themselves in terms of parameters stressed and the relative explanatory weight assigned to each. Even when they have been derived from the same paradigm, some will inevitably provide stronger explanations than will others. The model to be developed in the course of this discussion represents an expansion and generalization of Fried's (1967, 1975) model of the formation of tribes. Here also the fundamental problem is one of the

contact of and/or competition between societies at different energy—
and thus institutional—levels. Where Fried's problem is specifically
the expansion of states into zones occupied by non-state societies, he
concentrates heavily upon largely egalitarian target groups. The present essay asks what happens when the populations in contact with the
expanding states are ranked rather than egalitarian. One outcome in
fact is the formation of secondary states. The processes described and
analyzed by Fried continue to operate, but the results may differ from
one example to another. Although the same parameters are consistently invoked in explanation, they may vary in strength and relative
significance in different instances—a matter for empirical investigation—and thus in relation to each other within a causal system.
Alternatively, tribalization of such ranked groups may also occur,
involving a loss of complexity in the original ranked society. This
paper will attempt to develop certain predictions regarding these
alternatives. If the argument works, there is the potential that Fried's
original model can thereby be strengthened, through demonstrating
its applicability to a broader range of phenomena than that for which it
was initially developed. Ultimately it may be demonstrated to have
explanatory and predictive power in the total range of asymmetrical
contact/competition situations.

As previously implied, the evolutionary-materialist strategy requires the application of a hierarchy of function in order to analyze a
problem. A hierarchy of function is an explicit statement that some
traits are capable of bearing more explanatory weight than others—
and thus, that a statement of overall similarity and difference cannot be
reliably made on the basis of a simple trait list with equal weighting of
irrigation agriculture and magnetite mirrors. Most historical models,
such as the genetic model (Romney 1957; Vogt 1964), fall into this trap,
rendering much of the work produced irrelevant in systemic terms. In
the absence of a consistent assumption of the adaptive significance of
institutions it is too easy to treat them as passively transmitted from
ancestor to descendant like the family silver. Systemic explanation
demands that differential survival be explained and clarified—why
some institutions persist, why others are modified or disappear.
Origins, unlike survival, must be treated as random; questions concerning them are best treated as unanswerable in principle. What the
paradigm has done is to provide a clear statement of the dimensions of
comparison which will most probably be productive when consistently and noneclectically applied to a variety of examples. In the evolutionary framework of this chapter, these will be criteria of energy
harnessing, distribution, and control. The greater the energy encapsu-
lated in a piece of data, the more reliable will be its use in evidence, the

greater the number of problems for which its application will be relevant and valid, the more information it can store concerning the behavior stream which produced it. And therefore, the greater will be the probability of its potential contribution to the verification or falsification of a larger number of more diverse types of systemic proposition.

From these premises it may be deduced that the traditional archaeological criteria for establishing resemblance, usually based on evidence of ceramics, are of as little use to us as much of the traditional ethnographic evidence upon which culture areas or genetic models are constructed. The epistemological parallel here is very close. In both cases the traits upon which explanation and interpretation are based are largely or entirely secondary features and represent the expenditure of very few energy quanta. Stronger evidence of social, political, and economic processes can be derived from other kinds of material evidence such as architecture, assuming that it is its scale or mass rather than its style that is emphasized. Anything made by man represents the transformation of energy into matter, energy produced by and circulated in a human community. The transformation to some extent removes that amount of energy from general circulation by "spending" it, transmuting it into permanent material form. A pot fossilizes in this fashion a relatively minute quantity of energy; a building, proportional to its size, considerably more. The criterion of relative scale is thus the material isomorph of the capital and labor required for the energy transformation in manufacture or construction; like the energy-flow criterion itself, it is potentially universal in application. Monumental architecture—a diagnostic of nonegalitarian society—is a large chunk of fossilized energy permanently removed from general circulation. Concomitantly fossilized is the flow chart, or social organization—the division of labor of planners, architects, overseers, laborers, financiers, materials suppliers, judiciary, etc.—representing the process of energy investment. "A building," if appropriately analyzed, is thus theoretically capable of providing information on a fairly wide range of problems.

Probably the most powerful class of data to use in sociocultural explanation is settlement pattern—the arrangement of population upon a landscape. This may be taken as the material isomorph of the entire mode of production in its broadest sense, and of the core features of social and political organization. The greater the importance of any institution, the greater the number of contexts in which it should in all probability be manifest. Conversely it may be suggested that institutions and behaviors not reflected in this material form can be assumed with epistemological safety to have been unimportant.

It will therefore be primarily architectural and settlement data that will underwrite the discussion which follows, data capable on paradigmatic grounds of providing reliable evidence of sociocultural integration and processes of sociocultural change. By definition the processes of state formation—pristine or secondary—involve major institutional transformations resulting in turn from significant bioenergetic change. It would be illegitimate to postulate such transformation on stylistic, or other energy-poor, evidence.

Ranking and Stratification: Theoretical and Developmental Considerations

Because the present aim is to build a model of the regularities inherent in one form of asymmetric culture contact—that between states and ranked societies—some focus upon the characteristics of the latter, the target areas, is strongly advised. Several reasons justify the inclusion at this point of discussion which is only superficially digressive in what is planned as a treatment of the behavior of states. First and preeminently is the patent observation that the course of contact is determined not solely by the expanding state itself, but also by the organization (and the mode of production to which it is causally linked) of the target area. As a corollary to Fried's (1967, 1975) model of tribes, this paper suggests that egalitarian and ranked target areas will be differently treated by an expanding state, will show contrasting trajectories of development in contact situations. Second, more generally, ranked societies in some instances (pristine state formation) are transformed into states on an autochthonous basis. Thus in both pristine and secondary instances there is an intimate evolutionary linkage or association between ranked and stratified society, an association not impugned by the empirical fact that many ranked societies continue to maintain a stable equilibrium at this level of integration. The regularity of association of ranking and stratification is, however, sufficient to imply a fundamental continuity of the developmental process in both, and to warrant some expanded theoretical treatment of institutional stability and change. Third, therefore, the consideration of ranking which follows raises serious epistemological and methodological issues which must be addressed if any evolutionary analysis of nonegalitarian society is to produce remotely intelligible results; many of the recurrent explanatory problems of societies of this degree of complexity seem to be nomothetic ones not entirely amenable to lower- or middle-level solutions alone. The implications of this theoretical discussion for more general questions of the evolution of political systems—not necessarily explored at present—are accordingly broader and more tentative than might be expected in this context.

Within the more generalized category of "nonegalitarian society" there are serious definitional problems in the distinction of "ranking" from "stratification." In brief, the critical observation is that while the two contrast definitionally (Fried 1967), they appear operationally as a continuum, as quantitative scaled changes rather than as a presence/absence dualism. The economic underpinning of the definitions, moreover, suggests development rather than contrast. Fried defines ranking as a system with fewer status positions than personnel qualified to fill them; the differential access to strategic resources that defines stratification is absent in ranked society. But to the extent that the ranked society is based on a redistributive economy, and that the ranked nodes direct this economy, it is difficult to avoid some implication of differential access at least to those aspects of the economy which derive from the redistributive network. Some of these latter will of course be sumptuaries which, because of their limited circulation, cannot be effectively used in the control of capital (land, water, etc.) or of labor, but can be taken instead to represent a form of "payment" to the nodal individual for his management of the exchange system. Therefore their presence can be taken as an indicator that an economy is in fact of this type, although because they are not capital goods and do not, for the most part, increase local carrying capacities, they cannot in any sense be interpreted as the cause of the evolution of that system.

Harris (1968) has shown that exchange of subsistence goods and basic technology regularly accompanies exchange in sumptuaries, and that it is the former which in terms of natural selection can be held responsible for the maintenance of the system (cf. Parsons and Price 1971). The effect of such exchanges upon local carrying capacities—an empirical question—deserves more investigation than it has received. But it seems inescapable that the nodal position seems to have some sort of differential access to—or first crack at—any goods, however significant or insignificant quantitatively in terms of the local ecosystem, procured through redistribution. Some minimal element of stratification would therefore seem immanent in this type of ranked society. Were one to analyze and subsequently Guttman scale the behavioral components of stratification, it could be predicted that this extremely limited form of differential access would be bottommost. In practice of course it is severely restricted, in that this economic sector controls relatively little of the total energy harnessed and involves a comparatively small proportion of the total population. This economic sector grows differentially as—and if—the entire system evolves.

In the developmental range of ranked society from big-man to Tahitian or Hawaiian chiefs a major limiting factor in the absolute and relative position of the ranked nodes is labor. The evolution of ranking, as an inducement to increase productivity, is an intensification of production but one in which the central actor lacks control of this necessary labor component. Since he does not govern access to land or water, he cannot use these to attract or hold—much less coerce—the labor on which his productivity, and his continued participation in the system, depend. His only inducement is the redistribution itself, and he must effectively "bribe" his labor supply so it will not drift off elsewhere. Although data are insufficient to answer, it must be asked whether in the long run workers contribute more than they receive—a significant question in energetic terms. But to a greater or lesser extent, while the chief has first access to the fruits of redistribution much of this surplus is necessarily bespoke. On the basis of these considerations it becomes possible to regard this form of economy as the inception of the inequalities that characterize all nonegalitarian society. The differences between small- and large-scale ranked societies, and between these and stratified state-level polities, are based on the progressive addition of new behaviors, increasingly energy-intensive and differentiating.

It is therefore suggested that ranking and stratification be analyzed as a developmental continuum. The material counterparts by which these levels of social evolution can be recognized may be examined, given the premise that if institutions used definitionally are in fact important behaviorally they should be manifest in material terms. Site stratification (Sanders and Price 1968)—the contrast in size, plan, elaboration, and contents of communities which comprise a network—is the material isomorph of all nonegalitarian society. Such contrast implies nothing concerning the substantive contents of each community, only that there is an intranetwork difference. Site stratification patterns can be ordered in terms of their relative scale: numbers of levels, ranges of size of components, comparative demography (population size and density). From big-man to state the result is a continuum, without sharp contrasts except at the poles; any break in the continuum is ultimately arbitrary. From the standpoint of a cultural materialist paradigm, the conclusion of continuous scaled development from ranking to stratification is accordingly bolstered: a definition based on a sharp difference in principle should be paralleled by some operationalized present/absent criterion even if this one will not yield it.

Such a criterion has, however, been suggested (Price 1974) in the form of present/absent elite residences which contrast operationally in size, materials, and restriction of numbers with other residential structures. The underlying rationale is that these dwellings represent differential expenditures of energy. Any construction in any center of any size in any site stratification hierarchy represents energy first produced, then taken out of circulation. A civic center represents the surplus energy produced by a population and consumed or spent in this essentially public form (hence the scaled, continuum nature of site stratification). Differential housing, however, represents instead the differential ability of individuals or coresident groups to dip into the total energy flow and divert some of it to private use—i.e., a much more strongly marked differential access to strategic resources. But as previously noted, this ability is a more than/less than phenomenon; one could accordingly predict a continuum manifestation in the material evidence as well. Among the criteria needed to operationalize such a statement of internal socioeconomic differentiation would be the amount of energy differential (size, materials, labor-input assessment) represented in "elite" vs. "ordinary" housing, the relative numbers of each (in all cases far fewer of the elite than of the ordinary dwellings may be expected: all nonegalitarian society resembles the Eltonian pyramid), the degree of continuum shown by all housing together in a settlement or socioeconomic network of settlements (is there a sharp contrast between palaces and tenements, or is there also housing of intermediate character?). Differences in these parameters should reflect, and permit the reconstruction of, differences of sociopolitical organization.

The programmatic nature of these suggestions is granted: although they have been stated in operationalizable form, they have not yet been tested. They represent the consistent application of a single set of parameters (those demonstrably related to energy flow), the values of which should change in predictable ways with increased societal size and complexity, and serve in fact as a measure thereof. Certain material traits—residences, civic centers, the arrangements of population upon a landscape—can be taken as isomorphic, by deduction, of sociopolitical organization and of the mode of production. When ranking and stratification cannot be reliably distinguished on a comparative basis except at the poles of a continuum, then perhaps this fact is telling us something about the construction of a strong and workable set of definitions. In this case, it suggests one based explicitly upon a continuum of development, reflecting, as a dualistic contrastive one cannot, what must have been an evolutionary process; that the resulting taxa are less elegant is a lesser concern. Moreover, again by deduction, the course suggested opens a new set of empirical questions for research. What is the sequence in which particular rele-

vant (energy-distribution) behaviors are added? With what degree of
variation are these behaviors manifest (to what extent, for instance, are
extremes of ritual or sumptuary behavior definitionally necessary to
ranking? Can we have ranked society without, for instance, elaborate
tombs—indicating that "the money was being spent on something
else"?). To what extent do the ranking-into-stratification behaviors
scale and, in terms of our investigative strategy, why? A further advantage in the continuum model is the reduced concentration upon
taxonomy for its own sake, and concomitantly lessened danger of
reification. The present view of the ranking-stratification problem,
admittedly preliminary, departs to some considerable extent from
much of the literature. The terms have been retained in this modified
form because, interpreted expressly as a continuum, they retain their
usefulness in the analysis of developmental processes.

Processes of Secondary State Formation

Regardless of whether a given state is pristine or secondary (regardless, in fact, of whether that distinction is relevant to the problem
under study), the state in general constitutes a particular type of
political-economic behavior on the part of a population. States (Fried
1967) are defined on the basis of institutionalized power, first in the
form of socioeconomic stratification (differential access to strategic
resources), second, and supporting the first, in the centralized arroga-
tion and control of force. Such criteria are fundamentally material and
behavioral, capable of direct translation into energy-flow terms; they
can, in other words, be operationally identified on the basis of material
counterparts that are cross-culturally and diachronically consistent.
Pristine states achieve this level of integration through the systemic
operation of essentially autochthonous processes; secondary states, as
defined, reflect regular processes of interaction/competition of expanding states vis-à-vis non-state-organized populations. All by definition
are equally states.

As a central example of the processes of secondary state formation we may take the interaction of the state-organized polities of
Central Mexico with the ranked societies of the Maya area of Guatemala during the approximate period A.D. 300-900. Two principal areas
of contact, the Guatemala Highlands and the Petén Lowlands, appear to
illustrate the two subtypes, or continuum poles, of the processes which
occur under state impaction.

In the period under discussion a pristine state—Teotihuacán—
which had emerged on the Meseta Central of Mexico, undertook con-
certed expansion into Guatemala, characterized at the time by ranked

societies. Teotihuacán was highly urban (Millon 1973) with a diverse manufacturing and commercial economy (itself a stimulus to foreign adventures), underwritten by an extremely intensive hydraulic agriculture (cf. Price 1977). Following the decline of Teotihuacán as an imperial power it was replaced by three successor states ringing the Basin of Mexico; at least one of these (probably Cholula) resumed and maintained the political and economic interest in and pressure on the Maya area.

The patterning of the Teotihuacán impact upon Kaminaljuyú, in the Guatemala Highlands, is striking. As a ranked society Kaminaljuyú had been characterized by areas of dispersed settlement punctuated by civic constructions, including substantial adobe pyramids associated with other, often sculptured, stone monuments. Sumptuary goods, recognized on the basis of rarity and restricted associational contexts, are present. These are the hallmarks of ranked society, where a relatively high-energy redistributive economy (as this one seems to have been) generates sufficient surplus to divert into civic construction. Upon the incursion of Teotihuacán into Highland Guatemala a new, centralized civic center was constructed at Kaminaljuyú, its scale larger than the total aggregate of preexisting civic architecture and its principles of planning and its style entirely Mexican: plazas, temples, range structures, and associated residences. Following the withdrawal of Mexican pressure there appear to have been demographic decline and institutional devolution.

Colonialism seems to be reflected in these changes: the capture by a foreign elite of the capital and labor—the surplus energy—of an impacted population. Of this, the architectural evidence speaks clearly. Accompanying it of course are expected ceramic changes, observations of the burial of foreign objects in tombs, and other ancillary but consonant items of evidence. As presently used, the term "colonialism" need not imply a sequence of conquest and direct political annexation by the metropolitan power. Some military force or its threat was almost certainly applied, if only because people do not build civic centers as a form of recreation: the very presence of this type and scale of site intrusion reflects a differential power situation. The problem of formal political incorporation cannot actually be solved directly on the basis of material evidence—a fact that suggests some need for redefinition of a widely used and accepted, generally unquestioned concept which nonetheless cannot at present be operationalized. More significant is the unambiguous evidence of full-scale takeover of the non-subsistence economy; in contrast to annexation this can be materially defined. The visible overwhelming economic takeover may actually be a better indicator of what we call colonialism—

although its use leads to the conclusion that contemporary Guatemala is an etic colony of the United States regardless of the known lack of formal annexation.

Certainly Teotihuacán had ample motivation to control this particular economy. Kaminaljuyú is strategically located to exert control over a major adjacent zone of cacao production on the Pacific Coast, over a nearby obsidian mine, and over a pass leading to the Motagua Trench, a known source of jade. It had probably exerted some control, still as a ranked society, still based on redistribution, over most of these resource zones. Teotihuacán's "influence" preceded its takeover. If—and this remains unknown—the foreign incursion set off a local cycle of population growth, the present interpretation will be substantiated (see below): population increase would represent the results of pressures to intensify production of the relevant resources, and may be a regular component of the contact situation we call colonial.

Nothing comparable appears at Tikal, in the lowlands of Petén. As at Kaminaljuyú, contact preceded institutional transformation; but evidence suggests that the course of that transformation was different, less direct, not overtly associated with what we are calling colonialism. In addition to the customary ceramic data, there is at least one stela (#31) depicting a Mexican warrior—an interesting syncretism in that Teotihuacán lacked the stela cult. In architecture, one small masonry compound (5D-43) is constructed in a Mexican style, suggesting some permanent or long-term presence of Mexicans or some heavily Mexicanized group whose possible ethnicity is of less importance than its institutional implications. This compound is situated adjacent to, but is not a part of, the Central Acropolis, which remains entirely Maya in architecture and planning. Significantly perhaps, this one compound is situated near an area designated a market. An allocation of energy obviously different from that at Kaminaljuyú must be postulated.

Major sociopolitical transformations occurred in the Lowlands between the Early and Late Classic periods (Culbert 1970; Price 1974). By the Late Classic masonry palace structures, presumably elite residences, appeared in some numbers; all are stylistically Maya, and all contrast with the small residential structures built of perishable materials that constitute the most numerous building type. At Uaxactún Proskouriakoff (1963) traces the successive rebuildings of what began life as an Early Classic temple grouping into a Late Classic palace—civic, public space converted to private use, the direct material evidence of social stratification. These developments, not unexpectedly, appear to have been accompanied and underwritten by an intensification of the mode of production (Sanders 1973) and a concomitant demographic expansion. Such intensification assumed the primary form of a reduction in time in fallow, with perhaps some increased reliance on root and tree crops. Geographic conditions effectively preclude a shift (indigenous or introduced) in the mode of production. Given this intensification pattern, one expects a potentially precipitous decline in return on energy investment. Additional evidence (cf. Price 1974 for summary) of the shift in organization comes from the distribution of burials and from some intimations from physical anthropology—all consonant with the present interpretation and acting to support it. It remains to explain the causes of these changes.

A number of interrelated parameters have been differentially stressed to account for the emergence of state institutions. Among these have been environmental circumscription (Carneiro 1961), sociological circumscription (Carneiro 1970), population pressure (Sanders and Price 1968; Harner 1970), trade (Steward 1955b; Millon 1973), and hydraulic agriculture (Wittfogel 1957; Sanders and Price 1968; Price 1977). Much of the debate is complicated by the fact that all of these factors and more clearly play a role, and that few models have systematically linked them all by specifying their relationships within a causal explanation of real power. Most of the discussion in any case tends to refer to pristine states rather than to secondary ones—an acceptable procedure in some respects since states once formed are by definition comparable in their characteristics. But the processes of formation do differ, with that of the secondary state (excepting, once more, instances of historical succession) necessarily involving imposed external force, overt or veiled, including the alteration of its economic environment by the pressure of another state upon it.

Tolstoy (1969) argues that Teotihuacán diffused to the point of exporting its political institutions to the Maya, thus raising the latter to the state level of integration. Insofar as they constitute energy flow charts, however, sociopolitical institutions are by definition of limited exportability unless the infrastructure of the target area is demonstrably capable, or can be made capable, of supporting them. And while such institutions may be enormously profitable, they are also very expensive to support. Some explanation beyond the contact itself must be invoked to account for this type of transformation. A number of trade-based models exist—but it must be remembered that insofar as trade constitutes a lucrative resource, it is to that extent also capable of supplying a motive for the investment of force. Rathje's model (1971; but cf. Price 1977) treats trade as an independent variable for the

shift in Lowland Maya organization. At least in this instance, it seems
incapable of carrying so great an explanatory burden. Trade may constitute a resource, the control of which may serve as a power base
(Steward 1955b). It may elevate carrying capacity by raising a demographic ceiling imposed by what had once been a limiting factor and,
without the trade, may once again become so (Price 1977). Trade may
stimulate local economic development (Parsons and Price 1971) and
induce or stimulate demographic growth, especially in conjunction
with force (see below). But it may not do so; the conditions under
which it can or cannot must be specified and demonstrated. Often
however, it appears that trade may actually best be treated as a dependent variable, something to be explained with reference to the techno-
economic context of which it is a part. It is capable of great, and
regular, predictable variability in patterning; unless the relevant
conditions of its operation are stipulated, it becomes somewhat less
than informative to offer this parameter as an explanation. In none of
the senses mentioned, however, is trade equatable with diffusion,
because the latter postulates no consistent or lawful processes of
change and can therefore put forth no statement of cause.

Even where other factors or systems may be more powerful in
explanation, trade is obviously implicated along with them in the
organizational shifts throughout the Maya area. Even prior to state
formation the area was characterized by a sociopolitical system
wherein ranked positions derived their status as nodes in a redistributive network. Such societies are already trade-dependent. The
entry of a Teotihuacán into the socioeconomic environment may act to
expand trade volume and thereby increase the degree of dependence
of an increasing population upon it. Ranked positions would be
strengthened by having more work to do as more energy flows through
them, and mere status attributes and prestige could, under some circumstances, perhaps be transformed into real power. However, the
context in which this occurred in the Maya area includes force. It would
be to the advantage of a foreign power that order be maintained, even in
the face of the additional purely local competitive pressures caused by
intensification of production and increasing population pressure
upon resources (Sanders 1973). The necessity to exert such control
could perhaps help tip ranked positions into power-based ones. Comparable processes obviously occurred in some areas on an autochthonous basis—pristine state formation; in the Maya area foreign pressure appears to have been instrumental in setting these processes to
work. Essential similarity of dynamics—the demography-intensifica-
tion-competition force—is expectable in any emerging-state context.
But what sets off this nexus?

Most writers on urbanism (cf. Sanders and Price 1968; Jacobs 1969; Millon 1973) have emphasized the close interrelation between trade and the development of cities; such statements are of course based on principles known to Adam Smith. The relation between urbanism and the state, however, has been the cause of profound confusion for a variety of reasons, both scholarly and ideological. Childe's Mesopotamian data combined urbanism and the state in a single sequence and permitted the uncritical elevation of this particular association to the status of a generalization—they will always be associated and therefore equal the same thing—without comparative testing. All states, like societies at any other level of sociocultural integration, show characteristic ranges of settlement pattern which, as noted, may be taken as diagnostic of that level. Such ranges reflect the ranges, quantities, and patterning of the harnessing, distribution, and control of energy. The site stratification concept as previously used does not, however, imply anything about the nature or content of the settlements in question—only that they contrast systematically with each other and that these contrasts correspond to differential socioeconomic functions. The term "urban," on the other hand, describes the demographic and socioeconomic contents of the single settlement—a particular kind of pattern of energy flow. Thus it is possible to have a complex, multilevel site stratification hierarchy in which no single component may be demographically urban. No settlement can become definitionally urban, in other words, simply on the basis of its relative position in a contrastive network. However, on the basis of that network, and on the differential residence grounds already justified, it may nonetheless be obvious that a given set of material remains are those of a state level of organization.

In contrast with the Mexican states, pristine and successor, nothing in the Maya area can properly be called urban in demographic terms (Price 1977). There is a strong parallel with Classic Khmer (Coe 1961) in this respect, and with pre-New Kingdom Egypt. All of these are secondary states. Khmer, situated between India and China (both maritime powers at the time of the Khmer florescence), received "influences" from both. Egypt, more problematical and more customarily treated as a pristine development, may have been formed through kinds of pressures which were probably fairly indirect, emanating from Mesopotamia. A number of other aspects of Egypt's political evolution seem aberrant from the standpoint of the pristine state (Price 1977). But unless its nonurban character is a function of research efforts concentrated largely upon style and other secondary features, this lack of true cities may be taken as a strong suggestion of secondary status. Some secondary states, however, such as the Indus, are in fact urban; the presence of cities in no way precludes secondary status. But because known pristine sequences tend strongly to develop cities, and to do so in a homotaxially early phase of their evolution, the lack of urban settlements may be taken with some confidence to indicate secondary status.

One further observation of an occurrence which may be diagnostic of secondary status even though its incidence among such states is not universal: Major instability through time, including ultimate collapse not leading to the formation of a successor state, will differentially characterize secondary state sequences. Both this and the urbanism criterion relate directly to conditions of local infrastructure. The Maya Collapse is definitive and spectacular, perhaps an extreme case; not only do elite and large-scale energy manifestations cease, but the events in question are accompanied by almost total depopulation of the area. At an earlier period, between the Early and the Late Classic, a hiatus (Willey 1974), marked (in the perspective of most Mayanists) by a cessation of the erection of dated monuments and (in the emphasis of the materialist paradigm) by a cessation of all building activity, indicates considerable difficulty with the political economy. Less is known of the Khmer situation: the empire collapsed, though the loss of sociocultural integration does not appear to have entailed the scale of population loss of the Maya. Egypt, on the other hand, is practically a watchword of political continuity (at least into the Roman Empire). In the scale of its catastrophe the Maya state may be unique; but in terms of process certain of these devolutions are nomothetic. It is significant that both our comparative instances—Egypt and Khmer— are hydraulic in their infrastructures. The Maya, whose geography precluded a comparable shift in the mode of production, probably practiced a short-fallow swidden agriculture. Whether pristine or secondary, hydraulic agriculture on a large scale is capable of supporting, and may indeed require (Wittfogel 1957), state institutions. They should be more stable through time as a consequence.

It is accordingly possible to entertain the contention that all florescences in the Maya area and particularly in the Lowlands occurred in direct response to Central Mexican pressures and that the withdrawal of such pressures resulted in temporary decline (Willey 1974) or permanent collapse (cf. Webb 1973). The definition of "florescence" is based on materially inferred institutional structure, not upon stylistic traits; it involves the blanket question of the size and complexity of the sociocultural system. The transition from ranking to stratification apparently began under the aegis of Teotihuacán, was temporarily interrupted upon the fall of the latter, and resumed during the Late Classic under probable pressure from one or another of Teotihuacán's successor states, perhaps Cholula. In approximately A.D. 900—a time when there is a distinctive northward shift, at least temporarily, in Central Mexican attentions (Armillas 1969)—the Maya Lowlands Classic sequence ends.

Both the direct (as at Kaminaljuyú) and more indirect (Tikal) forms of state pressure leading to the development of secondary states out of ranked societies clearly require local ecosystemic support. This is stated as a necessary condition. The productive system must be capable of some degree of intensification, if only in the short run (evolution, including cultural evolution, is opportunistic). State systems, pristine or secondary, are by definition high-energy, demographically large—the conditions which favor the centralized control of resources and of power. States expand into areas controlling something they want; often such a resource involves labor in its production, and a mode of production capable of intensification, one in which an increase in labor supply will increase total output. Some areas into which the state moves are therefore inhabited by relatively large, complex groups of producers. And it may be universal in the behavior of states that their impact serves to increase numbers and densities; it is to the obvious advantage of the state to control and increase population in order to increase production. This is partially feasible simply by manipulating the market and thus stimulating increased numbers of producers and increased output of the desired commodities.

In the case of more direct forms of pressure actual political and military means may be applied. The behaviors involved etically constitute a continuum: even manipulation of conditions of supply and demand is a competitive process in a differential-power situation; economic and military takeover represents merely an intensification of this. Recent examples of this process, now called colonial and involving the overt takeover of capital and labor of the target area's population, are abundant. The British in India and the Dutch in Java both produced the effect of massive (excessive?) demographic growth. This growth seems analyzable less as a function of a decreased death rate brought about by the introduction of Western medicine than as the result of an increased birth rate in response to an insatiable colonial need for labor (cf. White 1973; Harris 1975). Much of the contemporary Third World demographic paradox may be explicable in terms of this model, which offers the further advantages of postulating at least one testable mechanism of change, and of allowing explicitly for a continuum of degrees of impact from less to more direct. On the assumption that these interrelated demographic and organizational processes characterized the instance of Mexico-Maya contact, then the observed Late Classic Maya population growth/institutional transformation feedback is accounted for and explained.

It is also apparent in terms of differential local resource bases of the target areas in question that a Teotihuacán should have expended more energy to exert direct control and impose at least economic, perhaps political, colonialism at Kaminaljuyú than would have been warranted in the case of Tikal, where a more indirect pressure seems to have obtained: Kaminaljuyú's location is strategic for the control of at least three of the principal commodities of interregional trade, where on the other hand Tikal's export work is more elusive to determine, to the point where one becomes concerned for its balance-of-payments problem. It is these considerations that are in part responsible for the earlier stated reluctance to consider as valid those explanations which are based upon trade as an independent variable. Even the analytical boundaries between "local" and "external" processes may be misleading: population growth, and too often carrying capacity as well, are customarily treated as local factors, contrasting with external ones such as foreign pressure. Such separation does not facilitate explanation. In sequences leading to secondary state formation all of these constitute interrelated aspects of the same system. The origins of secondary states, moreover—as in fact of all states—are functions of the expansion of scale of sociocultural systems, the coalescence of smaller systems into fewer, larger, more complex, higher-energy ones. As this happens, the nature and organization of the component parts are concomitantly modified.

Once demographic and productive intensification are under way, one must return to the question of infrastructure. It is no accident that the relatively "stable" secondary, like the pristine, states are hydraulic. A hydraulic mode of production in a paleotechnic setting is almost unparalleled in its capacity for intensification. In demographic terms this means that it has an enormous capacity to feed more people—and that the more people working, the greater the production. No such shift in mode of production ever occurred in the Maya area; instead, a basically swidden system was intensified by shortening the fallow cycle. But such intensification runs at an increasingly unfavorable ratio of return per calorie expended; further, in Petén, it incurs serious risk of long-run environmental degradation. This group of problems seems to have been one powerful contributor to the Collapse, but can be treated only in the systemic terms mentioned above, not as an independent variable. Obviously, however, the infrastructure could not sustain the processes leaned upon it over the long run, and the result was a collapse. What is of overriding epistemological significance here is that it has been shown that precisely the same constellation of factors caused the Rise as caused the Fall: In my end is my beginning.

Discussion and Conclusions

The noneclecticism of the foregoing suggests the basis for an explanatory model of secondary state formation. With the exception of situations of historical succession, secondary states are formed as a result of the expansion of other states, themselves either pristine or secondary. Underlying this statement is the assumption that states are inherently, institutionally expansionist—and that those empirically determined to be otherwise are merely unsuccessful in what is basically a competitive process. This inherent expansionism can be linked directly to the centralized control of force that defines the state. Operation of the processes of expansion is nonrandom: a state expands for certain interrelated reasons, including the neutralization of potential force on the part of others, and the control of resources (including labor) beyond its borders. These parameters should predict the direction of expansion and the differential energy devoted by the state to any particular expansionist adventure. On the basis of the model thus far, the fact that Teotihuacán and its immediate successors expanded to the south into Guatemala—and the fact that greater overtly colonial manifestations are visible at Kaminaljuyú than at Tikal—will be explicable, not as unique historical events, but as the expression of nomothetic processes. As states expand, therefore, the process and its effects are taken to be regular, although not necessarily uniform.

Secondary state formation is actually only one product of state expansionism. A statement of regularities must therefore include, even in the absence of proof as strong as might be desirable, some statement of the conditions under which different types of results might be expected to occur. Fried (1967, 1975) has postulated that tribes are formed from the impact of states upon non-state, largely egalitarian groups on their peripheries. Processes involving partial sedentarization and the more systematic institutionalization of leadership reflect the fact that states cannot deal consistently and efficiently with bands. This chapter has attempted to generalize Fried's model so that it may account in parallel fashion for the impact of states upon ranked societies. There two probable outcomes may occur: first, that the ranked society is transformed into a secondary state—the option thus far most intensively treated. But the second option too must be explored: the ranked society may be tribalized. The first type of transformation cannot be explained unless the probability of the second is also assessed.

It is hypothesized that where the ranked society is exploiting some resource desired by the state—and where production can be enhanced through the intensification of labor—the result of competitive pressure exerted by the state will be secondary state formation. The ranked society will thus be duly characterized by the "internal" processes of demographic growth and intensification of mode of production that underwrite, and the institutional centralization that defines, the state. Central Mexican impact upon the Maya area typifies this and serves in the process to illustrate the range of intensity of state expenditure of effort. Another illustration of this process may well be the Western opening of Hawaii. Although there is some debate concerning the organizational status of precontact Hawaii, the model developed here may fit. At contact it was at least a large and highly complex ranked society, with a mode of production partly based on irrigation (Wittfogel 1957); some case may legitimately be made for pristine state status—an analytically borderline situation which is per se not without interest. Under Western contact and with the introduction of firearms, however, an undeniable ruling house emerged very quickly (had it existed before, it seems to have been immeasurably stabilized and strengthened by the same transforming process). Further analysis is necessary to confirm or modify the analogy offered here as a possibly fruitful line of subsequent research.

If, however, the ranked society occupies an area containing some resource the state wants but is exploiting that zone in some other, usually more extensive way that competes with the state's "plans" for it, the course of events will be different. The result of state pressure should be tribalization, in Fried's terms, of the ranked society. Implicit in this general condition are two complex assumptions. First, the ranked society is for one reason or another incapable of the demographic/productive intensification required for systematic participation in the state's economic orbit. For this intensification to be successful, the local infrastructure must also be capable of a corresponding degree of intensification concomitant with that of the labor-demanding sector of the economy. Not all modes of production, in all types of environment, are capable of sustaining such development on even a short-run basis. The ranked society, in other words, particularly under paleotechnic conditions, must continue to feed itself; limited intensifiability of this sector may abort the changes in other economic spheres that underwrite state formation. Second, closely related, is the assumption of a relatively great quantitative differential between the state and the ranked society, specifically in the amount of energy harnessed. While itself not causal, such a situation may be strongly indicative of the existence of limiting factors such as those described immediately above, factors which inhibit expansion of a local labor supply. From the perspective of the state, a target ranked group of this sort constitutes far more of a potential threat than a potential economic asset. A prediction of tribalization is thus simply a logical outcome of the assessment of the costs and benefits involved in the expansion of the state.

In the more general terms set forth in the paradigm, it may be observed that when the conditions of contact involve direct competition for the same resource base (exploited similarly or differently), the higher-energy system will displace the lower-energy one, by competitive exclusion. In illustration, when hunter-gatherers and cultivators compete for lands capable of supporting either mode of production, the cultivators usually push back the hunter-gatherers. State-organized polities have consistently since 3000 B.C. expanded at the expense of non-state-organized groups. Once again, the distinction of local from external causes makes little sense in the analysis of this type of situation.

Tribalization under these circumstances offers a more effective neutralization of potential competition than secondary state formation when the latter cannot be efficiently or profitably maintained. Fried has noted that tribes, from the standpoint of states, constitute an almost uniquely controllable form of sociopolitical organization, with the effect that tribalization becomes an alternative to extinction of competing groups. Bison-hunters, in the American West, occupied at a low-energy and low demographic level land capable of supporting cattle ranching or grain agriculture (the last two also competing with each other). Most of the bison-hunters were of course band-organized, and thus fit Fried's original model. One may suggest, however, that Euro-American expansion into the American Southwest, which had previously supported ranked societies, may fit the present extension of that model. The Spanish conquest of the Southwest may well have caused the decrease in complexity of small ranked societies. While native Southwestern agriculture was intensive, irrigated, and capable of supporting high local population densities, each such group constituted an island: there was insufficient water to expand or coalesce such oasis groups—i.e., to increase the total energy content. Spanish mining and ranching interests, and Spanish plow agriculture, tended to displace any of these groups who were in the way. Similarly, ranked societies of the Northwest Coast seem to have been tribalized as a result of Euro-American institutional impact, particularly that of trading companies. The area suffered population losses mediated by introduced diseases, by emigration, and by economic disruption—infrastructural changes which underwrite and are causally implicated in the institutional devolution. In New Zealand, European introduction of commercial agriculture and commercial sheep raising seems to have had comparable effects upon the Maori.

Comparative material of this sort, even so programmatically presented, is essential for the treatment of nomothetic problems. Causality is regular, subject to the operation of the uniformitarian principle. Regularity does not, however, imply a correlation of 100 percent—merely one consistently greater than chance. A single contrary example cannot falsify. On the other hand, the better the model, the higher the correlations will be. Without comparative evidence there is no consistent nonarbitrary way to distinguish potentially nomothetic statements from the ad hoc, the unique, or historically determined characteristics of individual sequences. While the comparative data cited here are extremely preliminary, in some instances speculative, they suggest a direction of research necessary for the eventual testing of this model. They may constitute the raw material for the positive correlations that will verify, or the negative ones to falsify, our generalizations; if the correlations are weak, this fact will suggest that the model should be superseded by some other which will be more powerful. The strongest test of any theory, in other words, is against a competing theory.

The model developed here has been concerned with the problem of secondary state formation, a problem which raises far more general questions of institutional structure and evolution. All state organization, pristine or secondary, is expensive, involving high-energy infrastructures which, in order to function efficiently, require, and in positive feedback stimulate the growth of, state institutions. Because the institutional transformations described constitute a system, governed by feedback loops of various types, one expects a continuum of institutional development rather than mutually exclusive or contrasting categories. The transition from ranking to stratification is analyzed from this perspective; the results are supported by the material evidence of energy production and flow. Similarly, the opposition of "local" and "external" processes of culture change is rejected on much the same basis. Processes of change, whatever their ultimate origin, necessarily work upon, and through, the selective pressures of local ecosystems and the mode of production of the populations occupying them.

Thus there is a strong implication that institutions per se are not exportable. Yet quite obviously the competitive contact of cultures is capable of inducing profound differential institutional modifications in some, or all, of the parties concerned. Such modifications predictably show a continuum from direct economic and/or political takeover to the indirect alteration by one of the overall economic environment of the other. Evaluation of the substantive factors deduced as important from the paradigm permits assessment of the probable results: the costs and benefits of each course of action can be weighed. Therefore, the observation that one area is overtly colonized but another exploited only indirectly becomes explicable in general, nomothetic terms.

Reference to these same parameters similarly permits predictions concerning the probabilities of results other than secondary state formation under conditions of asymmetrical culture contact. The preceding discussion generates the following summary propositions:

1. If the non-state-organized target area has an infrastructure energetically capable of supporting state institutions, or one which under colonial or colonial-like impact can be intensified and rendered capable of doing so—and if this is to the advantage of the expanding state—the result will be the formation of a secondary state. If not, the result will be tribalization.

2. If the target area can maintain the appropriate infrastructure to only a limited extent in space and time, or can do so only under the economic and political modifications of its institutional environment caused by the expanding state, the secondary state that is formed will be unstable. Obviously this predicted instability is not expected to hold universally for all secondary states, some of which in fact are exceptionally stable and generate additional secondary states by historical succession. In paleotechnic contexts these very stable examples tend overwhelmingly to be, like pristine states, hydraulic. This consideration is the basis of the earlier statement that instability, where it occurs, indicates secondary state status, even though the reverse is not true.

3. If not only the total energy harnessed by the infrastructure but also the pattern of its distribution assumes certain levels and forms, the result, in a pristine or secondary setting, will be urban. If the total quantity of energy harnessed (necessary condition) suffices but the patterning of its distribution (sufficient condition) does not, the result will be a state which will be demographically and economically of non-urban character. Pristine states seem always to be urban, reflecting the growth of this energy-flow pattern on an autochthonous basis; their urbanism is one indication of their overall developmental precocity in a highly specialized type of ecosystemic and adaptive context. Non-urban states are always secondary, although not all secondary states

are nonurban. This difference appears to reflect the fact that, like state institutions, urbanism is profitable but also expensive—and may be expendable in some secondary contexts.

Acknowledgments

This essay began as an epistemological exercise that outgrew itself; it constitutes the last of a trilogy of related papers written between January and June of 1976. The first of these treats problems of pristine state formation, as this does the secondary state. The same paradigm underwrites all three papers.

Suggestions and comments have come from Eric Ross, Jane Ross, William Sanders, William Mitchell, and Michael Billig. Advice and encouragement from Marvin Harris have saved the paper from a comfortable—and doubtless more comprehensible—middle-level fate. I wish also to express my gratitude to Ronald Cohen and Elman Service for criticisms which have immeasurably sharpened and strengthened the principal arguments.

Thanks to Morton Fried are both necessary and sadly insufficient. My concern with problems of state formation and dynamics is largely a reflection of his initial stimulus and continuing influence. More immediately, the appearance of this paper in its present form is in very real measure the result of his support, trust, and good offices. I hope that he is not displeased at the present treatment of his own theoretical model, which is integral to this discussion even where at significant points our views show a not inconsiderable divergence. Insofar as one does not formally dedicate a paper: Dios se lo pague.

References

Armillas, Pedro
   1969   The Arid Frontier of Mexican Civilization. *Transactions of the New York Academy of Sciences,* Series II, No. 31: 697-704.
Carneiro, Robert L.
   1961   Slash and Burn Cultivation Among the Kuikuru and Its Implications for Cultural Development in the Amazon Basin. *Antropologica,* Suppl. 2: 47-67.
   1970   A Theory of the Origin of the State. *Science* 169: 733-738.
Coe, Michael D.
   1961   Social Typology and Tropical Forest Civilizations. *Comparative Studies in Society and History* 4: 65-85.
Culbert, T. Patrick
   1970   Sociocultural Integration and the Classic Maya. Paper presented at 35th Annual Meeting, Society for American Archaeology, Mexico, D.F.
Fried, Morton H.
   1967   *The Evolution of Political Society.* New York: Random House.
   1975   *The Notion of Tribe.* Menlo Park, Calif.: Cummings.

Harner, Michael J.
  1970   Population Pressure and the Social Evolution of Agriculturalists.
          Southwestern Journal of Anthropology 26: 67-86.
Harris, Marvin
  1968   *The Rise of Anthropological Theory.* New York: Thomas Y.
          Crowell.
  1974   *Cows, Pigs, Wars and Witches: The Riddles of Culture.* New York:
          Random House.
  1975   *Culture, People, Nature.* New York: Thomas Y. Crowell.
Jacobs, Jane
  1969   *The Economy of Cities.* New York: Random House.
Millon, René
  1973   *Urbanization at Teotihuacán.* Vol. 1. Austin: University of Texas
          Press.
Parsons, Lee A., and Barbara J. Price
  1971   Mesoamerican Trade and Its Role in the Emergence of Civilization.
          In R. F. Heizer and J. A. Graham (eds.), *Observations on the Emer-
          gence of Civilization in Mesoamerica.* Contributions of the Univer-
          sity of California Archaeological Research Facility, No. 11. Berkeley.
Price, Barbara J.
  1974   The Burden of the Cargo: Ethnographic Models and Archaeological
          Inference. In N. Hammond (ed.), *Mesoamerican Archaeology: New
          Approaches.* London: Duckworth.
  1977   Shifts of Production and Organization: A Cluster-Interaction Mod-
          el. *Current Anthropology* 18: 209-233.
Proskouriakoff, Tatiana
  1963   *An Album of Maya Architecture.* Norman: University of Oklahoma
          Press.
Rathje, William L.
  1971   The Origin and Development of Lowland Classic Maya Civiliza-
          tion. *American Antiquity* 36: 275-285.
Romney, A. Kimball
  1957   The Genetic Model and Uto-Aztecan Time Perspective. *Davidson
          Journal of Anthropology* 3: 35-41.
Sanders, William T.
  1973   The Cultural Ecology of the Lowland Maya: A Reevaluation. In T. P.
          Culbert (ed.), *The Classic Maya Collapse.* Albuquerque: University
          of New Mexico Press.
Sanders, William T., and Barbara J. Price
  1968   *Mesoamerica: The Evolution of a Civilization.* New York: Random
          House.
Steward, Julian H.
  1955a   *Theory of Culture Change.* Urbana: University of Illinois Press.
  1955b   Some Implications of the Symposium. In J. H. Steward (ed.), *Irriga-
          tion Civilizations: A Comparative Study.* Washington, D.C.: Pan
          American Union.
Tolstoy, Paul
  1969   Review of W. T. Sanders and B. J. Price, *Mesoamerica: The Evolu-
          tion of a Civilization. American Anthropologist* 71: 554-558.
Vogt, Evon Z.
  1964   The Genetic Model and Maya Cultural Development. In Evon Z.

Vogt and Alberto Ruz Lhullier (eds.), *Desarrollo Cultural de los Maya*. Mexico, D.F.: Universidad Nacional Autónoma de México.

Webb, Malcolm C.
1973   The Petén Maya Decline Viewed in the Perspective of State Formation. In T. P. Culbert (ed.), *The Classic Maya Collapse*. Albuquerque: University of New Mexico Press.

White, Benjamin
1973   Demand for Labor and Population Growth in Colonial Java. *Human Ecology* 1: 217-236.

Willey, Gordon R.
1974   The Classic Maya Hiatus: A Rehearsal for the Collapse? In N. Hammond (ed.), *Mesoamerican Archaeology: New Approaches*. London: Duckworth.

Wittfogel, Karl A.
1957   *Oriental Despotism*. New Haven: Yale University Press.

Aristotle's Concept
of Political Structure and the State

WOLFGANG WEISSLEDER

The classical Greek *pólis* as analyzed by Aristotle seems to fit only with difficulty into schemes of anthropological theory. Political anthropologists have tended to by-pass the topic, leaving it to classical scholars, historians, and political scientists. Those who have dealt with it at all have considered Aristotle's thoughts on political communities to be mainly philosophical idealization, though in fact he had taken pains to base them on systematically collected case studies. Aristotle was not really a dreamer who cerebrated about ideal political communities as Socrates and Plato had done. In his mature years, when he accepted the fact that he was not the second Plato and had learned to be himself, he discarded inclinations to conjecture about political utopias. He lived in politically eventful times and wrote with realistic and practical concerns in mind.

The last books of the *Politics*, VII and VIII, are the ones that contain most of the idealistic fantasies for which Aristotle has been chided; but they are also the oldest sections of the work, clearly conceived and written still under the spell of Plato (Dreizehnter 1970). Books III to VI deal at length with various possible forms of the *pólis*. The discourse here is quite pragmatic. The philosophical categories of rule and organization that had by then been applied to the *pólis* were separately discussed and analyzed. Thus, different forms of *pólis* governance were considered with respect to their appropriateness for specific situations, whether they were sociologically, geographically, or historically determined. If "ideal" can be applied here at all,

187

then it is only in the sense of conceptually "best suited to existent conditions."

Books I and II, which deal with structural elements of social life, are of the greatest interest to us. In these books, Aristotle systematically analyzed the components of social organization and of dominance.

Those who placed stress on Aristotle's philosophical method and ethical focus overlooked the fact that behind his dated idiom stands a well-defined analysis of social structure, not at all in conflict with modern typology. Aristotle seems to have been aware, perhaps intuitively, that political activity cannot be isolated from other social behavior but is a specialized aspect of the totality of social relationships. Here, we shall try to concentrate on the structured social interrelationships in the formulations that Aristotle gave. I suggest that this will reveal an inherent congruency and compatibility with modern formal statements of political systems.

Since Aristotle consistently phrased his analysis in terms of a system of social roles, I have found it useful to draw on Aidan Southall's "Typology of States and Political Systems" (1965), which invokes principles of political role structures. Southall offers three typological ranges of political systems: stateless societies, segmentary states, and unitary states. Each has a counterpart in the thinking, though not in the terminology, of Aristotle. We are primarily interested in the category of the segmentary state, since Aristotle sees the *pólis* as built up through the addition of inherently like units. To follow Southall further, the *pólis* thereby falls into the subcategory of pyramidal structures, those "in which the exercise of central authority depends on consensual delegation to it by the component units in each case, without any stable recognition of the right to enforce and maintain this by coercion" (1965: 126). Southall sees pyramidal structures subdivided, in turn, into two polar subtypes, each defined by the manner in which authority is delegated: associational or complementary.

At the very beginning of the *Politics*, Aristotle establishes three interlinked axiomatic concepts which he treats as self-evident facts not requiring demonstration. Every *pólis*, he states, constitutes a type of association (*koinōnía*), and all such associations are instituted for the purpose of attaining some good (*agathón*). *Agathón* in turn is soon identified with *autarkeía*, self-sufficiency and independence. The three pairings—*pólis* and *koinōnía*, *koinōnía* and *agathón*, and *agathón* and *autarkeía*—are repeatedly discussed, but their axiomatic nature is never questioned.

Human beings can live as such only in *koinōnía*, in conjunction with others, for they are "political animals." Aristotle wishes this to be understood as a characteristic of man's own nature and not as a result produced by the pressure of external necessity (Tomberg 1973: 18). *Koinōnía* should not be mistaken for an aggregation of undifferentiated individuals. This would be unrealistic, for it would run counter to experience. Rather, Aristotle sees *koinōnía* as ordered interaction among individuals in accordance with the prescribed roles they play in social life. Essential qualities of pairing, partnership, reciprocity, and interdependence, though almost regularly asymmetrical, define *koinōnía*—shades of meaning which are obliterated by the usual pallid translation "association."

The term *koinōnía*, in the sense of complementary interaction, is a vital one, for it constitutes Aristotle's working conception of a mutuality of expectations. It is well within the communal conception of *koinōnía* that members share equitably and fairly according to accepted and apprehended status. At the time when Aristotle wrote, individualistic ambition to obliterate status distinctions was not the main fuel of the sociopolitical dynamic, though the thought may seem heresy today. The universal desire to achieve equality or the self-image of being equal to others is a late-blooming flower of culture; to inject it into the Greek world view is an anachronism. An inward-looking community with socially differentiated membership may not have been the empirical norm even then, but neither would the empirical evidence have ruled out the appropriateness of such a view.

The *autarkeía* axiom represents the "greatest good" (*agathón*) that the complementary efforts of *koinōnía* may attain. Unluckily, *autarkeía*, translated as "autarky," is one of the many Greek words which found their way into English only after suffering severe compression of semantic content. "Economic self-sufficiency" remains as virtually the only meaning of a term which in Greek usage subtended a far wider range. Aristotle pays scant attention to the "economic" aspect of self-sufficiency, to a day-to-day or year-to-year operation of a domestic plant. His view of household economy is not that of the *Hausväterliteratur* of the post-Renaissance, which delighted in detailed instructions for agrarian and domestic management down to crop planning, instructions for caponizing, and cooking recipes. He expended no effort on detailing "daily recurrent needs" (1252b)[1] but dealt with social roles and social requirements almost exclusively. *Autarkeía* appears as the consummation (*télos*) of the various mutual role expectations that make up reciprocal dyads set forth in the *koinōnía* axiom. Therefore *autarkeía* is dealt with outside and above the level of production/consumption concerns. *Autarkeía* focuses preferably on internal interdependence and functional integrity. This emphasizes, beyond mere material needs, immunity from outside interference which neither invites nor permits the inroads of externally located authority (*arkhē*). The major sense of *autarkeía* emerges as "closure of the complementary role system."

The *pólis* axiom, in a sense, sums up the other two. It subsumes the elementary structures of which *koinōnía* is composed, so that nothing is (or could be) *pólis* that is not based on *koinōnía*. In turn, *pólis* is the only form of *koinōnía* that has *autarkeía* as its final goal (*télos*).

Once these *a priori* assumptions or axioms are granted as the outer limits of discourse,[2] we shall find Aristotle's social and political ideas approaching the empirical and theoretical formulations of social science rather closely.

Oikía, *the Model*

Aristotle arrived at his interpretation of political communities not through visions, conjecture, or wishful philosophizing but through the acceptance and analysis of social realities as data. An idiom of philosophical ethics partially hides a remarkably astute and solid structural analysis of actual social relationships.

Aristotle derived the political order of the *pólis* from a complex domestic unit, the *oikía*. *Oikía* stands for the minimal segment from which the supra-category of the *pólis* is elaborated. All higher orders are to be understood only through an analysis of the lower, since every *pólis* is made up of *oikíai* (1253b); conversely, every *oikía* is part of a *pólis* (1260b).

The place of the *oikía* in the construction of larger societal units is modular or, in Southall's terminology, segmentary: typologically like units add up to form a new and distinct order. (The alternative, in which the *oikía* model is employed in a paradigmatic sense, implying that the larger order is to be seen as its mechanical enlargement, is relegated by Aristotle to a different context. It invites comparison with Southall's unitary and hierarchical state and will be taken up in its proper place.)

Oikía, as defined by Aristotle, is a term without standing in social anthropology. Its customary translations, "household" and "family," are, of course, common enough in anthropology but tend to mislead in this context by evoking images of domestic establishments in which kinship serves as the sole or at least principal criterion for membership. Until relatively recently, in fact, we find "household" and "family" used interchangeably in the anthropological literature. Paul Bohannan introduced a clearer structural distinction between functionally discrete aspects of the familial role repertoire by segregating its psychological, social, jural, and economic components. "Family," in this sense, emphasizes affective and jural ties; the domestic bonds of the "household" stress economics and coresidence. But the common link between all the role players remains the biological network. All household roles are shown to be dealt out among kinsmen, and members of the household are identified as kin to one another. The household or family concept which Aristotle evokes under the term *oikía*, however, is not to any significant extent tied to the kinship aspect of family. Of the latter, in fact, Aristotle makes short shrift for a reason which, as far as he and the Greeks of his day were concerned, was quite valid: the biological network was not structurally meaningful.

The *oikía* enters Aristotle's argument from the outset as a complex composite which demands, and for which he supplies, a commensurately sophisticated analytical apparatus. Indeed, he introduces us to a rather sustained exercise in role analysis.

Aristotle bypasses the study of consanguineal-affinal kinship mechanism and defines *oikía* straightway as an entity composed of blood relations as well as non-kin members; i.e., he insists at the outset on incorporating slaves as a definitional prerequisite. Thus, while moderns may include non-kin as "economic persons" in the household, Aristotle demands their inclusion by definition. A complete household (*oikías de teleíos*) is made up of slaves (*douloi*) and freemen (*eleuthérioi*) (1253b). Slaves, then, are not to be construed as an accidental or adscititious part of a household inventory, a mark of wealth of those who were better off, but rather as a factor of social and economic structure in whose absence the definition of *oikía* cannot be properly applied to a domestic establishment. This inclusiveness places the *oikía* outside any continuum made up solely of kin-defined domestic entities of whatever size.

Our interpretation is not superimposed on Aristotle, and it was not even uniquely his insight. He gave credit to Hesiod, whom he quotes: "First house and wife, and ox to draw the plow"; and he continues immediately "for oxen serve the poor in lieu of household slaves [*oikétou*]" (1252b). Evidently, and in a commonly accepted conceptualization, slaves did not constitute, of themselves, a mark of wealth, but the absence of slaves indicated a form of social organization antecedent to even the minimal *oikía*. A normally complete household incorporated slaves; *not* to incorporate them would have been evidence of incompleteness, poverty, and marginality.

Although marriage was likely to precede the establishment of a full household, it was of itself insufficient to produce the new and distinct social entity which signified the *oikía*. At that stage a marital union would in all likelihood still have been considered the nested part of another, superordinate *oikía,* such as that of the husband's or wife's progenitor. Not until houseservants were assembled under a master had the foundations of an *oikía* been laid. An *oikía* would naturally include spouses of dependent children, cadet members of a lineage, and the mates of semislaves or slaves.

In Aristotle's view, the consanguineal family suffices to organize small-scale societies. He even allows for a mechanism to expand its membership: polygyny. Aristotle relies here on his favorite authority for a world antecedent to his own. Homer, he believed, described primitive kinship when he said of the Cyclopes that they ruled over their wives and children, "which shows them to live in scattered groups as men did in ancient times" (1252b). Whatever we may think of the ethnography of the Cyclopes, the citation states a principle, and marks a sort of hesitating at the brink of recognizing "levels of integration." Living in scattered groups is linked to social arrangements constructed solely along lines of affinity and descent.

The contemporary reality with which Aristotle had to deal was of another sort. His was a world of dense population, sustained by agriculture, manufacture, and trade, beholden to complex cultural institutions, literate and supremely innovative. The kin group was too cohesive, too narrowly conceived to give the flexibility with which viable units adapt to changing demands. Kin units expand and contract slowly—far more slowly than structures which include, as a matter of principle, such outsiders as members of collapsing lineages, adopted and semifree persons, bondsmen, and slaves. Greek society included a wide range of such statuses, though Aristotle made little mention of their existence in the *Politics* and none in his theoretical discussion there. He may have preferred to preserve an uncluttered typology and, therefore, to discuss only the "pure" extremes of a continuum, expecting that his contemporaries would fill in the spectrum. The numbers and types of non-kin can be adjusted to conditions and their efforts regulated, managed, and thereby turned into productive new channels. Aristotle reasons that the complexity of the cultural inventory in a complex population setting must be matched by a similarly complex societal mechanism under a common managerial rationale. The minimal order at which optimal integration can be achieved was, for him, the composite *oikía.*

Having rejected the simple conjugal or even the extended consanguineal family as paradigm for complex political organisms, Aristotle enumerated what can best be called the functional prerequisites of an *oikía.* He isolated three primary kinds of relationships as mandatory constituents, and it is noteworthy that he does not merely list the members of each but places them in role pairs, as egos and their alters. "The primary and simplest elements of an *oikía* are the bond [*koinōnía*] between master and slave, that between husband and wife, and that between parents and children" (1253b).

The order of the elements as here presented is significant, and the sequence is observed throughout most of the *Politics*. The primacy of the role pair master and slave is considered operant and distinctive of the *oikía*, and Aristotle did not seem called upon to argue the point. It was not a matter in dispute during his time and was recognized beyond Athens and Greece: *Familia*, the Latin equivalent of the *oikía* concept, "in classical Latinity means always a man's slaves," to quote Henry Maine (1885: 201).

Aristotle's exposition of the role system and of the role content of constituent role pairs must be seen in his own terminology in order to place it beyond the obscuring effects of translation. His terms for the three pairs are:

oikodespótes or *oikías despótes* (master)	*doúlos* (slave)
pósis (husband)	*álokhos* (wife, spouse, bedfellow)
patēr (father)	*tékna* (children)

The syndromic role assemblage of master, husband, and father is normally given as *oikonómikos*, which may be translated as "house-holder" if one carefully avoids overemphasizing the economic (production/allocation/consumption) activities. As Aristotle investigated each separate aspect of the *oikonómikos* role, he was mindful of its suitability for political magnification or augmentation. To anticipate: neither paradigmatic enlargement of the master role nor of the husband or father roles was ultimately found to be acceptable.

The situation of the *oikonómikos* toward his wife and children is clearly distinguished from the position he occupies vis-à-vis his slaves. After all, the former are free members of the *oikía*; the latter are not. The *oikonómikos'* position (*arkhē*) over his children (*tékna*) is likened to that of a monarch (*de basilikós*) (1259b). The affection to which a monarch is entitled and his seniority are the foundation upon which legitimate kingly authority rests. This, Aristotle feels, may be legitimately extended to encompass even Zeus, whom Homer, as he says, correctly apostrophized as Father (*patēr*) of Gods and Men, being king of them all. It should be noted, by the way, that the appellation father is here derived from the kingly status, not the other way round. Aristotle no less than Homer must have been aware of the purely symbolic nature of the comparison, since mythology depicts Zeus as father of neither the gods nor of men. Even so, the metaphorical linking of the *patēr* and *basiléus* (monarch) concepts is quickly reduced to its limiting parameters: A *basiléus* should naturally be superior to his subjects, *and yet of the same stock as they,* as is the case in the relation of age to youth and of parent to child. This proviso effectively eliminates the *patēr* role as a model of governance for complex, heterogeneous political structures, and Aristotle shares Plato's scepticism when it comes to believing that affection will keep heterodox populations in a state of voluntary obedience.

Aristotle speaks of the relationship between *patēr* and *tékna* where one might expect *huoi* (sons). Clearly, the *patēr* role gave the father active control over daughters as well. Authority over children was shared by both parents to a far greater degree than the presumed depressed status of women in Greek society would lead us to believe. The debate as to the relative placement of men and women arose as a problem mainly to literate Greek minds of philosophical-logical bent. It involved primarily the status of a woman's soul and whether the distinction between the souls of men and women permitted bonds of true *philía* between them. Perfect *philía* (i.e., affection unmarked by sexual passion [*éros*]) was thought to be possible only among equals. However, in matters of daily life, the social and legal position of the Greek woman was secure, whatever the arcane ratiocinations about her soul might have been. Women were no more "chattel" in classical Greece than in any society for which there is an adequate factual record.

Aristotle for one likens the primacy (*arkhē*) of a husband over his wife to "that of a statesman [*politikós*] over his fellow citizens" (1259b) and contrasts this with the age-hierarchical nature of the *arkhē* of a father over children. He elaborates on the marital-political metaphor and, far from invoking authoritarian modes of governance, analogizes that, where the true *politikós* exercises his function, a measure of equality tends to be maintained between the governors and the governed (1259b). He acknowledges, however, that even with a mutuality of interests and aims of equality, latent ambitions on the part of the dominant element tend to promote symbolic distinctions in outward forms such as modes of address or titles of respect (1259b).

Aristotle is quite firm on the point that the principal status differences attending the *oikal* roles of free males and free females are inherently of such a prestige nature and that the relationship of a husband to his wife is not one of predatory confrontation. The partnership between them (*koinōnía*) appears to him to be aristocratic, since the man exercises *arkhē* (primacy or authority) in accordance with his purposes—i.e., in matters in which a man is expected to lead—but he does not interfere with his wife's proper concerns (*Nicomachean Ethics*, 1160b-1161a). There is no implication that women's tasks are inherently unworthy, degrading, or to be relegated to inferior talents. They just did not happen to fall, in a cultural setting which was not of Aristotle's making, into the canon of primary decision-making processes which were reserved to the managerial province of an *oikonómikos*. (The chattel-wife of sociological fairytales does not appear in this scene either. Aristotle addressed live contemporaries. He must have had a measure of evidence on his side, for we know that he was sensitive to ridicule.)

Generally, in Greek social thought, the role pairs husband/wife and father/child carried no broad significance beyond that of designating sets of interpersonal bonds among individuals. "Kinship was then but one of several organizing principles, and not the most powerful one" (Finley 1954: 122). Therefore Aristotle could mention in passing and without regret that the Greek language provides terms neither for the parental relationship, for which he used *technopoietikē*,[3] nor for the marital relationship, for which he used *gamike* (1253b).

No such lexical lacuna existed regarding the roles of master and slave. *Despotikē* was a term firmly established in social and political discourse. But it goes without saying that, in classical usage, the word was burdened with neither the denotations nor the connotations which give "despotism" its current meaning. The Greek term designated the arbitrary, though legitimate, exercise of authority. In its realization, the authority might be benevolent or harsh, open-minded, or cruel. Credit or blame for these variations was attached to the specific situation or the personality or outlook of a particular *despótes*; *despotikē* was not automatically equated with oppression. The political ethic of a much later age would insist that arbitrary and unilateral decisions are of themselves illegitimate as well as self-seeking. The Greek view left room for good despots and bad despots.

Despotikē was accepted as a thing sanctioned in law and custom. *Tyránnis* was not so sanctioned, yet the term is used sometimes in the *Politics* and frequently in the *Nicomachean Ethics* to indicate "the rule of masters over slaves, since it is the advantage of the master that is brought about in it" (1060b19). The second clause differentiates *tyránnis* from *despotikē*. In the case of *despotikē*, nothing asserts that the actions and decisions of the master cannot be of mutual advantage to himself and his entire household. In fact, in the eufunctional model with which Aristotle operates to establish his typology, the ultimate aims of all the members of the *oikía* are assumed to be coordinate if not identical.

Aristotle entertains no doubts whether slaves differ from free

persons. They are, in fact, *ktēma*. This term, which usually finds its
way into translations as "property" or "wealth," originally had an
aura of meanings which tended to blur its outlines. The *ktēma* of an
oikía comprises its entire inventory, human and nonhuman, animate
or inanimate, spiritual and physical. In this sense, *ktēma* is the sum
of instrumentalities that serve the institution of the *oikía*. The items
of the inventory are typologically ordered, making slaves *ktēma ti
empsýkhon*, an animate part of the household, while all the rank and
file together (*hyperētes*) may be regarded as instrumentalities of a
higher order (*hósper órganon pro órganon*) (1253b). The term *órganon*
itself was not restricted to the narrow interpretation of physical
instrument or tool.

Clichés instruct us that Aristotle, true child of his period, un-
questioningly and callously accepted slavery as right and proper. He
did accept it as a reality. Yet he struggled with the philosophical and
moral problem—the opposition of *phýsis* and *nómos*, nature and
law—in a way to be expected of a Greek philosopher. Aristotle won-
ders and muses about the morality of holding as slaves freemen whom
war or other misfortune has brought to a state of servility, those who
by *nómos*, man-made practices and considerations, have been reduced
to slavery. He does not find a satisfactory answer to this, it is true, but
leaves the legitimacy of the practice in doubt. He is not certain that a
proper, socially constructive pairing of slave and master can exist where
there is no inherent reciprocity or complementarity of statuses as there is
where a relationship exists by nature (*phýsei*). Thus Aristotle condones
the institution of slavery without hesitation whenever he can construe it
to exist by nature—i.e., in all instances in which the master role and the
slave role rest upon the natural propensities of each: Anyone who, by
virtue of intelligence, is able to exercise forethought is designated by
nature as a master; those who can only physically carry out a design are
by nature slaves (1252a). Even slavery will then fit within the *koinōnía*
axiom. Aristotle evidently wished for an outward sign of the disparity,
for he believed that "it is nature's intention . . . to erect a physical difference between the body of a freeman and that of a slave" (1254a). Then
the slave would be given strength for menial work while the freeman
would be endowed with the prerequisites for political life. (However,
the freeman should not be thought of as characterized by weakness, for
political life encompasses not merely tasks of peace but also, and especially, military duties.) Realistically, however, Aristotle was aware of
the limited applicability of such ideational concepts. He notes that
"contrary to nature's intention" some slaves have the bodies of freemen
while others may have freemen's souls. He evidently feels that "if nature's intention were realized" we should all be able to agree that the

superior ought to rule the inferior, and we would know who is who beyond doubt.

Aristotle therefore felt himself to be on sure ground regarding the institution of slavery only when he perceived a community of interest and could justify even this practice as a relationship encompassed by the concept of *philía*—i.e., as a situation in which both master and slave merit the position one occupies toward the other. Then, and only then, did slavery appear morally defensible, because master and slave complemented each other.

Grave and insoluble doubts persisted in Aristotle's mind in the case of freemen who, captured in war, were thereby turned into slaves. In this instance, slavery lacks the sanction of natural propensities and does therefore not exist *phýsei*, by nature. It rests solely on legal sanction and superior coercive power (1255b).

Analyzing the *oikía* as structural model of the householding unit and as a module of the *pólis* structure, Aristotle adduced social but not economic role factors. Before we proceed to the political implications of the *oikía* concept, it might be useful to paraphrase the structure which Aristotle has erected at this point.

Oikía (meaning *familia*, household) designates the primary organizing principle of human groups at the integrative level of post-primitive society. It constitutes a composite organization made up of individuals who share kin and non-kin bonds. Minimally, three essential role dyads must be present: 1) *despotikē*, the master/slave bond; 2) *gamikē*, the marital bond of husband and wife; 3) *techno-poietikē*, the bond between father and children. Each dyad is characterized by *koinōnía* (complementarity). Jointly, the dyads create a superordinate *koinōnía* through which each achieves *autarkeía* (social closure).

In what sense the structure of the *oikía* contributes to the formation of a larger political system or systems of the sort to which the term "segmentary pyramidal state" in Southall's terminology might be attached remains to be investigated.

Oikía, *the Module*

Aristotle writes of the *oikía* as the minimal building block of the *pólis*. Every *pólis* is composed of vertical—i.e., segmentary—divisions, of which *oikíai* are the smallest discrete units with operational segmentary significance. Yet the *pólis* is anything but merely an enlarged *oikía*. And neither is one symbolically represented within the other. In fact, only one very general and abstract characteristic is shared by both institutions: internal diversity, produced through a diversity of role dyads with the *oikía* and through a plurality of *oikíai* within each *pólis*.

Were the *oikía* to be regarded as the model of higher political entities, its internal structure would have to be repeated at the higher level. Aristotle denies this vehemently and pointedly. At the very outset of the *Politics*—in the second paragraph, in fact—he asserts that the role of the *oikonómikos* is not to be equated with the role of the *politikós*, ruling out the naive analogy of the "father of the family" with the "father of the country." With a stab at Plato, he claims that it is a mistake to believe that the "statesman," the *politikós*, is to be equated with the monarch of a kingdom, or the manager of a household, or the master of a number of slaves. This would mean that each of them differs from the others not with a difference of kind but according to the number of persons with whom he deals. A man who is concerned with a relatively small number would be the manager of a household: one concerned with still more is a "statesman" or a monarch (1252a). The assumption that the *politikós* might relate to the *pólis* as the *oikonómikos* relates to the *oikía* would cancel any effective distinction between a large household and a small *pólis* (1252a).

Much of the first two books of the *Politics* is dedicated to the task of demonstrating that the individual subsystems of which the *oikía* is composed, and of which the role of *oikonómikos* is the syndromic summation, offer no role model that could be successfully raised to a higher political power. In Aristotle's system, none of the components of the *oikía* structure can serve, either alone or in conjunction with others, to generate a political community that would be anything but a larger and more populous *oikía*.

Patēr, *pósis*, and *oikodespótes* designate roles with inherent limitations. The poetic license whereby Zeus may be apostrophized as father of the gods, or the purely symbolic meaning transfer through which the term *patēr* may be applied to any dignified older man, forms no part of the argument. The term *patēr* corresponds first of all to the term *genitor* in present anthropological usage. Structurally the *patēr* role model could hardly be considered appropriate unless virtually all members of the larger community were to stand in recognizable genealogical relationship to each other.

Similarly, the politically significant content of the husband/wife bond, as interpreted by Aristotle (1259b), would seem to imply that in any extrapolation to a higher level, members of the larger systems would have to occupy essentially contractual and balanced positions toward one another, allowing for minor prestige distinctions. Aristotle seems favorably taken with this model: "The relationship of the male to the female is permanently that in which the *politikós* stands to his fellow citizens" (1259b). But by implication "permanently" introduces a significant new element into the equation: time. Aristotle evidently considers duration a major distinction between *pósis* and *politikós* roles. The significance will become apparent later.

The structured diversity of the *oikía* is the single most important and indeed the only element that Aristotle can see being raised to a higher (political) level. To the same degree that the complementarity of its components provided the *oikía* with its proper autarky-directed dynamic, systemic diversity should generate and preserve the autarkic potential of higher political institutions. Aristotle realized that absolute balance within any system would be unproductive since interchangeable equals have no expectations of each other and have therefore no social tasks to fulfill, and this a logical consequence of his role-based analysis of society.

In Aristotle's view, homogeneity of social structure was neither logically nor practically desirable because it would thwart naturally existing propensities and potentials. Distinctions present in nature ought to be preserved and drawn upon to assure a eufunctional and productive *koinōnía* at a level beyond the *oikía*. The new political entity is to be, according to Newman's annotation, a whole composed of parts (1253a20; 1328a21sq.), not a *mixis* or a *krásis* in which the mixed elements vanish, replaced by a new entity that is the result of the mixture. Still less is it a *sýmphysis* (126b10sq.) but rather a *synthesis* (1276b6)—i.e., a union in a compound form of uncompounded elements *(asýntheta)* which continue to subsist as elements or parts within the compound whole (Newman 1887: 43).

Aristotle was not given to postulative extremes. He admitted the need for some measure of homogeneity in the *oikía* no less than in the *pólis*. But he opposed such excesses and absolutes as those conjured up in the utopias of Socrates and Plato. Homogenization on all scores would cause the disintegration of political community. Aristotle offered quite non-idealistic, pragmatic reasons for this: after all, the *pólis* was not a conjectural or utopian construct to him. *Póleis* actually existed as "some sort of aggregation." But they were more than aggregations of numbers; they were made up of different *kinds* of individuals. Similars cannot bring them forth (1261a). And it followed, for Aristotle, that the well-being of every *pólis* had to rely on the reciprocal benefits which its members derived from their association. He weighed various constellations of interaction: whether, for instance, the reciprocal contributions would involve status-equals or persons of different societal levels. But he consistently maintained that absolute blending would be detrimental to the existence of the *pólis*, making it, to the extent that homogeneity was brought about, a worse *pólis*, as if harmony were turned into homophony and rhythmic diversity were reduced to a single pulse (1263b). Socialization turns such an aggregate into a community not through the virtually total obliteration of individualistic distinctions which Plato suggested but through (many-fold) ways of social behavior and mental culture. Far from being the ultimate good of the *pólis*, homogeneity is its destruction (1261). Aristotle reasons that, as an *oikía* will be more autarkic than an individual, a *pólis* will reach a higher degree of autarky than an *oikía*. Since he regards autarky as the product of internally diverse systems, the argument draws to an inevitable conclusion: "To the extent that the greater degree of *autarkeía* is desirable, the lesser degree of homogeneity is to be preferred" (1261b).

Oikía, *the Paradigm*

While *patēr* and *pósis* roles are rather strictly self-limiting, this is not true in the same sense of the subrole of the *oikodespótes,* the master over slaves. It contains an inherent danger, both to the partnership of *koinōnía* and to the role-sufficiency of *autarkeía.* Arbitrary rule can be imposed anywhere and can be extended over persons who are not slaves in any ascriptive sense. *Despotikē* can therefore give rise to a distinct system of domination and could logically be expanded without limit, engulfing individuals and population groups without respect to their specific statuses. There need be nothing symbolic about this, and those who regard centralization and absolute domination as principal characteristics of the "state" concept would search no further. This is, however, not the take-off point for Aristotle's conceptualization of advanced synergistic political structures; in fact, in his view, it leads to their negation.

Aristotle was not blind to the structured tendency of *despotikē* to expand and proliferate. He mentioned it several times in the *Politics* and the *Ethics* but entered into no detailed discussion. For him the reality of centralized, authoritarian political systems was graphically represented in the despotic empires of the Orient, in Persia and Egypt:[5] "among the Persians the rule of the father is tyrannical; sons are used as slaves," and "among the barbarians the female and the slave occupy the same position [so that] marriage thus comes to be the union of a female who is a slave with a male who is also a slave" (1252b).[6] All bow in servility before the king who rules autocratically over those subject to his *despotikē.* Hierarchical distinctions and ranks may exist at all levels but become submerged in uniform subjection to the one supreme regulating and controlling authority.

Aristotle thus deals only peripherally, as an aside, with what would be, expressed in Southall's terminology, the unitary hierarchical state. It is, in fact, as close as Aristotle can approach to the concept of the mass state. He sees it as the total obliteration of natural social diversity among members of the political community and the abandonment of autonomous segmentary subunits which, in his view, are the preferred guarantors of complementary relationships *(koinōnía)* and therefore conducive to producing true communal self-sufficiency *(autarkeía)*.

Monolithic centralization was incomprehensible and unintelligible to Aristotle. He must have considered it futile to expatiate on it—in contrast to Plato, who as a young man had seen the system at work in Egypt and had drawn much inspiration from it for his own conceptualization of State and Law. It was not so much the centralization of authority as the homogenization of society under the oriental system of government that was suspect to Aristotle. He could well imagine an enlightened and benevolent despot, but he was quite explicit on what he considered the defects and dangers of homogeneity: The creativity of balanced interaction would be curtailed. Societal distinctions and diversity exist *phýsei*, by nature, and "nature . . . makes nothing in vain" (1253a). They are, of course, expunged where *despotikē* replaces all other forms of social coordination. Some vast super-*oikía* might be so constructed but not political structures of higher and greater efficiency—i.e., productive of benefits not attained as well or better by the *oikía* as a module of a composite structure. As far as Aristotle was concerned, the results of a systematic blending of social roles were all in the loss column and offered no attractions to civilized Greeks. In fact, he did not hesitate to call such a super-household a perversion of political life. There could be either the *pólis* or else the primitive paradigm of an overblown *oikía* in which *despotikē* in its crudest and most tyrannical form had overwhelmed all the subtler aspects of a true *koinōnía*. *Despotikē* would be sterile as a principle of political community, since it would be unproductive of higher forms. Hence, the development *phýsei* goes from the *oikía* toward the *pólis*, which Aristotle conceived to be a synergistic composite, not toward the single maximized *oikía* he saw represented by the despotisms of Persia and Egypt.

Aristotle saw political structures of his day subjectively and, in a way, more clearly than we can, precisely because he was unaware of the "state" concept in its post-seventeenth-century form, which has come to color all later interpretations and analyses in the guise of formal or objective science. Neither was Aristotle trapped into believing that the great oriental empires were more highly developed political structures (further "evolved," had he known the term) than the Greeks' own localized polities, merely because the former were larger and more populous. Quite to the contrary, the *pólis* represented advancement and incorporated social pluralism, which to him was worth preserving against the monarchical-imperial anachronisms of Asia and the Nile Valley.

Insistence that functional pluralism be preserved urged Aristotle one analytical step further: to the recognition or discovery that the time dimension is a vital structural element of political communities. Time entered the argument as a logical *sine qua non*, locked in by the imperative of pluralism. Aristotle first suggested the time element peripherally in his discussion of the husband/wife role dyad. As cited before, he found a partial analogy between the *pósis* and *politikós* roles: "The relationship of the male to the female is permanently that in which the *politikós* stands to his fellow citizens" (1259b). The key word is "permanently." It implies that, in contrast to the husband/ wife bond, the relationship between the *politikós* and his fellow *polítai* must be of necessity impermanent.

Later, in Book II, Aristotle demonstrated deductively the notion of structured impermanence of political roles. I abbreviate and summarize:

1. The wellbeing of the *pólis* depends on each element contributing to others an amount equivalent to that which it receives [1261a].

2. In any sort of *pólis* there are more individuals available to fill ruling positions than there are positions [1261a].

As a consequence:

3. Where there is a surplus of equally qualified claimants, tenure of ruling positions cannot be permanently usurped; there must be alternation in the holding of office [1261a].

Aristotle reasons that there are two possibilities: Either everyone acts as a ruler in turn, as if shoemakers and carpenters exchanged their occupations now and then, or—and this he thinks might be better— the same men always rule wherever possible. Yet where this is made impossible by the *natural equality of all citizens* (1261b)[7] and because justice demands the participation of all, a compromise would be achieved by temporary tenure of all public offices (1261b). Every *politikós* must hold office for a year or some period of time, or there might be some other order of succession (1261a). Aristotle sees the impermanence of political relationships as an immanent consequence of equality and arrives at the intriguing conclusion that equality rather than asymmetric relations generates a dynamic of internal political change. He penetrates beyond the limits of static structures, designating as perversions those that seem to him inert and unresponsive to the exigent demands for internal adjustments or metamorphosis.

Notes

1. The parenthetic numbers here and elsewhere refer to the Bekker pagination of Aristotle's writings, a system that is adopted by almost all text editors, including A. Dreizehnter (1970). My translations generally follow those of Barker (1960) but occasionally deviate from them.
2. My interpretation of the three fundamental axioms is based on the introductory chapters of Tomberg (1973).
3. Actually, child-bearing or child-begetting.
4. More "wedding" than the civil state of matrimony.
5. A sense of political self-preservation may have kept him from pointing to the political creation of his wayward student Alexander.
6. For the present argument, Aristotle's or mine, it is immaterial whether this is ethnographically or objectively correct. We are solely concerned with Aristotle's own views of the political order.
7. My emphasis.

References

Aristotle's writings are referenced uniformly to the Bekker pagination which is adopted by almost all text editors, including A. Dreizehnter. My translation departs at times from that of E. Barker without special indication.

Barker, E. (trans. and ed.)
    1958   *The Politics of Aristotle.* London: Oxford University Press.
Dreizehnter, A.
    1970   *Politik.* Munich: W. Fink.
Finley, M. I.
    1954   *The World of Odysseus.* Harmondsworth, Middlesex: Penguin Books.
Maine, Sir H.
    1885   *Ancient Law.* 10th edition. London: Murray.
Newman, W. L.
    1887   *The Politics of Aristotle.* Vol. 1. Oxford: Clarendon Press.
Southall, A.
    1965   Typology of States and Political Systems. In M. Gluckman and F. Eggan (eds.), *Political Systems and the Distribution of Power.* ASA Monograph No. 2. London: Tavistock.
Tomberg, F.
    1973   *Polis and Nationalstaat: eine vergleichende Überbauanalyse im Anschluss an Aristoteles.* Darmstadt and Neuwied: Hermann Leuchterhand Verlag.

Political Expansion as an Expression of the Principle of Competitive Exclusion

ROBERT L. CARNEIRO

> ... the history of mankind shows us the grand spectacle of the grouping of man in units of ever increasing size. . . . Notwithstanding all temporary revolutions and the shattering of larger units for the time being, the progress in the direction of unification has been so regular and so marked that we must needs conclude that the tendencies which have swayed this development in the past will govern our history in the future. . . . The practical difficulties that seem to stand in the way of the formation of still larger units count for naught before the inexorable laws of history.
>
> —Franz Boas (1945: 100)

For the first three million years of human history, societies existed exclusively as autonomous communities. Archeology strongly suggests that during the long period of the Paleolithic,[1] political organization did not advance beyond the level of independent bands or villages. Not until after the invention of agriculture was the first step taken toward the formation of supra-community societies.

Once this step was taken, though—once village autonomy was transcended and supra-community aggregation began—political evolution continued at an accelerating pace. The result was that while in the Neolithic period the autonomous political units in the world numbered several hundred thousand, today there are only about 150. And of course as political units have become fewer, they have also become larger.

This process has operated so regularly that it may be expressed as a general principle of cultural development: Since Neolithic times there has been a *decrease* in the number of autonomous political units and an *increase* in their size.

As striking as the process has been, it is surprising that so few anthropologists have called attention to it. Fewer still have made any effort to account for it. But the regularity is too significant to be ignored, and the time has come to give it closer scrutiny.

It is generally agreed that the Paleolithic was a period of low population density and slow population growth. Thus, by the end of its three million-odd years, the population of the world was no more than a few million. The French demographer Roland Pressat (1971: 10), for example, has estimated that around 8000 to 10,000 B.C., the dividing line between the Paleolithic and the Neolithic, the population of the world was between 5 and 10 million.[2] These figures seem reasonable to me, and we can take their average—7.5 million—as a likely figure for the world's population at the start of the Neolithic.

Now, if we take the average size of communities at the end of the Paleolithic to have been 40 persons—a number suggested by the size of recent hunting-and-gathering societies—then the number of autonomous political units in existence as the Neolithic opened was something under 200,000.

The Neolithic revolution, which saw a shift from a wild-food base to a more reliable agricultural one, and which made sedentary settlements possible,[3] brought with it a sharp increase in human numbers. Yet this increase led to only a moderate growth in the average size of local groups. Community size rose from our estimated figure of 40 to perhaps 100. What the increase in population in the Neolithic did was to produce an enormous proliferation of villages. And undoubtedly this proliferation came about the same way it does today among surviving Neolithic peoples. Villages grew in size until, at a critical point, they fissioned. And the growing and splitting of villages occurred repeatedly, so that in the course of time one ancestral village gave rise to dozens of descendents.[4] Neolithic population growth was thus much more striking in the sheer number of villages that came into being than in any great increase in their size.

What was the political relationship between "daughter" communities produced by Neolithic village splitting? To judge from ethnological evidence, we must conclude that even though the two villages produced by a split were genealogically close, each was nonetheless politically fully sovereign. Indeed, splitting most often took place precisely to establish the independence of one faction from another.

We can see, then, that the creation of supra-community political units, which involves fusion rather than fission, was not typical of the Neolithic. The aggregation of villages into larger units was, in fact, the step that led out of the Neolithic and into the next stage of political organization. This next stage was that of multicommunity chiefdoms. The rise of chiefdoms was, in my opinion, the most important single step ever taken in the course of political development. The transcending of community autonomy was a long time coming—three million years—but once it occurred it opened up enormous possibilities. And these possibilities were quickly realized. Within a few millennia of the rise of the first chiefdoms—indeed probably within a few centuries—the first states emerged, and shortly thereafter the first empires.

Warfare as the Mechanism of Political Evolution

The question must now be asked, how was the great step taken by which local sovereignties were transcended? It could not have been an easy step since community autonomy was a stable condition, having prevailed for three million years. Drastic new circumstances must have been required. The invention of agriculture alone was surely insufficient to accomplish it, since present-day Neolithic peoples still live largely in autonomous villages. What happened in the wake of the Neolithic revolution to bring about supra-community organization?

Elsewhere (Carneiro 1970b) I have proposed the theory that village autonomy was first transcended, and supra-community political aggregates established, in areas of circumscribed agricultural land. Briefly, the theory runs as follows: As population density in such areas increased and arable land came into short supply, competition over land ensued. This competition took the form of war, and those villagers vanquished in war, being unable to flee as they might have done in areas of uncircumscribed land, had to remain in place and be subjugated by the victors.

The first step in this process, which saw stronger villages conquer weaker ones, led to the rise of chiefdoms. But the creation of chiefdoms did not solve the problem of land shortage or at best did so only briefly. True, it was chiefdoms that invented taxation and by this means forced the occupants of subject villages to till their lands more intensively, producing, for the first time, a surplus of food above subsistence needs.[5] However, since the population continued to grow, demand for arable land was scarcely mitigated by increased production, and warfare over land continued.

But in this stage of the struggle, instead of village fighting village, it was now chiefdom against chiefdom. The stronger again prevailed, and in this manner successively larger political units were formed. Finally, an entire circumscribed valley was unified under a single banner. The political unit thus formed, so much larger, stronger, and more highly organized than the small chiefdoms out of which it had arisen, warranted being called a state.

The emergence of states still did not put an end to competition over land. It merely increased the size of the competing units and the scale on which this competition was waged. State now fought state, and in many areas of the ancient world the result of this competition was the emergence of the still larger, stronger, and more complex political units that we generally call empires.

The Principle of Competitive Exclusion

The phenomenon so briefly sketched here—that of societal augmentation through successful competition—is, when seen in broadest perspective, neither aberrant nor unique. It is part and parcel of the struggle for existence carried on by all forms of life. Indeed, it is a perfect exemplification in the domain of culture of what biologists have come to call the *principle of competitive exclusion.*

Curiously enough, the principle of competitive exclusion, now recognized as a major factor in organic evolution, is scarcely alluded to by anthropologists. Only very recently, in discussions of the *Australopithecines,* have physical anthropologists begun to invoke it.[6] And cultural anthropologists, to the best of my knowledge, have still made no use of it at all (Carneiro 1970a: vi).

The principle of competitive exclusion, also known as Gause's principle,[7] states simply that two species occupying and exploiting the same portion of the habitat cannot coexist indefinitely. Sooner or later one of them will eliminate the other. Much experimental work has been carried out that substantiates this principle. For example, in a classic series of experiments, Thomas Park and his collaborators placed two species of flour beetle, *Tribolium confusum* and *T. castaneum,* inside a closed container. In the ensuing competition for food between the two species, one of them invariably survived while the other perished (Park 1948). Similar results have been obtained by many investigators, using a variety of animal and plant species.

The reader may object here that the principle of competitive exclusion, as biologists express it, is different from the form of competition I have described among human societies. After all, biologists apply the principle to competition *between different species,* while I have been talking of competition *within the same species.*

True enough. But merely because the principle is ordinarily stated in terms of interspecific competition does not mean that it does not also apply to competing groups of the same species. There is much evidence that it does. In fact, biologists agree that the stiffest competition of all occurs between individuals of the same species. Thus a corn plant competes for nutrients more intensely with a neighboring corn plant than it does with any weed (Billings 1970: 87). The reason for this is clear. The more closely related two individuals or two populations are, the more similar their food requirements will be. And if they are members of the very same species, they will exploit identical resources in identical ways. So if the resources exploited by the two become insufficient in relation to demand, the competition arising between them can be expected to be particularly acute. In this connection, Garrett Hardin (1961: 220) has noted that "as a species becomes increasingly 'successful,' its struggle for existence ceases to be one of struggle with the physical environment or with other species and comes to be almost exclusively competition with its own kind."

Perhaps more should be said at this point about the relationship of the availability of resources to competition, because it is crucial to the issue. Competition is no disembodied Platonic idea striving to realize itself. It is simply the outcome of two or more adjacent individuals or populations striving to survive under conditions of limited resources. Competition over land between human societies will thus scarcely occur as long as the societies are sparsely distributed over their habitat. Only when human numbers begin to press hard against the carrying capacity of the land will territorial warfare and its political consequences of conquest and amalgamation ensue.

This approach to war seems to me more realistic and useful than, for example, the equilibrium model proposed by Vayda (1968). To be sure, from a narrow ethnographic perspective, societies may indeed appear to be fighting to reestablish some kind of equilibrium or to restore certain systemic variables to acceptable magnitudes. But surely homeostatic control is not all there is to warfare, even to "primitive" warfare. Had homeostasis always been the outcome of competition between human societies, we would all still be living in Paleolithic bands.[8]

No, when we look at the full sweep of culture history, the most striking thing we see is not that equilibria were maintained but that they were overthrown. In studying varying forms of political organization, then, our major concern will not be with stability but with change. And the major change we see in political structure, the change from village to chiefdom to state to empire, is the direct consequence of competition between societies.[9]

The Evolution of Warfare

Conflict between human societies is probably as old as the species itself. At the very least, it must go well back into the Paleolithic. Among the simplest societies existing today, warfare is generally waged for noneconomic reasons such as the avenging of murder or witchcraft, and it is probably true that during the Paleolithic, when men lived in nomadic bands, warfare over resources was likewise relatively uncommon. There was, consequently, little dispossessing of a band or village from its territory.

The advent of the Neolithic thus did not create war, but during the later stages of the Neolithic, when human numbers began to press on the carrying capacity of the land, warfare became intensified and redirected toward the acquisition of territory. Though evidence of this intensification during the later Neolithic is widespread, it is perhaps best documented for northern and central Europe. Thus, V. Gordon Childe (1967: 74) wrote that "the earliest Danubians seem to have been peaceful folk," but "we almost see the state of war of all against all arising as unoccupied but easily cultivable land became scarce." Speaking of the same region, Grahame Clark (1952: 98) noted that "prehistorians have . . . vied in emphasizing the contrast between the early [peaceful] peasants and the later warriors."

The initial phases of this warfare over land probably led to the dislocation of an enemy and the occupation of his territory with no effort being made to subjugate him. This stage of fighting is well exemplified in contemporary New Guinea, occurring among such tribes as the Maring (Rappaport 1968: 144), Dani (Heider 1970: 131-132), Mae-Enga (Meggitt 1965: 81-82), and Chimbu (Brown 1972: 61).

As agricultural land became scarcer, warfare over land intensified still further, especially in geographically circumscribed areas. Here there was no easy escape, and the victors began to subordinate the vanquished. At first this involved only imposing a tribute on the defeated enemy so that the loss of autonomy by defeated groups was only partial. But as war became even more intense, the victors were no longer content with subordinating their enemies but began incorporating them into their own expanding political unit. This was a step of paramount importance in political evolution, for through the conquest of village by village, chiefdoms, the first supra-community political units, came to arise. Warfare, then, was the mechanism by which the number of political units in the world began to decline.

The rest of this chapter is devoted to tracing the history of this reduction and to projecting the trend into the future.

The Process of Political Evolution

The *stage* at which supra-community aggregation first occurred was very likely the late Neolithic. But the *date* at which it began naturally varied from region to region, depending on when—if at all—the region reached a late Neolithic stage of development. In areas where agriculture was practiced early and arable land was geographically circumscribed, this stage was not long in coming. Thus in Egypt and Mesopotamia supra-village aggregation may have begun by 5000 B.C. On the other hand, where agriculture was late in arriving or where arable land was uncircumscribed, as in Amazonia, supra-village aggregation did not begin until perhaps A.D. 1000.

Once the process of political fusion was under way, it tended to proceed rapidly. Thus in circumscribed areas the transition from autonomous villages to states or even empires took only a very few millennia. In Egypt, for example, sometime during the fourth millennium B.C., hundreds of villages were aggregated into some 42 chiefdoms that came to be called "nomes." These nomes were later reaggregated into the kingdoms of Upper Egypt and Lower Egypt. And finally, around 2900 B.C., Narmer (Menes), ruler of Upper Egypt, conquered Lower Egypt and for the first time unified the entire region.

The decrease in the number of political units in the world that began during the late Neolithic was not irreversible. Political consolidations were often brittle and short-lived. Newly created empires often fissioned back into their component states, states sometimes fissioned back into chiefdoms, and chiefdoms into autonomous villages. Nevertheless, viewed over the course of several millennia, the trend has been unmistakable: the number of independent political units in the world has steadily diminished.

This trend, which appears so clear to the anthropologist, is not always readily perceived by other scholars. A distinguished sociologist once remarked to me, for example, that the generalization could not be true since at the time of the Roman Empire a single state controlled all the land bordering on the Mediterranean, whereas today this land is in the hands of some fifteen different states. What this objection overlooks is the fact that while Rome was sole master of the Mediterranean, there were, in northern Europe, hundreds of small chiefdoms where today there are only 7 nations. The net effect for Europe as a whole, then, has been a substantial decrease in the number of independent political units since Roman times.

If we look elsewhere in the world, we see the same phenomenon. A few regions may be less unified politically today than they were a thousand years ago, but if we consider the entire inhabited area of the earth, the trend toward political unification holds good.

The Rate of Decrease in Number of Political Units

Given the fact that the number of autonomous political units in the world has declined, we would like to know something about the rate at which this has occurred. But determining this is no easy task. To do so, we need concrete figures to plot on a graph, and no such figures exist. We can make only the roughest estimates of what they would be. Still, the choice is between a gross approximation and no approximation at all, and a start must be made somewhere.

Before attempting such an estimate, we must take a closer look at the problems involved. The first problem is deciding at what date in history the total number of autonomous political units in the world was at its maximum. Even if we make the reasonable assumption that each region of the world reached its largest number of autonomous political units at the mid-Neolithic stage, before conquest warfare began to reduce that number, we must keep in mind that this "mid-Neolithic stage" was reached at different times in different areas. The confounding effect of this is that while the number of political units was decreasing in some areas, it was increasing in others.

Simple logic dictates, of course, that there must have been *some* date when the number of independent political units in the world reached its peak, and we must venture to guess what this date was. It must have been later than 3000 B.C., since most of the arable regions of the world did not reach the mid-Neolithic stage until after that date. On the other hand, the date was no doubt earlier than A.D. 1000, since by then conquest warfare had drastically reduced the number of autonomous villages in the world. For lack of any more elegant method, let us simply split the difference between 3000 B.C. and A.D. 1000 and take 1000 B.C. as the date at which the number of autonomous political units in the world was at its highest.

Up to this date (if our estimate is correct) the proliferation of autonomous villages exceeded the amalgamation of these villages into chiefdoms and of chiefdoms into states. Thus until that date the total number of autonomous political units in the world was increasing. Around that date—1000 B.C.—a balance was momentarily struck between proliferation and amalgamation; but from that date forward, amalgamation began to outstrip proliferation, and thus the total number of independent political units began to decline.

Having settled this question, however crudely, we need to consider next how many autonomous political units there were at 1000 B.C. To answer this question we must first know the population of the world at that time. Julian Huxley (1950: 39) has estimated that the world's population reached 100 million somewhere between 1000 B.C. and 500 B.C., so that at 1000 B.C. it was perhaps 80 million. If these 80 million persons lived in autonomous villages averaging 100 persons each (a reasonable estimate for Neolithic villages), the number of autonomous political units in the world as of 1000 B.C. would have been around 800,000.

However, by 1000 B.C. state formation was already well under way in several parts of the world, so that not all villages in existence were autonomous. Many of them formed parts of chiefdoms, states, and even empires. Thus the number 800,000 must be reduced. But by how much? Here again we must make a guess. It seems likely to me that at 1000 B.C. substantially more of the world's villages were still autonomous than were parts of chiefdoms, states, or empires. If we assume that three-fourths of them were still independent, that yields a figure of 600,000 as the number of autonomous political units in existence in the world at that time.

At last we have a figure to plot on a graph. Because of the guesswork involved, though, it seems specious to try to make a series of estimates of the number of independent political units at short intervals of time between 1000 B.C. and the present. Instead, let us make one more estimate for a date intermediate between 1000 B.C. and the present, namely A.D. 500.

Even though independent villages continued to proliferate after 1000 B.C. and indeed probably did so even faster than ever before, the rate at which these villages were being incorporated into chiefdoms and chiefdoms into states no doubt increased still more rapidly. The net effect was a very substantial reduction in the number of autonomous political units between 1000 B.C. and A.D. 500.

How great was this reduction? This estimate is again very difficult to make. It would appear that by A.D. 500 most of the densely populated areas of the world were at or near the state level of political organization. However, a number of large areas, such as Amazonia and North America north of Mexico, were still largely at the autonomous village level. Let us assume that in the 1500 years following 1000 B.C. there was a two-thirds reduction in the number of independent political units in the world, so that by A.D. 500 the number had diminished from 600,000 to some 200,000.

Between A.D. 500 and the present day the decline in number of independent political units has continued in almost every region of the globe. Europe offers us this striking example: "Before the Treaty of

Westphalia [1648] there were nine hundred sovereign states among the Germanic peoples, which afterward were reduced to three hundred and fifty. When the Germanic Confederation was founded in 1815, the number was thirty-six; finally, in 1871, there was only one" (Ogburn 1964: 151).

Arriving at modern times, we are at last able to place some solid figures on the graph. Thus, in 1939 the number of independent countries in the world was 76 (Hart 1948: 398), and for 1976 the figure was 157 (World Almanac 1976: 593-670).[10] Plotting our four figures on semi-logarithmic graph paper, we have the curve shown in Figure 1.

Despite the uncertainty of the earlier figures on the graph, the general trend is so obvious that it would not be seriously affected even if these figures were off by 100,000 or more. And not only has there been a decrease in the number of autonomous political units in the world; the tendency has accelerated. It is quite clear that the rate of decrease in the number of independent political units between A.D. 500 and A.D. 1976 was much greater than it was between 1000 B.C. and A.D. 500.

What accounts for this acceleration? Several factors were probably involved, but the most important one seems to be the following: As long as the warring units in a region were all small and of roughly the same size, the conquest of one by another was relatively difficult. But once conquest was well under way and significant disproportions arose in the size of neighboring political units, it became easier for the larger units to defeat and absorb the smaller ones. And this advantage became progressively magnified as the disproportion in size between warring units increased. Thus, for example, once the Inca Empire had attained a certain size, there was little real impediment to its becoming even larger.

The Increase in the Size of Political Units

In this essay I have focused on the reduction in the number of autonomous political units through time. The other side of the coin is that as political units decreased in number, they increased in size. It is this increase in size of states that has interested those few scholars who have looked at the long-term quantitative aspects of political evolution. Let us see what has been done along these lines.

Using a historical atlas, Hornell Hart (1948) measured the areas of successive record-breaking empires, and plotted these areas on a graph against time. By plotting the size of empires from that of Sargon II in 2400 B.C. to the USSR in 1944, he obtained a steeply rising curve which he interpreted as the rapid growth phase of a logistic curve that would ultimately flatten out as it reached a maximum size (Hart 1948: 309).

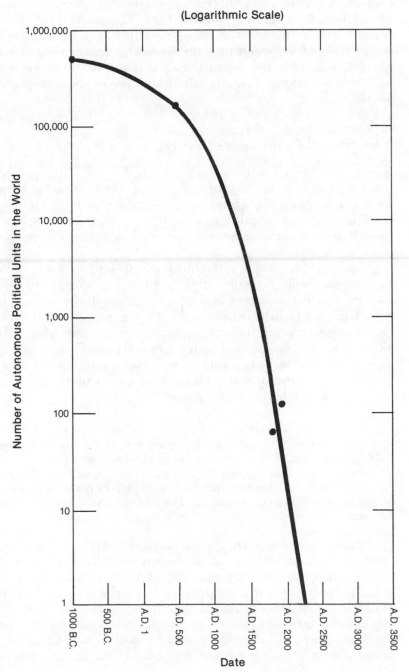

FIGURE 1

*The Reduction in the Number of Political Units
in the World since 1000 B.C.*

(Logarithmic Scale)

Raoul Naroll (1967) used an elaborate procedure which involved comparing the areas of the largest empires in successive 500-year periods from 2500 B.C. to the present. Louis Marano (1973) in turn took Naroll's data on the areas of empires, plotted them on a graph, and drew a series of regression lines for them. Both Naroll's and Marano's objective was to predict when complete political unification would occur and a world state emerge, and to this problem we now turn our attention.

The Political Unification of the World

Having traced very briefly the history of the decrease in the number of political units, it is time to project this trend into the future to see what we can anticipate. The culmination of this trend is, of course, the unification of the remaining independent nations into a single world state. Will this ever be achieved? And if so, how will it happen and when will it occur?

The idea of a world state has intrigued mankind for many years. In his famous poem "Locksley Hall," written in 1842, Tennyson envisioned "the Parliament of Man, the Federation of the World." Fifty years later, the French sociologist Paul Lafargue (1891: 160) foresaw the coming of "the political unity of human kind, a unity which will be founded on the ruins of the existing national unities." In recent years there has been much discussion of a world state, emphasizing the need for it but at the same time recognizing the impediments to it. For example, Leslie A. White (1959: 515) wrote:

> We are in a race today between national rivalries, on the one hand, with their precious sovereignties, ideologies, and ideals, which threaten to engulf us all in a desperate orgy of co-annihilation; and, on the other, with a tropismatic groping for an effective and powerful global system with which our present civilization may be preserved and a finer and nobler one built in the future. . . . The time of decision is probably not far off.

There is a feeling, then, that a world state is in the offing. If it does come, how will it be achieved? Only two possibilities seem to exist. One is that it will come through the voluntary surrender of existing national sovereignties to a single world authority. Those who believe in this outcome usually regard the United Nations as the logical organization to transform itself into such a world government. Yet in the 30-year history of the UN its member nations have given no evidence of being willing to surrender any substantial part of their individual sovereignties. On the contrary, they cling to them tenaciously. Even occasional attempts to investigate conditions within the borders of a state are quickly vetoed by that state as constituting "meddling in its internal affairs."[11]

Do the "newly emerging nations" offer any hope in this regard? Evidently not. The peoples of these nations, so long deprived of independence by colonial masters, have entered the UN intent on exercising their hard-won sovereignties, not in relinquishing them to some new supra-national authority.

If a world state is not to be achieved by the peaceful surrender of national sovereignties, then it can come about only through the same process by which states were created and enlarged in the past— namely, war.

But will a world state actually emerge through war? Even theorists who considered war to be the prime mover in the rise and growth of states have been reluctant to assign it such a role. Herbert Spencer, for example, wrote: "that [degree of] social evolution which had to be achieved through conflicts of societies with one another has already been achieved; and no further benefits are to be looked for. . . . From war has been gained all that it had to give" (1899: 665, 664).

And many modern writers, appalled by the enormous destruction that would result from an atomic war, resist any suggestion that such a war could advance political evolution.[12] Indeed, it is often asserted that the prospects of such a catastrophe alone are sufficient to deter it. However, the fact that, despite the anticipated consequences of nuclear war, the two major world powers came perilously close to it—during the Cuban missile crisis[13]—makes this argument unconvincing. The likelihood of another world war has no doubt been reduced by the existence of atomic weapons, but it has not been eliminated altogether.

Drawing on the theory we presented earlier, the principle of competitive exclusion leads us to expect that wars will recur as long as independent nations continue to exist. And this would be true of wars between the stronger nations as well as wars among the weaker. "Peaceful coexistence" would thus appear to be a temporary and unstable condition that sooner or later will give way to armed conflict between the major powers.

When Will Political Unification Come About?

The final question we need to consider is this: If major wars occur but nuclear annihilation is avoided and political unification of the world comes about, when will that be? Let us see what the three theorists we have mentioned have had to say on this score.

Although Hart dealt with the increase in size of nations through time, he made no prediction of when a world state would emerge. Indeed, he failed even to raise the question. Naroll did consider the question; in fact, estimating the time of arrival of a world state was one of his major objectives. His conclusions on this question are presented in the form of probabilities that a world state will have been established by certain dates (Naroll 1967: 98):

Date	Probability of a World State by That Date
A.D. 2125	.40
A.D. 2250	.64
A.D. 2375	.79
A.D. 2500	.87
A.D. 2625	.92
A.D. 2750	.95

Thus, for example, it is Naroll's prediction that by the year A.D. 2500 there will be 87 chances out of 100 that a world state will have emerged.

Marano uses Naroll's data on empires, but his approach to the problem is different. He asks the question, "If the trend toward larger governmental areas continues, at what future point can the land mass of the largest empire be expected to equal . . . the total inhabitable area of the planet?" (1973: 37). To answer it, he plots the areas of the largest empires, from the Akkadian Empire of 2100 B.C. to the British Empire of A.D. 1918, against time on semilogarithmic graph paper and draws the regression line. He finds that when this line is extended, it intercepts the figure of 134,680,000 (the total habitable area of the world in square kilometers) at about A.D. 3500. He concludes from this that "Naroll's projected date [a .79 probability of a world state by A.D. 2375] is premature by more than a millennium . . ." (1973: 38).

Our own procedure for determining the most likely date for the political unfication of the world is different from either Naroll's or Marano's. Instead of plotting successively larger empires, we have plotted the decreasing number of politically autonomous units. And in order to predict when a single world state will appear, we note where the descending curve intercepts the value of 1 on the horizontal axis. Looking back at Figure 1, where such a plot was made, we see that the curve intercepts the value of 1 at about A.D. 2300. Our prediction, then, is much closer to Naroll's than to Marano's.

The extrapolation of a curve into the future is always risky, especially when the points through which the curve is drawn are few and problematical. Still, to judge from the general trend of the graph, the formation of a world state cannot be far off. Indeed, its appearance must be a matter of centuries or even decades rather than of millennia.

Viewed in its broadest perspective, the tendency of political evolution is striking. For 99.8 percent of human history people lived exclusively in autonomous bands and villages. At the beginning of the Paleolithic the number of these autonomous political units must have been small, but by 1000 B.C. it had increased to some 600,000. Then supra-village aggregation began in earnest, and in barely three millennia the autonomous political units of the world dropped from 600,000 to 157. In the light of this trend the continued decrease from 157 to 1 seems not only inescapable but close at hand.

Acknowledgments

I would like to express my appreciation to Barbara Bode for reading this essay in manuscript and giving me the benefit of her wise counsel.

Notes

1. I am using this term in the broadest possible sense to encompass the period between the beginning of culture and the end of a purely hunting, fishing, and gathering mode of subsistence. Thus, at one end it includes any cultures that may have existed before implements began to be fashioned out of stone, and, at the other, the Mesolithic cultures that were transitional to the Neolithic.

2. Julian Huxley (1950: 38-39) estimated a total world population of 10 million, with a lower limit of 5 million, for the time immediately prior to the invention of agriculture, the date for which he took to be 6000 or 5500 B.C. but which today is recognized to be closer to the 10,000 to 8000 B.C. employed by Pressat.

3. In my opinion, Sussman (1972) is correct in suggesting that it was the sedentariness made possible by agriculture, rather than its enlargement of the food supply, which, by reducing infanticide, changed the very slow increase in population during the Paleolithic into the relatively rapid one of the Neolithic.

4. The most carefully documented study of village splitting among present-day Neolithic peoples is that made by Napoleon A. Chagnon (1968: 70-72) of the Yanomamö of southern Venezuela.

5. The possibility of producing a food surplus is inherent in virtually every agricultural village. Proof of this is afforded by the fact that villages in preindustrial states were very commonly forced to pay a tax in kind which ranged between 10 and 25 percent of the food they produced. (For Rome see Bloch [1942: 131], for Egypt see Petrie [1923: 57], for India see Altekar [1955: 321], and for Burma see Sangermano [1843: 93]). This indicates that among

autonomous Neolithic villages there is always an unactualized margin of food production, amounting to from 10 to 25 percent above subsistence, which can be squeezed out of them once they are conquered and taxed.

6. Specifically, the question has been raised as to how the "robust" and "gracile" forms of *Australopithecus,* if indeed they were separate species, could have avoided competition fatal to one or the other during the million or more years they coexisted in southern and eastern Africa. See Birdsell (1972: 302-309) and Howells (1973: 25).

7. So called after the Russian microbiologist G. F. Gause (1934), who conducted a number of experiments on competition between two species of yeasts and between *Paramecium* and *Didinium.* But this is a misattribution. Gause never generalized the results of his experiments, never expressed "his" principle explicitly, and in any event acknowledged the priority of others. See Gilbert, Reynoldson, and Hobart (1952: 312) and Hardin (1960: 1294).

8. In the discussion that followed the presentation of Vayda's (1968) paper, David F. Aberle (1968: 100) remarked: "in terms of scientific yield we are likely to get further, faster with concepts like competition, expansion, and domination, than with concepts like function, equilibrium, homeostasis, and reduction of inequalities."

9. Attempts to explain the origin of the state through non-conflict means, such as through religion (Steward 1955: 62-63) or trade (Wright and Gregory 1975: 277-283) have not borne fruit. Some years ago (Carneiro 1970b: 734) I wrote of "the demonstrated inability of autonomous political units to relinquish their sovereignty in the absence of overriding external constraints," and nothing I have learned since has caused me to change this opinion.

10. Because of the wholesale decolonization that has occurred since the end of World War II, several dozen new nations have come into existence. This, of course, is a reversal of the general trend. Nevertheless, viewed against the enormous reduction in autonomous political units that has occurred over the last three millennia, this reversal appears as little more than a small back-eddy in an onrushing current.

11. Discussing the possibility that the UN might play a major role in the formation of a world state, Leslie White (1949: 380) remarked: ". . . the goal of a single world organization embracing the whole planet and the entire human race is now almost in sight. But if it is reached it will not be the work of frock-coated diplomats in a United Nations' *opéra bouffe.* . . ."

12. Thus Arnold J. Toynbee (1966: xi) wrote: "In the Atomic Age it will be impossible to found any future 'world state' by force. A 'world state' . . . may now be the only alternative to mass suicide, but it will have to be established by voluntary agreement."

13. Robert F. Kennedy (1969: 23), who was at the very vortex of that crisis and thus in a position to give a realistic assessment of its seriousness, described it as "a confrontation between the two giant atomic nations, the U.S. and the U.S.S.R., which brought the world to the abyss of nuclear destruction and the end of mankind."

References

Aberle, David F.
  1968   General Discussion. In M. Fried, M. Harris, and R. Murphy (eds.),
          War: The Anthropology of Armed Conflict and Aggression. Garden
          City, N.Y.: Natural History Press.
Altekar, A. S.
  1955   *State and Government in Ancient India.* Banaras: Motilal Banar-
          sidass.
Billings, W. D.
  1970   *Plants, Man, and the Ecosystem.* 2nd ed. Belmont, Calif.: Wads-
          worth.
Birdsell, Joseph B.
  1972   *Human Evolution.* Chicago: Rand McNally.
Bloch, Leo
  1942   *Instituciones Romanas.* 2nd ed. Translated by G. Zotter. Barcelona:
          Editorial Labor, S.A.
Boas, Franz
  1945   *Race and Democratic Society.* New York: J. J. Agustin.
Brown, Paula
  1972   *The Chimbu: A Study of Change in the New Guinea Highlands.*
          Cambridge, Mass.: Schenkman.
Carneiro, Robert, I.
  1970a   Foreword. In K. F. Otterbein, *The Evolution of War.* New Haven:
          HRAF Press.
  1970b   A Theory of the Origin of the State. *Science* 169: 733-738.
Chagnon, Napoleon A.
  1968   *Yanomamö, the Fierce People.* New York: Holt, Rinehart and
          Winston.
Childe, V. Gordon
  1967   *What Happened in History.* Harmondsworth, Middlesex: Penguin
          Books.
Clark, Grahame
  1952   *Prehistoric Europe: The Economic Base.* New York: Philosophical
          Library.
Gause, G. F.
  1934   *The Struggle for Existence.* Baltimore: Williams and Wilkins.
Gilbert, O., T. B. Reynoldson, and J. Hobart
  1952   Gause's Hypothesis: An Examination. *Journal of Animal Ecology*
          21: 310-312.
Hardin, Garrett
  1960   The Competitive Exclusion Principle. *Science* 131: 1292-1297.
  1961   *Nature and Man's Fate.* Mentor Book. New York: New American
          Library.
Hart, Hornell
  1948   The Logistic Growth of Political Areas. *Social Forces* 26: 396-408.
Heider, Karl
  1970   *The Dugum Dani.* Viking Fund Publications in Anthropology No.
          49. New York: Wenner-Gren Foundation.

Howells, William
  1973   *Evolution of the Genus Homo.* Reading, Mass.: Addison-Wesley.
Huxley, Julian
  1950   Population and Human Destiny. *Harper's Magazine* 201: 38-46.
Kennedy, Robert, F.
  1969   *Thirteen Days: A Memoir of the Cuban Missile Crisis.* Signet Book.
          New York: New American Library.
Lafargue, Paul
  1891   *The Evolution of Property.* London: Allen and Unwin.
Marano, Louis A.
  1973   A Macrohistoric Trend toward World Government. *Behavior Science Notes* 8: 35-40.
Meggitt, Mervyn J.
  1965   *The Lineage System of the Mac-Enga of New Guinea.* New York:
          Barnes and Noble.
Naroll, Raoul
  1967   Imperial Cycles and World Order. *Peace Research Society Papers*
          7: 83-101.
Ogburn, William F.
  1964   On Inventions and the State. In William F. Ogburn, *On Culture and
          Social Change* (ed. Otis Dudley Duncan). Chicago: University of
          Chicago Press.
Park, Thomas
  1948   Experimental Studies of Interspecies Competition. I. Competition
          between Populations of the Flour Beetles, *Tribolium confusum*
          Duval and *Tribolium castaneum* Herbst. *Ecological Monographs*
          18: 265-308.
Petrie, W. M. Flinders
  1923   *Social Life in Ancient Egypt.* London: Constable.
Pressat, Roland
  1971   *Population.* Translated by Robert and Danielle Atkinson. Baltimore: Penguin Books.
Rappaport, Roy A.
  1968   *Pigs for the Ancestors.* New Haven: Yale University Press.
Sangermano, Father
  1843   *The Burmese Empire a Hundred Years Ago, as Described by Father
          Sangermano* (ed. John Jardine). Westminster: Archibald Constable.
Spencer, Herbert
  1899   *The Principles of Sociology.* Vol. 2. New York: Appleton.
Steward, Julian H.
  1955   Some Implications of the Symposium. In *Irrigation Civilizations: A
          Comparative Study.* Social Science Monographs No. 1. Washington,
          D.C.: Pan American Union.
Sussman, Robert W.
  1972   Child Transport, Family Size, and Increase in Human Population
          during the Neolithic. *Current Anthropology* 13: 258-259.
Toynbee, Arnold J.
  1966   Foreword. In Garcilaso de la Vega, *Royal Commentaries of the
          Incas.* Part 1. Translated by Harold V. Livermore. Austin: University of Texas Press.

Vayda, Andrew P.
  1968   Hypotheses about Functions of War. In M. Fried, M. Harris, and R.
          Murphy (eds.), *War: The Anthropology of Armed Conflict and
          Aggression.* Garden City, N.Y.: Natural History Press.
White, Leslie A.
  1949   Ethnological Theory. In R. W. Sellars, V. J. McGill, and M. Farber
          (eds.), *Philosophy for the Future.* New York: Macmillan.
  1959   Review of Hans Thirring, Energy for Man: Windmills to Nuclear
          Power, and Norman Lansdell, The Atom and the Energy Revolu-
          tion. *American Anthropologist* 61: 513-515.
World Almanac
  1976   *The World Almanac and Book of Facts.* New York and Cleveland:
          Newspaper Enterprise Association.
Wright, Henry T., and Gregory A. Johnson
  1975   Population, Exchange, and Early State Formation in Southwestern
          Iran. *American Anthropologist* 77: 267-289.

Index

Aberle, D. F., 220
Abubaker, S., 142, 150, 153, 159
Adab, social organization of, 42
Adams, R. McC., 27, 39-40, 52, 57, 72, 81
Adams, R. N., 3, 14, 78
Africa
   agriculture and state development in North Africa, 10
   slavery in, 14, 145, 157
   state formation of West Africa, 8, 12
   state and non-state forms in, 3
Agathón, 188, 189
Agricultural production
   and conflicts between sedentary and nomadic societies, 9-11, 24, 29, 181; in Borno, 142-147, 155; defensive reactions in, 155-156, 157; in Fombina, 142, 150-154, 155; in Iranian Baluchistan, 125-139; and nomad-initiated state, 155, 156, 157
   in Egypt, 219
   in India, 219
   irrigated. *See* Irrigation agriculture
   in Mesoamerica, 105, 108
   military barriers affecting, 29
   in North Africa, 10
   related to state development, 59; in Iran, 59, 63, 65, 125-139
   in Rome, 219
   significance of invention of, 205, 206, 207
Ahmed, A. G. M., 137
Al Idrisi, 144
Alland, A., Jr., 141
Altekar, A. S., 219
Amazonia, supra-village aggregation in, 211, 213
Architecture
   and development of state, in Teotihuacán, 171, 172, 176
   as evidence of sociocultural

integration, 165, 166, 168-169
Aristotle, 13-14, 22
   concept of political structure and state, 187-203
Armillas, P., 107, 177
Asia, Southeast, irrigation agriculture in, 70
Attolini, J., 89
Autarkeía, 188-190, 197, 200, 201

Bagehot, W., 24-25
Baluchi government of Iran, development of, 9, 11, 125-139
Barker, E., 203
Barth, F., 138
Barth, H., 144
Basseri, centralized chieftainship of, 138
Bellow, S., 35
Billings, W. D., 209
Birdsell, J. B., 220
Biu, development of state in, 12, 142, 144, 147-150, 154-157, 159
Bloch, L., 219
Boas, F., 205
Bodin, J., 24
Bohannan, P., 190-191
Borno, 158-159
   nomads and agriculturists in, 10-11, 142-147, 155, 156
   as secondary state, 11, 154-155
   stratification in, 157
Britain, effects in India, 177
Brown, P., 210
Bujra, A. S., 136-137
Burgoa, Fra. F. de, 106

Capitalism, and social stratification, 41, 43, 45
Carneiro, R.
   on circumscription related to state development, 28, 31, 173
   concept of evolution, 18

225